Aufgabe

Number 13

Molly Zuckerman-Hartung, "What's in the front, whose in the back"
2011, oil, enamel, glitter, detritus, & cut painted canvas, left: 9 x 10 inches, right: 15 x 12 inches
Private collection, Oakland, CA

EDITORIAL BOARD | E. Tracy Grinnell, Jen Hofer, Paul Foster Johnson, erica kaufman, Nathanaël, Maryam Parhizkar, Jamie Townsend, and Zandra Ruiz

GUEST EDITORS | Biswamit Dwibedy, Olivia C. Harrison, Teresa Villa-Ignacio

ART EDITOR | Ashley Lamb

TYPESETTING & COVER DESIGN | HR Hegnauer

COVER & INTERIOR ART | Molly Zuckerman Hartung

FRONT COVER ART | "The Necessary (Blushing For Now)," detail, 2012-13, oil, acrylic, and dropcloth on canvas, 70 x 60 inches, Private collection, Minneapolis, MN.

BACK COVER ART | "Shit and Space," detail, 2009-11, enamel, pil paint, pigment, and denim on canvas, 60 x 48 inches

INTERIOR ART | "What's in the front, whose in the back," "Scalps in French," "Readymade Mood," "Petit Four Arp," "To the Detriment of the User (Finally)," "The Impossible," "Bird & Bird (Broad advisory, transactional and contentious capability)"

All images courtesy of the artist and Corbett vs. Dempsey, Chicago.

Aufgabe has been published annually by Litmus Press since 2001. The journal has presented the work of nearly 1000 writers, translators, editors, and artists from 23 countries. This is the final print issue.

Litmus Press is the publishing program of Ether Sea Projects, Inc., a 501(c)(3) nonprofit literature and arts organization dedicated to supporting innovative, cross-genre writing with an emphasis on poetry and international works in translation.

Litmus Press / *Aufgabe*
925 Bergen St. #405
Brooklyn, NY 11238
www.litmuspress.org

All Litmus Press publications are distributed by
Small Press Distribution
1341 Seventh St.
Berkeley, CA 94710
www.spdbooks.org

ISSN: 1532-5539
ISBN: 978-1-933959-22-1

Aufgabe is made possible by the New York State Council on the Arts with the support of Governor Andrew Cuomo and the New York State Legislature. Additional support for Litmus Press comes from the Leslie Scalapino—O Books Fund, individual members and donors. All contributors are fully tax-deductible.

Contents

Essays, notes, reviews | edited by E. Tracy Grinnell, erica kaufman, Jamie Townsend & Zandra Ruiz 309

After/words: an editorial exchange | E. Tracy Grinnell & Jen Hofer 413

Contributors 417

About the Artist | Molly Zuckerman Hartung 434

Feature

Poetry from Seven Indian Languages
guest edited by Biswamit Dwibedy

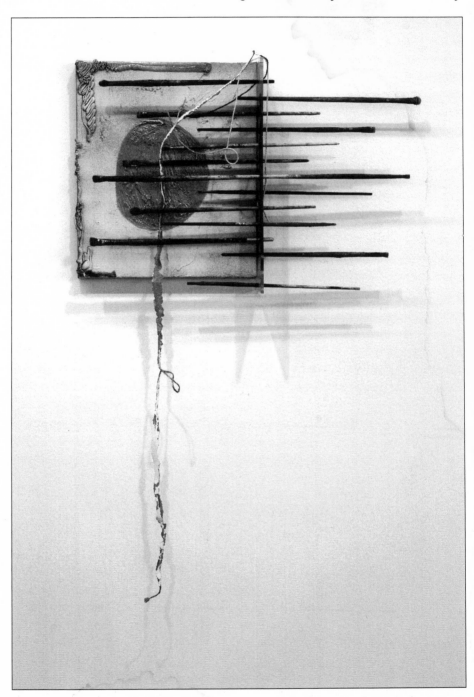

Molly Zuckerman-Hartung, "Scalps in French"
2011, oil, spray paint, caulk, Plexiglass, old paintbrushes, and string on canvas, 16 x 34 x 5 inches
Private collection, Brooklyn, NY

Voice and Voyage: Mapping Contemporary Indian Poetics

Biswamit Dwibedy

The fact that India is a land of many cultures and languages is not unknown. There are twenty-nine states in India and twenty-three official languages. These can be divided into two umbrella groups: Indo-Aryan, spoken by about 75% of the population, concentrated in the Northern and Northeastern parts of the country and Dravidian, spoken mostly in the South. Individual mother tongues number several hundreds, of which a couple hundred are endangered.

Many Indians are multilingual; other than their mother tongue they are also likely to know either Hindi or English. It is not uncommon for someone who's been to school to be trilingual, with a working knowledge of both Hindi and English along with their mother tongue. Unfortunately, as children move through the school years, they find themselves immersed in Hindi and English, and they begin to lose touch with their mother tongue. They speak it, but can't read or write it.

For a young generation of writers, English remains a popular language of choice; it promises a wider audience, better remuneration and international exposure, if you are lucky. However, literature in regional languages continues to flourish, thanks to strong local poetic communities and independent presses. Government organizations such as the Sahitya Academy, also continue to publish work in regional languages from across the country. In fact, of all the books published in India, about half are in the regional languages and the other half in Hindi and English put together.

And where does poetry feature in all of this? As is the case anywhere else, poetry is generally ignored across curricula in the country; I remember having to read only about twenty poems during my time in high school, and that hasn't changed much. Unless one is a student of literature or has strong interests of their own, one doesn't really encounter poetry in the schools. The past years have seen a huge surge in publishing in India, especially if the work is in English, but poetry still remains in the domain of small presses and government-funded publishing houses. The concept of an MFA in Creative Writing and especially Poetry is practically unknown in India.

Compiling this collection has been a lesson in how poetic communities in India work. It took me three years to put together this dossier. Numerous emails to poets were sent of which a majority remain unanswered. I was asked to do the project shortly after I had moved to India, and my knowledge of regional poetries was admittedly limited. It took a year or two to do the groundwork: finding poets in each language and going through the work. It wasn't until last year that I finally found the translators, many poets themselves, who acted as my key into the poetics of each regional language. If it weren't for the translators featured here, I would not have come across many of the poets included.

I had two main objectives while making the selections for this dossier. I wanted to seek the unfamiliar, the as-yet-unseen, in the writing that I was going to present. To me it seemed that poetry in India, particularly in English, is under a lot of pressure to maintain a certain identity—the subject of the poem is always the poet and the place he or she is from: India. I wanted to seek out poetry from India in which the subject was not India, but the being *there*, the becoming that depends on geography. Going through the translations I feel that each set of poems, each language has an inherent rhythm, a speaking that marks territories, which each poet tries to both preserve and push further. This is what I wanted to represent in this collection, an aura, a mood or tone perhaps, that marks the rhythm of a particular regional language. I am grateful to have found translators who were sensitive to the same.

I begin with a collection of Kashmiri poetry because it addresses the relation between a becoming and its geography. The collection in Kashmiri is from the translator Sonam Kachru's forthcoming *Make Humans Again: Voices from Kashmir.* They represent, as the translator himself puts it, a mental climate of the place. Kashmir has been a place of great political turmoil and the poets here represent both sides of the politically fractured valley—Indian-, and Pakistan- claimed Kashmir. In a language where so much of the poetry is about the violence and turmoil of that place, I found Kachru's selection unique because he brought to attention poets whose work aims, as he puts it, "to show that Kashmir can function as a principle of poetry for Kashmiris, who write for Kashmiris, when Kashmir is not the only subject of their song."

Hindi is one of the most widely-spoken languages in India, with numerous poets doing very interesting work, most of which remains to be translated. For Hindi, I chose the poet-couple Rustam (Singh) and Teji Grover, and the young poet Vyomesh Shukla, translated by Rahul Soni, all of whom are at the center of a great effort to fortify contemporary poetry through translation, publication and international exchange. Grover, Singh and Soni have all been involved with the magazine *Pratlilipi,* home to some of the best contemporary writing in Hindi, and some of the finest translations from other Indian languages. Shukla is one of the finest poets writing in Hindi. Rustam and Teji Grover are also activists; they're environmentalists, interdisciplinary artists and translators of Norwegian poetry. They travel internationally and work closely with several poets in the country, and these different involvements influence their writing. Shukla, a much younger poet, lives in the small town of Varanasi, yet his work, like Grover and Rustam's work, is a marked departure from mainstream Hindi poetry. Sachin Ketkar, the poet I have chosen from Marathi, also lives in a small town, Badodra, but he has been instrumental, along with fellow poet Hemant Divate in making contemporary Marathi and Gujrati poetry available both in their original and in translation. These poets best represent the heart of a contemporary experimental poetry scene in India.

There are state-systems and then there are nomadic war machines. If Hindi and English constitute the language of the majority, functioning around the metropolis of Mumbai and New Delhi, then poets working in Kashmiri, Bhojpuri, Bengali, Assamese and Malayalam form nomadic groups that move around and navigate that majority. Always at war in order to retain one's own identity, these regional poets have managed to establish their own poetics that are markedly different than those in Hindi and English.

The two best examples of such would be the poetic communities working in Bengali and Malayalam, and I have included several poets from each language. Each one has a strong literary tradition to uphold and a strong local community that supports emerging new voices. Working away from the metropolis of New Delhi and Mumbai, the Bengali and Malayalam writers represented here cover a range of poets, most of them living in small towns in West Bengal and Kerala. Like their counterparts in Odisha, Assam, Tamil Nadu and states across the country, these poets strive to maintain what it means to be a part of a larger apparatus (of Indian poetry) and still maintain one's own identity and autonomy.

The Bengali selection represents a younger generation of poets such as Sanyal and Bandopadhyay who have found an audience and recognition, thanks to the support of an emerging, wider readership, both local and online. Aryanil Mukherjee, the primary translator of the Bengali section, is a poet based in America who writes in Bengali, and then transcreates the poems in English, breaking both linguistic and geographical boundaries. Most of the Malayalam poetry selected here is edited by the renowned poet K. Satchidanandan, who has consistently produced radical work in Malayalam and helped bring to the forefront emerging voices as well. Poets such as Sarju, Jayan, Raman and Rose Mary are a new generation of poets who work in different fields, artistic and other. They represent the range of creative work being produced in regional languages, just as the whole collection represents the range of poetics in Indian languages across the country and beyond.

The selection of Bhojpuri poems from the translator Rajiv Mohabir's collection A Veil You'll Cast Aside, also addresses the idea of physical and linguistic migration. These are folksongs that are as popular in India as they are in the Caribbean. Mohabir has given a contemporary avatar to folksongs that have transformed through the years and yet manage to maintain their musical force and cultural relevance. They recreate mythology, give poetic shape to ritualistic utterances that are still performed today. Because Indian literature has historically been an oral tradition, I wanted to include something that is also sung. These poems "make present" the ancient, the traditional. They are relics of an oral tradition that has survived centuries and transgressed boundaries to exist as a part of a culture's contemporary everyday practice.

I end with a small selection of Tamil poetry from two very important young Tamil poets, Malathi Maithri and Sukirtharani. Maithri grew up in a fishing community of strong, independent women. Determined to educate herself, she passed high school in spite of her parents opposition, worked in Auroville and is now a political activist working with human rights and environmental issues. Sukirtharani, a dalit poet who could barely afford to go to school, is very much an autodidact, a well-known poet now thanks to a chance encounter with poetry through small press literary "little" magazines several years ago. I would have liked to include many more women poets. The very small number of women poets I was able to include in this collection disheartens me. In a country where rape and violence against women is an everyday occurrence and where women live under unthinkable oppression, it is admirable that new young feminist voices are using poetry to express themselves and be heard. The issues they address through their poems are important, their concerns of utmost priority if India is to progress as a culture. While a majority of the poetry written in India by women takes these issues as their central theme, the poets represented here address these issues to differing degrees, always using language in new ways, be it the formal invention of Grover and Mahjuba or the perceptual inversions and word-play in Rose Mary, Maithri and Sukirtharani's work. I have covered seven languages in this dossier. That is barely a third of the many official languages and only a small fraction of the many languages alive in India today. For this I must apologize, as I must for the lack of women poets represented here. My search to bring focus to more experimental feminist poetry in regional languages continues. However, I do hope this fault of mine motivates people around the world to seek out these voices, to surpass the many barriers and help them be heard, for we cannot let their voices pass in silence.

— **Biswamit Dwibedy**

Bangalore, India, January 17, 2014

A Poetic Prelude

Chaman Lal Chaman

Translated from the Kashmiri by Sonam Kachru

And the poet Mahjoor knew him at once, and gathering him in
close embrace, said to the visionary company:
"He was to be the guide of us all, words his kin, his mouth
the wellspring of cascading speech."

Then the Teacher of the World arose and drawing his hand
over Nadim's face, bade him be seated near him, and asked:
"Are the lights still lit to burn on the day the river was born?
Do flowers yet grow
on our houses thatched with mud and the bark of birch?
Is spring the same? Do the leaves of the Chinar remember all
their colors?"
    Nadim broke into a sweat:
      "The trees you planted in your time stand
     To this day: but they are as blades of grass
     Lost in thick fog."

Being a Fragment on the Poet Nadim's Arrival in Heaven from *Nadim Nazrana*
by Chaman Lal Chaman, offered here as a fable of Poetry in Modern Kashmiri

Night's Triptych

Dina Nath Nadim

Translated from the Kashmiri by Sonam Kachru

Night   obscured sighs

  The moon   a cold hearth

    The cold   needlefine

  The shade   Mutable mist   The garden   A head, bared

  Beds   of flowers   Skin, leathered

  The orchard   A flock of birds in the grip of grief

  Long   The mortal road Tall maples the bones in this room

    Nests   moth-eaten   The crow   a stain indelible

Night   pregnant message

  The moon   congealed pus

    The cold   breath brittle

  Expectations Smoke in sleep stirring The dark A close sky foreboding

  Mountains   Swell of love   Unyielding What lasting is hidden

  A Clue This stillwater deep Desire   A knotted riddle

    A Cry The soft strangling Languor The sudden serpent's bite

Night   a fairy tale

      The moon   warm light soft to the touch

           The cold   whitesparks in new fire

     A dream   Kohl brightened eyes   Life   breath loaned;

     Death   The abrupt dive of a hunting kestrel   Tears   Warm consolation

     Hope   A stoneriver of hail   Spring   Greensweet hope

A flower   Composure   The cock's crow   Opaque envelope of morning

Untitled

It came to pass that time came to rest
On a picture: and the bold, green lines
Grew long, and there was a forest.
He who took the road through
Found home—and there was breath.
Where is the forest? What place, mind?

*

It was love: when the highest branch
Was shaken in first light and could see
The far shadows it cast to the ground.
Though after it grew to face the close sky,
Its heart was given entire to the broad earth.
And when the wind came it tasted of pain.

*

Through fields I knew a path to go
A long way until it came to rest
By water. To the other shore, however,
From a far village, men paved a road.
Now across the stream short messages are sent
While the waters shudder and gibber under,
Overhearing the news of men on either shore.

*

A little of the broken mirror still glittered
From where it lay under the refuse and cut-grass.
A cow passed by without looking at it; and a dog
Stopped long enough to sniff, clouding it with air.
A crazed woman was next, and she stooped to it,
Wrapping the broken glass in folds she made of her rags.
None here know what became of the mirror after.

*

A vessel that drops of rain have loved can look you in the face
like the face of a woman with a face like water,
whose sins, like the surfaces of water, are etched clean by rain.
But someone was here, and has broken the vessel. Its pieces
  are everywhere. Two days on, the children will come, and
  play with what pieces they find.
It is said that there are only two and a half steps to heaven
  from hell

Two Poems

Abdul Rahman Rahi

Translated from the Kashmiri by Sonam Kachru

took flight—

> patience, a cup, spills over.
>   They hid
> in a cave
>   one hundred years under
>
> sleep: dreamfathomed.
>
> And the lightsleepers?
>
> The dog,
> unblinking
> time,
> overtook Decius
>
> and the cave—waste
> of dream
>   of dark
>   cobwebbed—
>
> the cave is dragonhoard.

Mood

The fog—
       Outside—
              The silence,
                     And cold.
There is not a rag to wrap naked trees.
       Mud walls beg, surround me.

I have seen grey ash in the oven
And I have stood by a window
Without fire, shadow-spurred
 To ask the lengthening road —
Where are you going?
       Won't you take me with you?

— There was fog and silence and cold.

I sat back down again
by a corner in the granary.

A Request

Moti Lal Saqi

Translated from the Kashmiri by Sonam Kachru

You

    Who bear the flute,

Inclined

    To lie

By Gunpowder

    Hills,

Strike up

    A mood,

Attune us

    To rain

To the wet earth

Colors,

Win for us

    A smile

From blueblanked

    Skies.

We are

These many generations

On fire.

You

       Who

              Play

                    The flute,

The relief I crave

Is not

At home

In all that is the case,

My body kindling

To fire

More intimate

Fires.

You

       Who bear the flute,

I pray—

       This palette dulls

       To dusk's ends,

        Do not

Play

        Time's fool,

Do not

        Strike up

A mood,

        Attune us

No more

        to the burning

Colors,

        To new

Fire.

Come Into View

Rosul Pompur

Translated from the Kashmiri by Sonam Kachru

In time,

       Passage—

Inside of rock

There will come

Into view:

Waterfalls,

Blossoms

At roots.

Past sand,

The waters,

Feet and sail—

To not waste this day,

Or the next,

To keep heart.

Do not stir

Your conscience

Awake;

Heaped, the ash

Shall come next

In view:

At one

With fire

Of Chinars.

Time's hand

Is grown illegible:

I cannot make

A word of it—

Dwell and too long,

And the shades will pass you by.

They say "He was,

Is,

And will endure"—but you,

You have let yourself go

Unto ruin,

        and the magic plays

Out, to fade.

Two Poems

Akthar Mohiuddin

Translated from the Kashmiri by Sonam Kachru

New Disease

He's out of his mind, I said.
He will get to his house and then not walk through the door. He will just stand
there, as if in queue,
sometimes for over an hour: he stands
there, waiting for who knows what; and then,
he will not enter. But turns at last his back
to his door, if you please, and turning, softly walks away.

No, no, no, he said, there has been some change for the better. He has been to
the doctor.

And what did the doctor do?

He said that as soon as the patient returns home
someone ought to perform a search of his person. Then one must wait
to see whether he will enter his house, or, even
walk through the gate.

TRANSLATOR'S NOTE

Nav Byamar—there is no way to capture the manner in which this title, with its two words, and three stress cadence, rudely echoes and refuses a title beloved of so many authors before, in what must seem today, but was not necessarily so, a happier time, time when it was possible still to hope for 'new Spring' (*Nav Bahaar*). (I stress, however, that Nadim already spoke in the fifties of refusing to sing of new spring, youth or idle dreams of one's first, wild longings). Now, no 'New Spring' any longer, but 'A New Disease'. The choice of articles is always a burden for the translator when the source languages have none. I have chosen the indefinite. A vain hope that the condition is not a true disease distinctly its own.

And they did, just as the doctor prescribed; and now
he will enter. The doctor said that ever since
we have had searches performed on us
at every possible door, outside every possible gate,
this new disease has proven catching.
Some are even compelled, he said
to perform a search of themselves
before they can walk through gates,
            any gate,
                        or enter a house,
                                    any house.

Terroriste

Old Mother Dearest was walking home along an alley when there before her a patrol walked in; and even as little Shafiq saw the soldiers, he started to cry. He lay down; he rolled around; he tugged at his mother's sleeve; and would not be moved.

The officer thought: "the moment their children get a glimpse of us they start in fright." He said to the boy not ungently: "Not to be scared, mein Junge."

Old Mother Dearest replied as best she could: "What 'scared'? He cries because he wants to hold your pistol. Er sagting 'gib me deine pistol'."

The officer started and fell silent. He was silent a while, and his teeth were clenched.

"Verdammt Terroriste," he spat out in the end and hurried his patrol past.

TRANSLATOR'S NOTES

The original narrative is, of course, in Kashmiri, but employs a highly skilled use of an argot of Kashmiri-inflected Hindustani in the desperate, proud speech of the mother to the officer, who speaks Hindustani and not Kashmiri, though nevertheless attempts it when consoling the boy, betraying his situation only by his term of endearment, a reflex of his native language. I have attempted to convey the effect with German, and German spoken poorly by someone used to English, respectively. I chose these two languages because of their etymological kinship evident in the verb 'to give'. Hindustani and Kashmiri share a root for the verb to give from the Sansrkit '*da⁻*' as well, and it is the most important verb, I feel, in this tale of these distant, yet related, langauges and speakers in the original.

To render the effect consistent, I have replaced 'Kashmiri', which qualifies 'children', with 'their', in the officer's thought that the children are scared of them. The imprecation in the original is in a third language, English, alien and so common to both: "Terrorist Bastard!" I have tried to suggest the effect by allowing 'terrorist' in a stranger garb to stand in for a word alien and yet that might become common to both languages. It goes without saying that you would know everything you need to know about these people from the texture of their language. And that is an effect I have not been able to convincingly bring across—for it creates a surreal effect in translation and a forbidding abstraction (inviting thoughts of counter-factual histories), which the original does not intend. It does not invent, but documents the unhappy condition called 'normalcy' in political, journalistic speech: and what it suggests, by way of literary effect, it suggests under the sign of a grim, ironic, feelingly considered recognition of how things really stand.

A Snow-Wind

Fatima Mahjuba

Translated from the Kashmiri by Sonam Kachru

On a day not unlike today, or any other

In a season not dissimilar, in an hour

Not quite unfamiliar—

    A snow-wind bucked

Like a deer:

    Unstill, now here, and then again

There:

    The noise of its breath was fear

'Til a hand—my hand,

    At contact—our touch—

Was a step

    back into quiet.

A snow-wind was here

A little like filaments of light

A traveler who has fore-suffered

The sun, burnt in unrelieved heat,

Could not be more pleased to see:

The Light threshed

Through a willow-bound grove

Under a cloud-closer sky.

And then I was seen

His road obscured,

And the season—and still,

The snow-wind swept.

O Fatima,

Are you scabbed yet

in the scathing wind?

Don't open up your wounds, nor list your sorrows

Yet—It is madness,

All.

Eight Poems

Rustam

Translated from the Hindi by Rustam and Teji Grover

On the white stone

In this image of

'the black stone on the white stone'

which I have just now read

or in that image of

the white stone on the black stone

which I have just now crafted

'dies a thousand deaths'

the light which captures its life

or the hand which holds this light in place.

Restless life in imagination

Discontent

the rose

grows

without the memories of past lives

In the transparent mirror

the transparent tear

is held up

on the edge of the transparent eye

The shadow

looks at its own shadow

Is almost real

Almost

alive

Once again you are in the mirror

Once again

you are in the mirror

Once again I shatter you

in the liquid body of the mirror

The body

is shattered too

and

in the cracked mirror

is liquid

I have to think with great patience

I have to think with great patience

about the fact that you are nowhere, the fact that you will

    not turn up.

You are not there, you will not visit me—I have to let this

knowledge simmer in the pot

with great patience,

I have to let it turn into a liquid I can savour.

Then I have to

let the liquid

settle into my soul,

slowly,

with great patience.

Inside the brown rock

Inside the brown rock

Inside the brown red rock

Inside the red green rock

Inside the green blue rock

brown red green blue

yellow sun was

fashioning itself

in which there was a

thousand-coloured rock

which in the beginning

appeared to be only brown

and had stung me

Translated from the Hindi by Teji Grover

Images

Images

tire even of me

and

of being images

Surely

their patience has a limit

for this insolent stranger

Surely

they dream

of another world

in which they are suffixes

Then

they dream

of not being suffixes

either.

In the mirror you're not

In the mirror you're not

the mirror

in my imagination

Black leaf

green flower

a drop of snow on blood

eyes that are clear and stone, a thing

                        out of

                        this world

Then eyes that are clear and stone, a thing

                        out of

                        this world

                        and within it

the mirror

that's now blank

            and pure.

The rock

The rock

was turning into fire

which was already fire and

looked like rock

among many other rocks

which were already fire and

looked like rocks   in a way that

among many fire-like rocks

at many a place

rock-like fire

was burning

Three Poems

Teji Grover

Translated by the author

Untitled

I must avoid writing earth in my poems

— **Miranhshah**

It's not that you don't feel at home anywhere, or you haven't got roots anywhere. Nowhere does loneliness ever leave you. It's just the opposite. You feel at home everywhere. You've got roots everywhere. Everywhere, there's closeness, affection, companionship.

On this planet filled with intimacy, who can I tell that it's like this ...

Who's going to believe me?

(With/Without A Poem)

At the hoodwink-doorstep to the mind
what at this moment waits there
this drop
that pools with its desire to drench
let's call it Sambari[1]
let's see
what'll happen, if we do say it.

OK then, let's say, Sambari
Let's see
if the fruit juicens instantly, or not
greenlings ripen in the sunlight
right up to the point of deception, or not.

Say!
Sambari
dew-fed
droplet
wandress
will you make me end up sobbing
to the point of doubt
and delusion in love?

You
who fills cucumbers with inconsolable froth[2]
and then, on your own, stops dead
at the peaceful taste of evanescent sweetness.

Sambari, Oh Sambari!
like a rabid dog
stops in its tracks just before the bite

NOTES

1 Sambari : Benign sorceress.
2 Refers to the foam or froth which is forced to emerge from a cucumber
   when one rubs a thin slice from the blossom-end in a circular motion
   against its cut edge; this is done ostensibly to remove any bitterness.

glimpsing the morning of infancy
in a pup's dew-like eyes
silenced
like the taste in cucumber.

Are you listening, Sambari?

From fruit to cucumber, from there
dog and silence
The image, panting, goes on changing
and still, the spirit, unable to thaw
do you see how bitter this is?
So sad
that to call it sad
is the desire to drown in the river.

Sambari
Ah!
Sambari
openhanded sister of uncertain hour
you're drying up already,
aren't you?

How can I tell you what'll come out of the blue in the end
—What dissembling to be gone through
How drowned in incense smoke
How drowned in pleasure

What *lilas* of doom will be played out forever
here
where the drop vanishes into thin air.

The Last Love of a Dramatic Woman: In Four Prose Scene Songs

SCENE 1:

Time: A morning four years after Amana's death.
Place: The foyer of Amana's husband's house
Characters: Amana's children
                      Amana's make-believe presence in place of dust-motes in
                                                                                                      a sunbeam
                      Amana's husband who's never on stage
                      The woman

It's seven o'clock.
The curtain in this room has risen, Amana.
Let's imagine you're here in the room
In the place of dust-motes in the make-believe sunbeams
                  the un-dead
                  A—mana
                  is here

And this being here is welcome.

Your children are home, and you see a woman there, too.
Your husband is making her tea.

So early in the morning
the little yellow butterflies are already worn out.
In the fragrance, their wings are heavy
but light too like a strand of thought

The children playing houses in sand
draw lines in water
Their feet are cold, Amana
The woman's there only speaking your own thoughts aloud

This being here is welcome.

This is not the month of rain that the cloud must put on a show,
Even so, like a novice, she helps your children on with their shoes.

How effortless, their hands on her shoulder.
How fine, wholesome.
How complete this picture is
How inevitable this morning, like a splash of color descending a few
                                                            steps

In her mind, she kisses your husband's eyes with her tears.

At seven in the morning which ancestors does she beg for love

Over what bridge did you come
Over what bridge did she

One is death, one a great love.
You came, chatting away like sisters
from far away,
as if from the same land.

In the rays of the sun, in the place of dust-motes
            un-dead
            A-mana

The scent of tea wafts in the air
            and look—
an inkling of love has crossed the stage

Can it be called one of the characters

SCENE II:

Characters: He who is never onstage speaks out in the woman's dream about his wife Amana.

The woman sleeping near the wall.

He (in her dream):
> My children are only the relics of her not being there
> For me, every child on earth is an echo of her not being there
> Every woman is a seed lodged in her not being there.
>
> Tell me,
> can I sow this or can't I?
> *(Suddenly, in sleep, the woman's head bangs up against the wall)*

Woman:
> In his dream he has banged my head up against the wall
>
> This man, he who is never onstage, has banged my head full of his dream.
>
> Can I lay it in your lap and sleep
> Can I tell your children a story
> Don't you think this stage is just the right place to die
>
> This stage, that has appeared for me
> right through the aisle
> of your grieving

SCENE III:

Time: An evening long after the morning in the first scene.
Place: The living room of Amana's husband and their children.
Characters: The woman in an almost black costume
               A blue envelope in the middle of papers scattered on the table

The woman comes, and sees that there's no one there. She's already learned that there's no difference between being and not-being. That being sits like a seed in not-being. That this way, parting is illusionary. In the mind, you can go on kissing those eyes, with all those tears, go on begging love from your ancestors, and finding it all, then it's like the message in that blue envelope which lies there in the light from the lamp. She knows everyone knows what is bound to be written there. She knows that even so, the words of this message will be something new, that she'll fall into a faint from the unique texture of the words.

Like the poor, she weighs these things in her mind. The hypnotic spell of words on the one hand, the withering away of love on the other; and even so, she lifts the envelope, brushing the fine paper against her cheek and eyelashes, tosses it onto the table as if before its time she were breathing out her very life.

To her it seems those children's books are falling apart.
To her it seems she should mend them.

To her it seems the windows are closed.
To her it seems the mirror is coated with Amana's dust.
To her it seems the universe won't rise or set.

She suddenly goes out of the room
stopping at the threshold, knocks at the door
For a moment she thinks maybe those people are still inside
Maybe she has read the signs of the end all wrong.

Hard for her to believe
that she stopped on the threshold to try and remember his face
Hard for her to believe
that she touches her own face trying to remember his.
Hard for her to believe
that death could ever take this form
to get some sense of love, you end up touching your own cheek.

She starts running towards the oncoming night.
Her almost-black costume raging like a storm,

Dogs bark at the ripples in the falling curtain.

She turns in the direction of the bridge.
Those viewing the stage know the name of this bridge.

To her turning in the direction of the bridge,
it doesn't seem as if she's turning

Place: The bridge

Against the railing of the bridge that black costume leans like a hollow statue. From a distance, you can't tell if there's someone there in the robe or not. Up close, you can't tell if there's anyone there or not.

In the sudden stilling of the storm robe, the folds in layers, as if the last pangs of labor had been halted in mid-thrust.

Look into the water, and the waves won't tell.

Five Poems

Vyomesh Shukla

Translated from the Hindi by Rahul Soni

On the Wall

circular, oblique, wavering
going in all possible directions and angles
or returning from there
shapes that have emerged from the nucleus of childhood mischief

even well-behaved kids become devils while writing on a wall

phrases from the lexicon of slightly older children
like 'Rama is a ghost,' etc.
traces of turmeric, tea and pious past deeds
arcane abstractions at every step
where one wild animal runs
a second screams a third lies down
unconnected compositions

the cries of an utterly white wall
are present in the noise of this scarred and spattered wall
grease, Mobil, coal tar and some other such suspect stains
whose origins whose reasons cannot be gauged
phlegm sweat piss shit semen and betel juice stains
flaking plaster moss going from green to black

a laidback poet sat in the shade of this wall
sitting right here he wrote
that some poet sat in the shade of some wall

What I Wanted to Write

the eye and the invisible are related
I've felt that all scenes occur
drawing a curtain over the invisible
whatever wasn't seen is all in the scene
and can't be seen

Vijay the motorcycle mechanic's shop is open on Saturday
and in its being open the shop's being closed on Sunday
wasn't visible but its being open on Monday was

the opposite of this happened on a holiday
the shop was closed
but in the vision of its being closed the shop was invisibly open
and who knows why people
were happily getting their motorcycles repaired that day
I only have a beat-up scooter not a motorcycle
but I too was getting a Bajaj Pulsar repaired as I smoked a cigarette

unsettled by the invisible I walked into the visible
and started asking a friend about this shop
so he said he'd been thinking a lot
about the shop today who knows he may even have been smoking
half my cigarette in the shop open in his memory

coming home I thought Pondicherry I've never been there
its entire architecture I told myself
lies behind the sound of the word Pondicherry
but it's there for sure

then I wanted to write a sentence
in writing intent is invisible words visible
the shapes of the words are here
but what I wanted to say is nowhere to be found
perhaps it's behind the curtain of the sentence
it isn't it is
it's not at all what I did not want to write

The Boy

all that can be said is that the boy has gone into the balloon now but
it's hard to live there shunning the world
for eating bathing sleeping loving
even the boy has to return to the world

the boy's portrait, if anyone should make it, can only be made in black
he keeps the other colors in the balloon now
it's there that he will put on makeup for his Hamlet Hori Ghasiram
there's great poverty here the company's curtains are soiled and wounded
Hanuman runs a coaching center by day a bhang shop by night
Hori is in debt again
and this time he should kill himself
some irrelevant old unsuccessful faces say without being asked that
a long time ago the boy used to play Hori's part or someone else used to play it
amidst all this he was telling me something one day or asking me for money
the unsuccessful people remember or don't remember
the boy told me something or didn't tell me
the theater is trouble you have to burn your house to feed it

spectators come or don't come
don't come or don't come

Bhartendu's stage is on fire people panic and run in English
seeing this the boy stuffs tobacco into his portrait's mouth and disappears
he's always been a spendthrift now he spends his breath blowing up balloons
he had a good voice he fills up the game of balloons with his ragas
children fly Yaman Ahir Bhairav Tilak Kamod in their part of the game
there's too much time and too little of the boy
persisting in the habit of breathing
singing

Whom will the Country Never Forgive

our sleep uses roots for pillows
and dreams like trees
I consider my city my river very old
and others' cities others' rivers mine

outside dreams on the riverbank smoke rises incessantly
an old man playing the shehnai rested his head on a step of the ghats and
    fell asleep
his sleep used stones for pillows
and dreamt of rivers
his shehnai sang songs of water
music rained on the country
and the fires went out

mother tells me everything is on fire now
the river's on fire the city's burning
sleep rains from our eyes like fire
our world is defeated and full of venom
and people look at people with suspicion born of unfamiliarity

now home is not for friends but for relatives
fattened they come tumbling down the slope of happiness
girls haven't been getting wed since forever
and love for them is not a democratic right but an underground activity

you can't draw a map of your city
because the city's changing faster than even you
and maps are made across the seven seas
at such times, some blunt words tend to be written or spoken
about unexpected occurrences
such as, 'the country will never forgive the heinous acts of terrorists'

The New

(Remembering a jugalbandi by the
renowned percussionist Kishan Maharaj)

in a proud arrogance
the margin will ring out like the mainstream
people will think it is the center of power of beauty
the center will look on respectfully
it will be assumed that things are changing
many old lines will break in these moments
the configuration of many things will be rethought
a new understanding will now be required

Three Poems

Sachin Ketkar

Translated from the Marathi by the author

Significance of the Mosquito Net

A net to entrap humans

We drift towards it
Trying to save our skins
From mosquitoes
Its maniac probing
Ensnares us

Mosquitoes make an aerial survey
Like our political leaders
And discover the way to our blood

When I stretch out in the net
A lush green bonsai banyan
Grows from my mouth

Tube-light filters through the sieve
A ceiling-fan air
Breathes silently
I sleep
In the shade of the bonsai

My subtle body
Struggles to escape
The sieve

In the darkness of night
Arrives the impish mutant spider
Weaving this World Wide Web

My subtle digital body
Has already escaped
Having been filtered
By the mosquito net

Preliminary Lessons in Cheirology

I)

Walking alone and aimless
On the deserted streets
Of the lines on my palm

I watch
The automatic shoes on my feet
Taking me along with them

II)

My fifty thousand male fingers
Rise erect
But a bit late

Like a submerged river
My ambiguous Line of Destiny
Runs over
The mount of Apollo
Over the geographical map
Of your body

III)

I walk all alone
Over the blue desert palm of the sky
On the trail of the Line of Head
Over the Mount of the Eclipsed Moon

There I gather
The hollow skulls of words
And blow them like conch shells

IV)

In the train that goes
Over the tracks of the lines of my palm

A night with pitch black eyes
Stares at me
With wide open eyes
From the window

When she closes her eyes
I caress her
Wet eyelids

Then I take her palm in mine

And tell her fortune

A Hymn to be Chanted at the Time of Rebirth

With the mysterious laser saw
Of my breath
I want to hack
The dire eclipsed banyan
As its seismic cyanide aerial roots
Penetrate every speck
Of my salvation-seeking soil.
In that opened space
I want to sow
The ejaculated sperm of the sun
The radioactive egg
Of the chicken-eating moon
I want to take harvest
Of poems
Which are purposeless
But having golden wombs.

Then I will have the luscious red fruits
Of the intense desire of bats
To be absorbed in the sun,
Of the taste of flesh,
Of the Eucharist lust for blood,
Of the desire to pluck
The white mushrooms of Time
Grown on the damp rotten wood
Of my lungs,
Of the blanched dreams
Of turning into the bleached cranes
Flying away from these wilds.

I want to transmigrate
To my own body.
I want to draw cryptic good swastikas
On every iota
Of the world's body
On every moment
Of the every world
On my body.

I want to kill
The old mahut
Who rides the diaphanous backs
Of the vanished rivers
Since he prods
With his desiccated goad
Concealed in his loin cloth
The blue thousand-petalled-lotus
Of the disappeared rivers
And blows out
The orphic eyes
Of the invisible rivers.

I want to wipe off
The tales of the non-self
Of the graveyard night
Scribbled in Chinese
On my Yorick skull.

I have resolved
I, by all odds, don't want to become
The headless aghori
Wandering dressed in night
With a beautiful useless trident in my hand
Wandering around with an inventory of unsolved questions
Written on my skull.

I surely don't want to become
An *aghori* baobab tree
Vulturing near the naked corpse
Of the paddy field
Which sits up with raised ears
At the slightest noise.
The salivating cadaver of grainfield
Drooling with its pink tongue.

Therefore I want to perform
The ravenous austerities
To appease the occult sun
Concealed deep inside the womb of earth
And the occult earth
Concealed deep inside
The womb of the sun.

After cremating
The carcass of God
In the laser crematory
Of my breath
I want to worship
The active godhead
Of the famished cosmos
I want to fly away
Transmuted into a bunch of perfumed aureate butterflies
When the silken winds blow.

Three Poems

Pronob Pal

Translated from the Bengali by Aryanil Mukherjee

The Falsity of Language

Blossoming sculpcolor. The falsity of a language that was meant to demythify. Expansion hollow. Blue filling the blanks of an extended truth. No stoppageade no stationation, only desolating emptily hands. Essay of head descending to feet feather. Crimps of earth opening to croppety milking rice. Transmitting symphony grain by grain. Materialis goes waterating in the high drain. Weaving inflation finger to finger a nonchalant extension treads uncontinuously. Print it or mint it, open the landscape in its house. The altered *Baul* is unerred, actually vacationing.

TRANSLATOR'S NOTE

Baul—The spiritual nomad-minstrels or bards of Bengal

Poetrariet

In the traffic signal of picture writing finger, a magic of sky. Going over the fragments of a fractured moon seamed wavily to its light. Glitterati laced on the frills of fullmoon. The green turbulence of returning songs in abscondic brain. In atomic splinters, I destroy bits of momenthome. The plurals of an open reindeering me and its possibilities. Sleeppen speakatoo, the sun on clock wings, distracting shenanigans of written shadows.

Brushfires tresspassing on chessboard. Euphoric body language of a mannered *anchal*. How far is afar! In the indolent camps, the whispwind of poetrariet in Mrs. empty now. Walk feet before me, leading a headathon. In the empty hour of a mystic afternoon, night feels like an antonymic myth of cooked lies. Hand copying the mechanics of head. A slice of greening Youland, as the last bornvictor of all greynessing defeatist humans.

TRANSLATOR'S NOTE

Anchal—The portion of the saree that wraps the upper torso

Fogville

Loverinas candlecarved. Over grimaced words in a sorrowed war. Pettyvilles go back, sexy moontango hanging from the multiplex, awards and friendly delicatelier. The boytrain of running girls merrily on track. Earth wetting in station dew before the hilltunnel deglutition. Gurgling cobblestones open mineral lexicons in the waterexcite of Ms. Mindvine.

Rockdecade hands, undeterred, follow friendly rules. Engraved periods without reincarnation, life's lushroom melted by vibrating pendulums. A melting solestar therm, in one madworld of lovable fogville.

Vigo's Song
(in part)

Sabyasachi Sanyal

Translated from the Bengali by the author

Bitter man, bitter man

This is where we stop
Bitter man, the snow'll wash you off

So the world has moved on
Leaving its fallacies dry
What are you without them
An image forever wry

Bitter man, bitter man
Here the feather will drop
Bitter man, the snow'll write you off

(Vigo's song)*

—

So it's winter where Vigo went down
On his haunches
A still aroma of a repressed trigger is all that's going to remain

White walls, a white street, white waters and a distant enamel
ship
We claimed that we could talk, but no sounds came out
The glass rattled, whisky sloshed
A feather dropped and detonated
Smokes and mirrors

Wish you were here to witness my absence
From all those that mattered
Wish I were as well ...

—

Your suddenness and repetitions
are the few things I have come to like

Removing gravity from a lump of metal
Requests, imploring … etc … immaterial miniscules … anything … everything … al …
Time speeding along the tree line
Hesitations stumbling after it—
these are what I can call my own—an owning, a vulnerability that you fail to part with
How could I castrate my obligations to myself?
And my subordinate complexities

Think, someday our eastern hearts too would be easily digestible
In a jelly-jar filled with brine
Even our stories, our generation's headaches
will be displayed
How can I not feel good about this … all this?

*(Who is this Vigo?
Vigo is a barrier, kind of a dwarf-demon
Whose shadow eats dirt and grows under the abandoned bridge
and his body toils in salt-mines of Sumatra, Madrid
Dreams of a legitimate snowstorm rising somewhere in the north
His are the sorrows
that sit with our shadows
and watch how they crack-up laughing … lighting penumbras)

I'll bite your tongue off you fuckwit if you tag this work as surrealism.

Anyways
Oh my tales, Oh my genre headaches
Are we basically the meowings of a starved cat
loitering beside a fish-curry-recipe
Symbols! Logos! you buggered fragrance
don't you have a language of your own?

Does the darkness speak of tangibility? When the ship sinks
Waves crash against the beach
The language of a catfish faced with a gutting knife
Sting-pains from barbs to finger-tips
What you know is just a cover up—a protocol of stratifying one pain with another
A color-blind explosion showering hell
On terse neurons

—

Get documented you fuck, become a theorema
Ride a raincab in a fucking desert
Crawl up the gypsy frocks, crawl up their tattoos
Cry out loud like the conscience of a snake, loud moans
of moonshine fucking, empty the horn
Stir fry me in a wok,
Spice me up with ginger, sage
Dip your bread and banjo in the goulash
Celebrate, celebrate my fucked-up tangibility ...

Your suddenness and repetitions
are the few things that I have come to like

And I am not just a redneck about love
I know the precise—where to put the pillow while making love
Those who live in vineyards
still hum while sucking crab shells
soak their wounded fingers in lemon juice
when there is not much of anything
not much of a house, a home
no car beside the reverberating honk
in an irritated parking lot,
returning from the graveyard of dear ones
battery down
as if the news of the ship came
A loneliness starts gyrating within our shells
All our concerns about tears
bookshelves covered in cobwebs
complexities of snow-covered houses

—

People who suffer wounds
are the ones who talk about past
reinstall them in a future
bellbottom pants sweeping the city
sailor caps from yonder
in the city of deserts

Our shadows will attack our shadows
That's the only reality I believe in
I still await a penance
looking at a humorless light
I like to believe good times for all ...

—

Bitter man, bitter man
It's a life not to be
Bitter man, we'll sail off to the sea

So the world has moved on
And its songs turned to dirt
Oh what are you without songs
Merely a withering gust

Bitter man, bitter man
Here the feather will drop
Bitter man, the wind will dust you off

(Vigo's song)**

So this is the summer where Vigo went down
on his haunches
A still aroma of lavender is all that's going to remain

Green fumes emanating from meadows, a green balustrade
mosses gather on marble tombstones
The glass rattles, whisky sloshes
green detonates, it rains green ...

It's a life we all wanted
It's a life we're never going to live

Wish you were here to witness my absence
from all that mattered
Wish I were as well ...

—

Your suddenness and repetitions
are the few things that I have come to like

I like people who turn blind
when they visit nature
Distance becomes a mountain
where depressions get horded
The grasping tiredness when fishing gets over
After the anticipation is rolled-up and towed

**(Who is this Vigo ?
Vigo is a beyondness, a demon-dwarf
whose minty shadow hangs out in butcher shops
snatches entrails from hogs
makes aberrant sausages
His body sweats in the coal-mines of Borneo, Dublin
and dreams of a tangible desert within a penumbra of rainforests
It's his sorrows that taught us to measure
the quicksand of clock)

So, this is the mango grove ... this is its limitations
and this is the cat that defines the limit
so what're your worries about not having a door somewhere?
I open the windows—call-out the cat's dreams
Call out the fears of the birds living here
put my hunger under lock & key
suspended in a void
I have always had a house
my house has never been good ...

Even after all this you cast away my sarcasm
grabbing a pair of subjective balls
you try to inspire me to be comprehensible
An inspired mango grove
worried about the silent wanderings of a limiting

Your suddenness and repetitions ...
return

History of Indian Literature

Subhro Bandopadhyay

Translated from the Bengali by Aryanil Mukherjee

1

So much so following which I'll lay down beside pain and the stained sunbeams will alight on me I clearly understand it's my head that tries to deny that ancient constellation which, by the way, is conjuring up, and the archaic span of our language pioneers, where *Faiz Ahmed Faiz* writes—*wheatish fragrance of my beloved*, ah! how much love can sustain in conflict, in competition the trembling leaf, the sweet press of soft hands so longingly prolonged, and the archaic span of our language opening up, its devotional music—its *kirtan*, *kheur*, touring the city, as if we are sitting in front of a freshly invented heap, some scavenger digs out his long-lost stained blanket, cannot come any closer to the antiquated rusted pain I lie down flat on my back and watch the flight of old friends, those good old poetry bookcovers, good old days of street rallies, and I certainly knew that around the pond outside, a root anchors, although trunk missing and the entire tree seems hollow, lying beside the heap.

Next, some more people come along again digging; pressed under the weight of expectations; on the greater blackboard a less greater chalk making impressions, and now we move to the side to notice that those empty branches are no longer vacant, as though we have not looked at it with enough attention, branches of the non-empty roots stand upright yet shaking, and on each branch glistens unused words—of a near-extinct hunter and the claws of birds; on the side our monogamous selves opening their jaws wide, saved genitals, intoxicated by the odor of a pet climate, the sticking onto the tongues of fashioned scavengers, coming to dig in winter, carrying ornate flasks of warmth where shadows begin to accumulate.

And we are stalled, the carriage not listening to the brakes on an unmended road, the ambition collapses, some professors have mulled—*I have trodden this path over and over*, but there's no point, the zeal has faded, and with it the weight of our dreamless heads of days and months, and a saffron-coloured horseman goes by, we are surrounded by a group of people strangely robed, the survey continues, of our land, somebody just chopped off the head of a poisonous snake which had advanced, to entwine and lie around the bamboo shoots, as if metal pellets are flung towards a flock of *munias*.

Ah how beautiful this cluster of black alphabets, oh where are you wanderer, yet let my doors be open wide, ah how wonderful is this silence, and my marrow immersed in the intense fossils of white page, all my books remain open, all that I have written, all that I want to write for posterity, and how brightly lit, how whitely illuminated my death on these pages, but did I write all this! I didn't want to, merely an all-pervading silence

And in the meanwhile from within this medley someone writes a letter so much silence is undesirable; quietly eating into the blued body of dawn to open eye-lids higher above silence flapping against the Gothic tower—one who sat with a predilection for rain, could not even imagine—the temptation of strange words bringing blue sand pine trees to scrape the body of language, reincarnations of 15th century, cacti burning nearby, in sleeplessness

And we are now dismantling this heap, its dust and stone, a new fighter plane encircling above, its thoughtless brain, and songs of the 20th century bringing out their fervour, Kolkata of rallies and tram-cars, all sorts of poetry, their indelible marks, the lonely boy covering up the heap again

Asking for silence is in actuality asking for alphabets, a language calm, long stretch of November moonlight falling on a sprawling field, and a few rickshaw-pullers and their wives playing cards in the corner after a round of daily chores, hidden in half-darkness a cluster of black alphabets come to gather around them, with a dryness retained through ages, with everlasting gaps

TRANSLATOR'S NOTES

Faiz Ahmad Faiz—20th century Pakistani lyric poet
kirtan—Hindu devotional songs
kheur—Parody-songs performed in 19th century Bengali theatre
I have trodden this path over and over—A line from a popular Tagore song/poem.
Munia—A variety of Tiger Finch found in Bengal, multi-colored

No longer is Ayan Rashid the lonely reader of Ghalib's poetry, Suman, too, has arrived in the Lodi Garden few dimmed songs in the interior of a gaping brain, past Puja and Id, ragpickers arrive at Metiabruz to lift heaps of cloth-shreds, their frolicking children, hiding inside the heaps, Darbeshbaba to arrive any minute, he needs those shreds to hide the color of his black garb and the children will pounce at the lure of baataashaa

in fact many a times I have myself taken Ghalib into the long, mysterious hairs of our rustic womenfolk, into the secret of their red ribbons and mustard oil and there their intrinsic rivers are on the verge of an overflow, a letter from Hason Raza goes by proclaiming—why did [you] leave [me] behind now at sea

alone Ghalib sits forlorn, his listless hand on my shoulder, perhaps a little calmer inside from the passage of time, *if love didn't breed melancholia, work would have brought the suffering for sure*

upon translating this line, Abu Syed Ayub shuddered, Gauri, his wife, has gone out, Kolkatan darkness of evening 8 pm in the early 1970s

TRANSLATOR'S NOTES

Ayan Rashid—Ayan Rashid Khan, Urdu litterateur and auteur, lover of Mirza Ghalib's poetry
Mirza Ghalib—One of the greatest 19th century Indian (Urdu) poet
Suman—Kabir Suman, contemporary Bengali retro-modern singer
Metiabruz—A predominantly Muslim settlement of seamsters near Kolkata
Darbeshbaba—A Muslim peer
Puja—Durga Puja, five day Bengali Hindu festival (worship of Goddess Durga) celebrating harvest, peace and prosperity.
Id—EId-Ul-Fitr, Muslim religious festival signifying fast-breaking.
baataashaa—cheap sugar candy offered to the gods/deities first in prayer and then distributed to the people
Hason Raza—Early 20th century Bangladeshi folk poet
Abu Syed Ayub—A Bengali Muslim literary scholar, professor, translated Mirza Ghalib from Urdu
Gauri—Ayub's Hindu wife

3

There's always a railway track over and above pain on its side and a hand spread out to a heavy goods train passing by and with a gradual sprawl of paddy fields on both sides, the goods train at the centre, slowly softly approaching zero, halting at a prolonged red signal now gone defunct in the rain, the driver comes out yielding to it from head to waist

And nearby, the tribal woman sits with her little girl inside the barber shop, nose-pin of golden metal bulging out on her blunt black nose, fragmented sunlight, at a distance, Tagore working on the play of wintry light, afternoon post just arrived, the first letter opens the same trembling, Balliol College, Oxford, mailmen of numerous forests stumble on Amiya Chakravarti's letters, even now the Express train etcetera of so many poem series by Auden, Spender arrive, is Tagore moved the same way, little by little he wants to write down this kind of poetry—a poetry of experience, just these are not part of the escapade, but what will come of all these letters, it has been a few years since Amiya passed away, a flock of parrots fly by, the poet raises his head, a bright dazzling sky, a few squirrels come and sit on the lap of the tribal woman this winter afternoon

We know when an asphalt road spines through a poem leaving stains of raindrops on its brilliant black margins, and in the middle of that road all wetness is denied, heaps of used furnitures rise, some unfinished multi-storeyed buildings their brand new structure-style, gradually moving closer to the (heap of) furnitures some people standing up for discarded political festoons of our civilization forced to rot, or do we all live there, a sharp-clawed eagle tries to hold on to the ground to stand, guns are fired, following a lyric poet's grimcrack imagination futile and heartless the bird lies smithereened in the middle of the road, destruction is a neighbour, and through the middle of that wet road, on a long line of brown chairs and tables someone has shoved a knife into a fat book to hold it up, and not too far away lays a naked Rabindranath Tagore, solitary, on a wintry afternoon

Rail tracks on the side of pain, a hand spread out over it, a heavy goods train passes; and nearby, the tribal woman waits with her little girl inside the barber shop, shuddering at the thought of spurting blood, but sheer weight crushes the hand is chopped off the pin of golden metal that bulges out on her blunt black nose, falls and after stripping our clothes three-fourth fold we confront a question, which if pronounced as truth, brings back a swarm of Amiya Chakravarti's letters, continuous streams of alphabets stamped on it, incessantly filling the mailboxes installed on these open fields

FROM **Code Memory**

Aryanil Mukherjee

Transcreated from the Bengali by Aryanil Mukherjee from his book, *Smritilekhaa*

a fleet of rose petals drifting upstream prompted me to write after Derrida

when a river is memory
it loses its source
there is an anxiety to shed old skin
and show a rawer self   a disquieting
like the shaking gumballs in the dispenser
bringing on a certain anxiety of self-expression
like solitary water that descends on the flower
as a drop
and that a flower too   is a kind of weed
is perceived through evaluation
and suggestion

the weed-thought could remind one of a flower's
bright washy lukewarm lunar yellow
could remind one of yellow parchment scroll
where the transparent fish from the river arrive

fish made from mud or dust   or flesh & blood
but in a shape of its own
goldfish that light up the table
swirling in a glass bowl
making me hear the song of the golden sun
and green leaves

my green leaf
unfurling
to make legible my signatory consciousness

let's relaunch a barter system

I promise you the human voice
you return me the moans of nature
of animals
nature   as an animal   but not mother
mother   who is an animal   like the ma-penguin
hundreds of them returning in line
like black words on the page
a single relentless sentence in never-ending winter
sinking under snow   under the rock and grime
ossifying into layered parchments

somewhere under that snow   under the rock
I know there's a flat cardboard man
the ashen consciousness of burnt meteors   the I-self
metals in the crevices of laterite
the frozenness of fluid history
fossilizing the dead fly of flower bouquets
that's there too

at some point everything was water
the *Om* sound bearing its elements
the floors wet everywhere in the house
one of the funeral singers slipped and fell
it was a terrible blow

thick yawns highlight the seminar room
where an old woman sobs constantly like riverflow
talking about a death from childhood—
a young sister

there are ideas without handles on them
even the flower has
an idea about the garden
the waves   about an island
knowledge transpires across galaxies
the little dwarf holding the string under a mammoth
balloon
is me—the explicator
the beholder of metaphor

fish fly over it
having misplaced its hidden egg the emu is mad
it shrieks

a scream like fire   a scream like hot paint
like fuming fluid lava that lost all color to turn into
colorless ejaculate   completely demented
with a rage that burns the canvas   scorches womb
the name escapes us   the form   shape   deed

the ashen consciousness of burnt meteors   the I-self
metals in the crevices of flowing laterite
frozenness of fluid history
a dead fly stuck to the flower bouquet

today is a birthday

▲ ▶ ▼ ◀ ▲ ▶ ▼ ◀ ▲ ▶ ▼ ◀ ▲ ▶ ▼ ◀ ▲ ▶ ▼ ◀

it is the sea under the microscope
amoeba turning into a murderous whale
to remind us of our self-devouring afflictions

there are places where pain is statured as the mother of poetry
who is constantly smearing on us
its tender poultice of mud
and *life goes on*   *and that is progress*

there is a bridge in the painting
arched over white lilies
we think of them with such intensity
that new memories can form
and the vase can discharge its red lilacs
it's an ancient bridge   rusty
painted according to ancient principles
with a color that is now detritus
dust to dust   ashes to ashes

the little chicken bore a littler chic
an egg buoys up in between
upon which I stand
and separate son from mother

▲ ► ▼ ◄ ▲ ► ▼ ◄ ▲ ► ▼ ◄ ▲ ► ▼ ◄ ▲ ► ▼ ◄

As a child, I was always scared of human beings stuck to
other humans. And not just humans—chameleons atop
chameleons, dogs attached to dogs in late summer. Years
later I got the logic and logos of the natural phenomenon
of affixation. Of white feathers to a swan, the nib to sacred
papery white, fingers to the keyboard etc. The same message
gradually spoke out with greater plural strength accumulated
from each event. The same finger that knows the sticky
touch of gum, sends warm imagination to the cold core of
life's dead stars. Every search reveals a want for familiarity.
For something that's accomplished, felt, dense, scaly, warm,
unspoken, open, empty, smooth and silvery. Succus or
blood. Oreic and oneiric. Clove-like and love-like. Constantly
brushing against the other. Ceaselessly intersecting.

▲ ► ▼ ◄ ▲ ► ▼ ◄ ▲ ► ▼ ◄ ▲ ► ▼ ◄ ▲ ► ▼ ◄

not yet dusk.
backdrop of a cornered tree
a stream of black eyes cut-out from the sky
without any visible crease left by the scissors
wondrous unseen of a cloud's scribe

and beyond the unseen   crickets hum
a not seen longtime breeze
of mindful sea
smothered star fish following a dragged dinghy
staggering

breaded in a sand zone
of miniscule time

many of your letters lay open here
like eyes of dead fish
crabs lettering in *Brownian motion*
my words for you on yellow sandpaper
replying to an ancient note
any flashing countenance still missing
despite an electronic vocabulary
all silvery sheen rubbed out

I used your face like wine
keeping it fluid with age
reflected afar.

minimalist salt of pithy text
smeared on the brim of rolling waves.

▲ ▶ ▼ ◀ ▲ ▶ ▼ ◀ ▲ ▶ ▼ ◀ ▲ ▶ ▼ ◀ ▲ ▶ ▼ ◀

Anima is the inner side of a mask. Persona, its outer. But the puppeteer has no mask. He is without a face, without a figure. We observe that absence. From where the wire descends and then appears the floaty spider. The art of weaving is all about of an understanding of this buoyancy. Of staying afloat.

I have at times likened the puppeteer to a ventriloquist, sometimes a magician. One day, he wondered if the puppet-hands could grow longer, longer than life; if by habitual error, they narrated the stories behind the stage; if the doll quietly stood before the mountains, and when she stood; if two monstrous muddy hands came down and squelched her into earth, clay and stone to remind us of the origins of life.

▲ ▶ ▼ ◀ ▲ ▶ ▼ ◀ ▲ ▶ ▼ ◀ ▲ ▶ ▼ ◀ ▲ ▶ ▼ ◀

Michael, you spoke with so much elegance that morning
all that humor and icing
but that it was borrowed speech
we realized decades later

a language was inhaled in silence
while we thought about its mechanics
as a kiss
the labor-pain of speech born between jostling muscles
saliva and lava

you provide lip service to my song
and the audience can tell it is immiscible
aligns but doesn't unite   disproportional shadows
man walking his dog

Michael! Michael! the tall sisters lean over you

—Why doesn't he talk now ?
—He is asleep, my little darlings

the ventriloquist said.

what is complex   is pure
and purity is most complex of all
water wind and stone are its axes
the barely visible red thread on the beach
and the locus of trembling gulls
define the equation of utmost visibility
of impossible and impure
mathematics

poetry remains close to lament   or is a lament's wick
and lament is not necessarily related to loss

before we are taught to make flowers, lizards or the human teat
with blue and red plasticine
won't you show us how to make a plasticine lump
with plasticine lumps?

could you separate colors from mutilated bodies?
some people can't find them

are never comfortable in melting pots
rather they prefer to follow isocontour lines on maps
alongside their holiday trains
at the end of elongating summer
when under the salty gull's feet
our meager waves have shallowed
to their best transparencies

as recall becomes the second nature of
underwater photography
I can better figure out submerged coral islands at times
an unconscious within which the litmus changes
phases move in and out
smoke rising from the tribal tents
and songs
that continually shrink into a singular being
inside my receding window

I prefer landscape drawings
that have thought about bone structure
the anatomy of geography

so much of our writing technique
comes from the philosophy and adaptations
of a maskmaker
an understanding of obscurity can come
from the study of its construction

the two white lizards living behind the wall-photo
know how to become
perfect guardians of poetry
know   where the rainbow will rise
the length of its service
and if that day comes when
I can find out more   about the rainbow
like how wet it is
I'll have to say—

bye bye poetry

Three Poems

Anvar Ali

Translated from the Malayalam by Rizio Raj

Yin-Yang

The Han, a loom:
upon the surging water's Yin,
the warp of Yang emerging
from a thousand night lamps.

The Han:
Memory of an era of weaving.

Yin-Yang
Yin-Yang,
A woman had sung incessantly on the loom:
the Yang of the starfish laying its yarn
upon the Yin her canoes strummed by night.

*

The harvest came: Season of blood.
The *Yin-Yang* turned into wailing and bellows.

Wrapping the rags of Seoul about her,
gathering the top-burnt *Sans* in her hands,
she roared towards the Yellow sea.

No one ever saw her afterwards.

(Lee Si-Young says: She is there,
in the cage of her son's apartment in a huge block,
breathing only the breath that she holds, and
her grey hair resembling the leek root)

*

Yet,
she will come tonight, and
read the curvature of my *Malayalam*
in the *Yin-Yang* of her *Hangul*.

We shall weave,
a Yi-San poem, a prison uniform worn by mistake,
a Kim Ki-Duk film, a reckless nightdress,
the Bharathappuzha, a threadbare bath towel.

Sun Bin

The barmaid at Yo Bar—

A cocktail of weary smile
chitchat and beer

A yellow moonbeam body
stuck to the attire of darkness

She, the Daejon[1] sorrow
filling herself by midnight
that scribbled love all over my notepad:

"Mr. Ali and Sun Bin, friends ...
Quenchonoyo?"[2]

"Quenchonoyo."

Three O clock at night—

In the cold,
extracting herself from the cocktail
and draping around,
over her darkness-attire,
a Sun-Bin-dream
of joining a fashion designing course
for the next year ...

from the Bar in Chon Min Dong
an hour's walk
to the apartment in downtown
where Appa and Omma slept

"I lonely ... Ali lonely?"

---

1 Daejon is one of the ancient towns in South Korea.
2 "Is it okay?" and "It is okay", in Korean

Four a.m.—

It is the return for me
along with dawn clouds;
watering the Mukumhwa[3] petals
that she folded out of a tissue paper for fun,
by drizzling a dream of slender Sun-Bin-fingers
blooming upon
some boyfriend's night flesh next year;
the return
to the monsoon abode in Kerala
where my little ones, bed and mate
are all inundated

   "Sun Bin lonely ... no boyfriend"

   "But, Sun Bin eppoyo[4] ... will get a boy friend,
   sure"

In the apartment where *Appa* and *Omma* slept,
the darkness-attire fell loose ...

... over the plain's yellows
red saan[5] nipples ... its
Daejon autumn ...

In the notepad, our ants keep traveling on—

   "Sun Bin, when will your autumn end?"

   "Ali, when the flood-waters recede from
   your monsoon home, and the sky clears ..."

----

3 A bush flower in various colours widely seen in Korea
4 'Sun Bin is beautiful'
5 Saan: Hill. During autumn, most of the hill-tops in Korea turn red.
   The plants in the valleys and plains will turn yellow with red patches.

"Sun Bin, will you send my children then
the sunshine-dresses you designed?"

" hmm ... I will send your girl
 my red nipples too ...
Quenchonoyo?"

"*Quenchonoyo*"

The Song of Songs

It went off startling the cities.
The scattered bones
didn't become the destination
nor the stones a punishment.

From measured distances,
each city heard it bark.
Each channel was filled with its foam.

Since there was no more distinction
between the body and the soul
it passed
formless
as incarnate speed.

*

Renuncees of the future, know
one day
this journey will end
on the tip of a rubbish heap.

The nervous system
that had been circulating
the anarchist electricity everywhere
will that day reverberate
as a single string.

It will hug and crush
and explode the last vowel.

From then on
the rubbish dumps of earth
will give birth to
rivers that will drown
heaven and hell.
Love's army, all nude,
Will stand guard to it.

Nothing that is not mad
will have entry there.

Three Poems

P. M. Govindanunni

Translated from the Malayalam by K. Satchidanandan

Shadows

The eyes that drop in the woods
turn into spotted tigers
The eyes that drop in the river
turn into spotted deer-boats
Reaching the sea
they
turn into whale-battleships.
The pathways that lead
from the feet that had once
conquered the mountain
will now lead my blindness
into the elephant-trap.

House

This is
that memory:

razed
roof

broken
doors

the last
horses
launched from
the moist walls.

Bathing

As you descend the steps and touch water,
Your toes become fish.

Only the two of us
in this ancient pond.

We have nothing to tell
the water-snakes and the frogs.

Our faces snap and fall
into the slimy green water.

Let us identify ourselves
with the left-over bodies,
finish before the fish
Eat them up whole.

Why did we meet
in this green eye?
This moment's
fatal perfection and purity,
whose sin is that?

Five Poems

P. Raman

Translated from the Malayalam by K. Satchidanandan

Elegy

Lord Siva, whom
even poison trapped in the throat
could not kill,
look at this child, gone,
with a whistle trapped in its throat,
the old man, with sputum
the fishermen, with fish,
and the poet
with a word trapped in his throat.

Lord Siva, whom
even poison trapped in the throat
could not kill,
the child is gone,
with a whistle trapped in his throat.

Farewell

Some words
I spoke years ago
have to be read
with these my gestures now.
Some dreams I saw years ago
are fit only for this nap.

Still,
o, prophet,
don't condemn me like this
when I shed tears years ago
I didn't know you'd
go away like this.

Untitled

1

To the chill
brimming on the trees outside,
the deadbody played
host.

As the pyre took hold of him
it returned too
to the same trees.

2

O, depth,
on your core
all over
the fish
engraves.

Every Hole

every hole is choking
with the tales of the great.

like the giant beasts that live in burrows.

its mark
is a letter that sticks out.

try dragging it out
your arms will
turn tiny
and give way.

like mine.

Scared to Name

Got a charm
from a place
I fear to name.

The magic hands
of that place
tied it round my waist.

Now I don't
fear anything
even a whole year
without a job.

Except
that one place
whose name I fear to recall
let alone utter

Two Poems

Rose Mary

Translated from the Malayalam by K. Satchidanandan

Obituary

Rosa Maria: the one who
came alone to this earth,
mostly traveled alone,
and suddenly one day
put an end to her journeys
and went back alone,
one for whom
change alone was changeless,
one who had wandered
in search of secure,
eternal love and failed
one who looked for hearts
and reached only bodies,
frail sleep-walker ...
Sh! No noise! Let her
sleep forever.

The Sparkling Sword

Started killing at three.
The first victim was
a poor grasshopper
day-dreaming at the tip of
a blade of grass.
A single strike with a coconut frond
tip-toeing from behind:
there lay still
those slanting green wings.

At six the soulmate was
Kunjuvakkan, a little chick.
One day he came while
I was sitting dazed in fever
under the mulberry tree.
Gently, very gently,
I wrung his throat.
As life was leaving his frame,
I saw a drop of tear
dangle from those tiny eyes
At another time a gecko lost her tail
Thanks to my carelessness.
Then the family of ants,
residents of the Champa tree for generations.
I threw the whole clan into fire.
Burning bodies. Exploding skulls.
The long procession of ants
ever alert, on the wall.
I had but stretched my hands
and the scared ants ran helter-skelter
before vanishing into a hole.
Only one tiny stray ant was left roaming,
madness in his eyes and despair
on his bent little head.

How many more stark murders,
genocides, collective sacrifices ...
The days were easy with moralising sermons
And hearty laughters. But
in the silence of the night
a sparkling sword dangled overhead
in the still darkness.
O, Lord of insects,
when will that sharp sword
of judgement find my neck?
Fear chokes me like
an invisible shadow-snake.
The fierce drums of the day of judgement
begin to drown me in their hellish sound.

Two Poems

Sarju

Translated from the Malayalam by K. Satchidanandan

The Pen-knife

The iron in the blood,
an invisible knife
in the depths.

It won't rust until death;
yet life has managed to dissolve it.

Unknown to the shirt's pocket,
not hidden on the waist-belt
an artist's care without a cover
or the beast's instinct,
as an inner strength
in the turns of the road,
in our rowdy times.

Still during the security checks
at the airports,
raising my hands in a gesture of surrender,
pretending to be tickled.

With the poets with
smuggler's faces,
along with the cutthroat evenings.

Instinct

Nothing is as deceptive
as the mirror.
It maintains an unbroken
silence about depths.

The scents I apply daily,
—the after-shave lotion,
the hair oil, the perfumes of Arabia
on the body and the clothes—
to make me appear someone else,
the mirror wouldn't know.
So much of smoothness
does not go well with the instincts;
still it reflects the nose
shrinking from my own smell.

Two Poems

Jayan K. C.

Translated from the Malayalam by K. Satchidanandan

The Crucified

A prayer that
sharpens its eyes
towards the sky

Kindness that
opens its arms
sidewise

Nakedness that
pierces the earth.

The Tree's Gender

A tree in front of me.
Don't know its name.
Just kissed its trunk,
branches, leaves,
blossoms, flowers.
A tree in front of me
as I wake up from the
scorching nightmare of a desert.

Is it a male tree or a female tree,
male branch or female branch
male leaf or female leaf
male blossom or female blossom
male flower or female flower ...
I don't know.

A tree that extends love
like a Bodhi I front of me.
I just kissed.

Three Poems

V. R. Santhosh

Translated from the Malayalam by K. Satchidanandan

Autobiography: A Book

At the end of everything
time will forget him;
only the common iron
of oblivion will remain.

The chill of silence
the sea first chose
will be stuck on his face:
he will not know.
Its monochrome painting
will come in search of you
from the mined out building.

His invisible chill
the world will never know.

The Elegy and the Sign of Life

There was none, never.
Only kisses lived instead.
Time built a ship
with its clock,
and the West wind of commerce,
a captain.
As the earth grew round,
some from the East were
deputed to the desert.
None rode a donkey,
And the house they were after
was no manger.
The air was full of red lips:
The signs of having lived.

Blood oozing on the sand.

Marking the Wind

A grunt passed this way
in search of a name.
A drop of leaf fell
as in a realist's tale.
Gold racing on a needle-point;
sun for the ant and the grasshopper.
Objects fell on their heads
like the dead in a battle.
That name did not get recorded in the F.I.R.
Kilometres lived
in its glory.

Three Poems

P. P. Ramachandran

Translated from the Malayalam by K. Satchidanandan

Language, Arithmetic

Reduced to fractions
arithmetic is easy.

So much of sand, so much of water,
if we measure them,
the river is an easy sum,
can do it in the mind.

There are no more boats in the ferry
no more currents to flow
no woods in the mountains
no abyss left unfilled
Malayalam is just one desolate expanse.

I gave a hoot with my
meaningless tongue
reduced to a hollow sound.

A boy on the third bank of the river
saw everything from the branch
of a tamarind tree.

He has no grammar at all;
the hooting at the ferry is sweet poetry to him.
He does not know simple arithmetic.
To him, many ones together make
just a very big One.

Watching

A train derailed by
a wrong signal
stopped in the low lane
going down to the fields.

As it came to a halt with a screech
the dogs began to bark at the scream
the strange iron wheels raised.
Cats readied their hair-bow of alertness.

The village raised its head
guarding its chicks
under its wings.

The skin of the AC sleepers
got bruised with
the barbs on the fence
and the branches of trees.

A squirrel was reading out
the names on the reservation chart.
A fowl smell, bored by the unending trip,
peeped out yawning from the compartment door
to see at which station
the train had stopped.

The driver, impatient,
waiting for the signal
jumped down from the cabin
to the nearby compound,
picked up a ripe betel-nut
and opened his pan-box.

The curiosity wore away
in front of my eyes;
everything grew familiar;
dogs sniffed and pissed
turning the train into
a house verandah.
 Cats curled up and straightened up
and turned the berth
into a fireplace.

Chicks began to cry
from under the huge bogeys.

Don't know when it got the signal.
There, it runs along
the bank of the canal.
No smoke nor steam;
not even sound.

A row of ants
is hurling it along.

Simple

To let you know
I am here,
a sweet cry,
enough.

To suggest
I was here
drop a feather,
enough.

To prove
I will be here
the warmth of brooding,
enough.

How can birds
express life
simpler than this?

Three Poems

Chhannulal Mishra

Translated from the Bhojpuri by Rajiv Mohabir

The World is Such a Thing to See

You've come and you will depart, remember this, proud heart.
Wake up now! The day has come to awaken.

With your hands give alms, with your lips chant Ram's name.
When the crow comes to your door you must go.

You will never cross that bottomless river—
stuck halfway, growing old, what use is remorse?

O proud heart, illusion runs the world.
You came fists clenched and will leave empty handed.

This world is a thing to see.

Actions ferry everyone across the river,
be they guru or student.

Caressing each stone, you build a palace.
People say *This house is mine!*
This house isn't mine, it's not yours,
it's a bird's perch for the night.

You've built a mahal, limed a great fort.
Everyone will play this game;
will have to depart at dawn,
will go alone.

You brought nothing here, brother.
Nothing here is yours.
Kabir says, *Listen, O Saints,*
not even a penny will go with you.

Dasrath's Request

O my queen, take the kingdom of Ayodhya,
but don't ask my eyes for their sight.
Ram will go, exiled to the forest, Bharat will be king,
but don't ask for the finger that wears the gem.

After many attempts as an old man
I have four sons, finally;
a baby's rattle hangs in the courtyard,
don't ask for the peacock of my line.

In darkness has passed my time,
now the sun shoots reddish rays from the east,
take all the royal treasures of my kingdom, but
don't ask for the source of my life.

This dusk will soon dawn outside
and Dasrath will keep to his word,
if you ask, I will waste my body, but
don't ask the dawn for its peaceful light.

A Backward Wind

Admonishing his mother to forgive
those who wrong her,
a son slashes his father's throat.
Everything stews in wickedness—
a backward wind ravages the earth.

A wife curses her husband's mother—
all respect and propriety, inverted
like this wind.

A father sells his daughter; without guilt,
he counts his profit before her.
his morals scatter in a frenzied dance
into a backward wind.

Wives nightly betray their husbands
wrapping limbs tightly about their neighbor's thighs.
Caught in a cyclone,
what god can save them
from a backward wind ravaging the earth.

Three Poems

Pintu Rai

Translated from the Bhojpuri by Rajiv Mohabir

How Will I Go to My Beloved

With each breath take the Name, don't waste it.
Who knows if this breath will come or not.

How will I go to my beloved,
I just don't understand?

The body is but a rag, a veil of smoke,
how could I show this to him?

I do not know the rules of this "love"
alluring him is unthinkable.

Kabir says, I am as a filthy vulture,
a crow, not a boatman—

Padmakar says, Call the Name
so that our likes may cross the river.

The wicked lie that besmeared Sita
is nothing compared to what I have become.

Kabir says, Listen Saints! You will cross
if you hold the Name in your mouth.

The Bow Bearers

Two brothers set off from Awadh,
archers clutching bows to their chests,

archers gripping arrows
in their fists.

Ram walks before, Lachiman behind.
after the two princes, mother Janaki follows.

How shall I tell of their splendor?

Sita sees a golden glint
on the outskirts of the forest—
this is the beginning
of the song's end.

What will they eat; what water will they drink;
where will they spread their mats
when the heavy rains begin to fall?

On the outskirts of the hermitage
Sita sees a golden glint.

On the Battlefield in Lanka

Lachiman fell faint and Ram prayed,
Brother, please open your eyes.

I am determined to serve you,
when one hand breaks, what becomes of the other?

Father's departed for the next world,
and now Janak's daughter is lost,
tell me how will I bear separation from you? ·

What shall I tell them when the others ask
all of Ayodhya will ridicule the fact
that for the sake of a woman I lost a brave man.

From the Ayurved's medicine
Lachiman rose. With both hands,
Ram held his brother close.

Three Poems

Babla and Kanchan

Translated from the Bhojpuri by Rajiv Mohabir

Today is Your Wedding

Today the groom's procession leaves his home
to collect you—it comes.

You won't wear your veil indoors,
so why do you take such care to cover your face?
You should know better—
you will leave for your beloved's home.

Your veil is soiled with indelible stains,
—this veil is your body, it will always be stained,
it will betray your union with the One.

Cast it off
you must leave for your real home.

All the saints leave paper trails
while wrapped in your silks, your unfaithful fabrics
you will never understand, though you read
and read till your eyes grow sore

today. Today you will go to your beloved's home.

At Night I Dream

A dream shows me my love.

In my courtyard, not a single neem tree
breaks the fiery glare of the sun.
In the shadow of my home, he lays a sheet for us.

In his home, neither a brother's laugh
nor nephew's frolicsome footfall.
I shoulder the hope of my love's lineage.

At night I dream—

His home, with no other son's marriage,
the shehenai wails only for us.
My love, sailing this music, steers us into celebration.

I Will Not Go

Don't send me to my in-laws
for there I will not go, Baba.

Each day my love's mother jabs me while I rest.
His lustful father drinks too much rum.
Don't make me go, father.

Each day that man's tongue,
lolling, drips when she displays
her wares—don't send me there, Baba.

She rocks him to sleep,
he's the jewel in her lotus—
an ornament on her lap.

My love's father pummels
his wife in their lean-to,
with his wood, he hammers her—

Don't send me there, Baba.

Four Poems

Malathi Maithri

Translated from the Tamil by Lakshmi Holmström

She who threads the skies

As the sky fills
the empty shell
after a bird has hatched,
so desire fills
everything.

My daughter threads together
pieces of the sky
scattered by the wing-beat
of migrating birds

like a mysterious game.
The blue sticks to her hands.

She who ate the apple

I arrive at an unknown place somewhere.
Slowly I open eyes of hunger
and gaze outward,
clutching the rim of the boat.
And now, suddenly, I see
a shining apple, shedding
a pale red light.
I pluck it and bite deep,
continuing my journey.
After this
I will never return again
to my own dark lands.

Language Change

Endearments become rain
childish prattle becomes birds
gibberish becomes grass
deference becomes a river
tenderness becomes dewfall
humility becomes a moat
requests become curses
entreaty becomes a grave
dreams become cruel gods
abuse becomes chosen gods
desires become demons
silence becomes love
the language of God becomes the night
the language of Satan becomes the day
changing from one to the other
in our dictionary
as if a glass of wine ripples
becoming the wide sea.

Demon Language

The demon's features are all
woman
woman's features are all
Demon.

Demon language
is poetry.
Poetry's features are all
saint
become woman
become poet
become demon

Demon language
is liberty

Outside Earth
she stands:
nilli, wicked woman.

Three Poems

Sukirtharani

Translated from the Tamil by Lakshmi Holmström

Infant Language

I need a language
still afloat in the womb,
which no one has spoken so far,
which is not conveyed through sins and gestures.
It will be open and honourable
not hiding in my torn underclothes.
It will contain a thousand words
which won't stab you in the back
as you pass by.
The late dreams I memorized—
hoping to share them—
will not be taken for complaints.
Its meaning will be as wide as the skies.
Its gentle words won't wound
the tender surface of the tongue.
The keys of that unique language
will put an end to sorrow,
make way for a special pride.

You will read there my alphabet, and feel afraid.
You will plead me in words
that are bitter, sour and putrid
to go back to my shards of darkened glass.

And I shall write about that too, bluntly
in an infant language, sticky with blood.

Translating Her

In the bedroom
scattered with sunlight
like crumpled balls of paper,
they stir, waking up
to the sound of a tuneless song.
She walks past,
shrunken buttocks swaying,
beating out a rhythm
on the small drum she holds.
They ask me what the song means,
prying, eager, as if checking out
the sex of a newly born
I translate her poverty
the hunger she eats,
the hunger she expels,
her dwelling place
whose hair is sprinkled with untouchability
her oppressed community.
I speak the words, becoming her.

A faint smell of meat

In their minds
I, who smell faintly of meat,
my house where bones hang
stripped entirely of flesh,
and my street
where young men wander without restraint
making loud music
from coconut shells strung with skin
are all at the furthest point of our town.
But I, I keep assuring them
we stand at the forefront.

Special Section

A selection of poetry originally published in the Moroccan journal Souffles
guest edited by Olivia C. Harrison & Teresa Villa-Ignacio

Molly Zuckerman-Hartung, "Readymade Mood"
2011, graphite, hardware, tee-shirt, and pinwheel on canvas, 28 x 20 inches

The *Souffles* Poets

Olivia C. Harrison & Teresa Villa-Ignacio

Founded in 1966 by Abdellatif Laâbi and several other avant-garde Moroccan poets, *Souffles* (in French, literally "breaths", figuratively "inspirations") was one of the most influential literary, cultural, and political reviews to emerge in postcolonial North Africa.[1] *Souffles* was also the first venue to publish the work of some of the most important postcolonial Maghrebi and Middle Eastern writers, including the poets featured here: Abdellatif Laâbi, Abdelkebir Khatibi, Tahar Ben Jelloun, Mostafa Nissaboury, Mohammed Khaïr-Eddine, Mohammed Ismaïl Abdoun, and Etel Adnan. Initially devoted to Francophone Moroccan poetry, the quarterly journal quickly became a transnational, interdisciplinary, plurilingual, and multimedia venue. It featured literary texts and artworks from the Middle East, Africa, Europe, and the Americas, hosted debates about Third World Cinema, Négritude, Francophonie, and pan-Arabism, and published editorials on the Portuguese colonies of Africa, Vietnam, and Palestine, among other topics. In 1970, Laâbi and his co-editor in chief Abraham Serfaty founded a clandestine Marxist-Leninist party, Ilal Amam ("Forward"), leading to the banning of the journal in 1971 and the arrest of Laâbi, Serfaty, and dozens of fellow leftist activists the following year. Though the *Souffles* adventure was short lived, the journal served as a vital repository of revolutionary and experimental texts in the late 1960s, and continues to be celebrated as a pioneer of the Moroccan radical left.

Each of *Souffles'* twenty-two issues presents a wide range of genres, from experimental poems, literary manifestoes, and abstract art to political tracts, open letters, and interviews. The selection of poetry and fiction presented here varies prodigiously in style and tone. From the dense block of unpunctuated prose that constitutes Khaïr-Eddine's lamentation *Bloods*, to the paratactic chaos driving the rage against neocolonialism in Nissaboury's and Ben Jelloun's poems, to Laâbi's majestic and mythic invocations of solidarity with Palestinian refugees, these texts' formal innovations suggest new discursive modes through which to explore, valorize, and debate the meaning

---

1 *Souffles* was first made available by U.S.-based scholars Anne George, Carol Netter, and Thomas C. Spear, who digitized all twenty-two issues of *Souffles*. *Souffles* and its companion Arabic-language journal *Anfas* are available in full on the website of the Bibliothèque Nationale du Royaume du Maroc. *Souffles* may be consulted at: http://bnm.bnrm.ma:86/ListeVol.aspx?IDC=3; *Anfas* at: http://bnm.bnrm.ma:86/ListeVol.aspx?IDC=4.

of subjective experience in colonial and postcolonial contexts. These poems share an investment in provoking the reader and upsetting the political and aesthetic status quo through what Marc Gontard calls "the violence of the text,"[2] breaking all social and religious taboos, peppering their texts with scatological, sexual, iconoclastic and even blasphemous figures and themes. The irreverent tone of this poetry is the hallmark of experimental, youthful artists, to be sure, but it also serves a decidedly political function, never straying far from the decolonizing thrust of the journal. What these poets are after is, on the one hand, stultified Moroccan culture—what "colonial science" dubs tradition, according to Laâbi[3]—and, on the other, contemporary forms of neocolonialism and cultural imperialism. The narrator of Mohamed Ismaïl Abdoun's prose poem "Palma," for example, recounts his journey with a fantastical frog—an allegorical figure of the burdensome colonial past, or perhaps of the weight of tradition—who, by turns, fascinates, infuriates, and ultimately dies, leaving the narrator at once relieved and melancholy. Instead of lamenting a national culture that is trapped between the forgetting of precolonial culture and colonial acculturation, the journal thus brings these poems together in a democratic experiment in which imagination and the power of singular wit are brought to bear on the events of everyday postcolonial modernity. The diversity of the works selected for translation here forcefully captures the creative effervescence and revolutionary rage of the Souffles poets.

Souffles has enjoyed increasing visibility in the past few decades thanks to its enduring political and cultural legacy. Recent scholarship on contemporary Moroccan literature credits Souffles for paving the way for the recognition of popular culture in a context in which cultural production in the Moroccan dialect, Darija, and in Tamazight were sidelined.[4] The journal presciently recognized the role of colonial science and Orientalism in stultifying folklore, and condemned nativist or traditionalist attempts to "return" to precolonial high culture, consisting mainly of Islamic art and classical Arabic texts, at the expense of popular theater, so-called naïve art, and crafts honed over the course of centuries. The editorial team also insisted on recognizing Morocco's ethnic and religious plurality, including not only Imazighen but also Jews.

---

2 Marc Gontard, *La violence du texte: études sur la littérature marocaine de langue française* [*The Violence of the Text: Studies in French-Language Moroccan Literature*] (France, L'Harmattan, 1981).
3 Abdellatif Laâbi, "Le gâchis" ["Waste"], *Souffles* 7-8 (Morocco, 1967).
4 The term *Berber* derives from the ancient Greek *barbarós*, which signifies and onamatopoetically portrays those who speak a language not understood by Greeks. Muslims adopted this term to designate the indigenous populations of North Africa. Against this prejudicial etymology, we follow the usage of "Berbers" themselves: Tamazight is the umbrella term for the languages spoken by Imazighen (Amazigh in the singular.)

Yet if *Souffles* was a trailblazer in celebrating Moroccan diversity and popular culture years before the 1980s Berberist movements, the journal's Marxist-Leninist and pan-Arabist discourse sounds somewhat dated today. More problematically, *Souffles-Anfas* neglected entirely a political issue that has taken on pressing importance in Morocco and the Maghreb since the heyday of Third Worldism, which, like Marxism, has traditionally sidelined minority issues: women's rights. The journal published only one poem, "Jebu," by a female writer, the Lebanese writer and artist Etel Adnan, included here in Adnan's self-translation.

The poems that appear in this special section of *Aufgabe* form part of a critical anthology of selected translations from *Souffles* and *Anfas*, which we are in the process of editing. While a handful of texts excerpted from *Souffles* have been translated into English, no authorized translations of the journal have yet appeared. Our anthology aims to address this gap by making available, to an English-speaking audience, historically significant conversations on the future of postcolonial nations, a unique archive of innovative literature and critical writing, and a judicious assembly of texts that allows for the study of the literary journal as a genre in its own right. It will join a growing community of Maghrebi literary texts in English translation, including a selection of Abdellatif Laâbi's poems entitled *The World's Embrace*, the compelling collection of Moroccan poetry published in the fifth issue of *Aufgabe* and guest-edited by Guy Bennett and Jalal El Hakmaoui, and *Poems for the Millennium, Volume 4: The University of California Book of North African Literature*, a monumental anthology, edited by Pierre Joris and Habib Tengour, that spans twenty-seven centuries of Maghrebi literature, representing oral and written traditions of cultures and languages as diverse as the Tamazight, Phoenician, Jewish, Roman, Arab, Ottoman, and French.[5] In the wake of the Arab Spring, *Souffles*, an early example of cross-regional, multilingual, political and cultural militancy, beckons to be rediscovered in the English language. We hope, with this issue of *Aufgabe*, to offer our Anglophone readers a foretaste of *Souffles'* remarkable poetry.

The editors and translators express their gratitude to Abdellatif Laâbi for granting the rights to translate and republish these works.

---

5 Abdellatif Laâbi, *The World's Embrace: Selected Poems* (City Lights, 2003); Guy Bennett and Jalal El Hakmaoui, eds., *Aufgabe* 5 (Litmus Press, 2005); Pierre Joris and Habib Tengour, eds., *Poems for the Millennium, Volume 4: The University of California Book of North African Literature* (University of California Press, 2012).

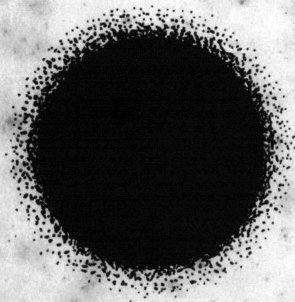

revue poétique
et
littéraire

Bloods

Mohammed Khaïr-Eddine

Translated by Teresa Villa-Ignacio

i eschew myself and it's not inadvertently that blood extradites me i go to the clashes in the cities that have no real name and everywhere i trudge along atom-sized clouds on all the telephone lines dishonorably intentioned stars and downpours are placed i only address these words to you because we remain unseparated you say we are inseparable we are separable i retort on oath at the very hour that i was assassinated i constructed you according to my sense of propriety according to the agility of traps without omitting anything of the magic of voodoo dethroned by the european with teeth so sharpened with hands so long with the science of a smiling reptilian the father of fathers of the old fish fabricated by the old sacred tarantula before the father of fathers and the mother of fathers i have not made you to measure up to God have not raised you to the height of the globe i gave you my voice we are even you say and i object i claim to be from a civilization of mongooses and anarchic vipers i do not know Asia hearsay and fat books sentences rhymes coups d'état stirrings of the heart blood like a rosary dedicated to political insurgencies of my blood cutting off breath and rations from whomever wants to be drenched in it of course i'm disappearing blood-pyre blood-oil blood-bath blood believe me i see clearly the bad conduct of bloods and leukemic eyes i don't pass by without noticing the barrages of blood the blood and the black sardine of blood i was present at bleedings operated on the nape of the neck and the pubis it was on a throne of schist and on the adjoining void of delirium the old maid embittered by the work in the fields and by all the wells she had dug sinking down until only her head appeared above the rock and laughing half-asleep while above her and at her level the doctoresse sketched the deluge smoke snow war death was present i said to myself does she have a heart of blood a body capable of enchanting me it was not true death had long grey hair rather death was all black very sharp hair death not described death of invisible blood crouching in the storeroom of our sorrows of our devastations i held her against my soul i gave her my heart she made a bird of it a bird who accompanies her everywhere she assassinates and undresses where she eats and gets drunk death has favorable intentions death justifies without punishing and we made sacred love without my knowing why i made her an excellent cake with my sperm and my floury blood she will not forget my caresses my stay-don't-leave-i-am-your-spouse-you-are-my-Great-Chosen-One not soon in any case she will return perhaps one night and it is not from my viscera that she will spring she will applaud will hail me oh Master like Caesar oh Owl like the filibuster or the Tornado come so that I may poison you come so I may dress you in a white and delirious toga ah forgetting no longer believing loving dying sparingly milestones pedestrians automobile drivers cyclists kings but you logical writers customs raids the evening opens cafés light bulbs eat sun man rots his liver they patch up my blood it hurts where i glow red they see me running under the draperies and the tables in a flow of magma i infect the mosaic i lacerate the couches i destroy the flowers block the toilets i don't respect money that falls from the holey pockets of these poor fellows who are afraid of you my iguana blood and me always calling into question my blood which i treat as a garbage dump as rats pestilent with an epidemic of malodorous moons of negation as all that makes one happy and avid to hold on to during the rain when coal costs as much as blood my vomited blood my blood that does not go to the lobsters of two ingots' worth of incense up my nose and the Italian hairstyle my blood that wobbles chips ages my scoundrel blood my ordinary blood my tergal winter blood in which i learn to hide myself to better count the black ice and hail my sidewalk blood my bastard blood docile and devious not a salon dog not for the ladies with the copper red smiles the real smile of the helianthus it's you proper blood that always skids toward the roots of disorder my leper blood my blood like Saint-Just on the scaffold my blood your tremble my blood you consecrate a real evildoer my blood you gun down my blood you have the eye of a terrorist my blood you fled from the protuberance on the bejeweled hand of a master my blood in which clang chains and real palace bells my blood which spends a bad afternoon and will spend a bad night and a monday of wrinkles my blood you do not win the lottery my blood you drag your juicy spurting sauce from a base of sap of stars whose throats were cut by flint and the carob tree on the last scrolls of vertigo and from a renunciation deferred my blood you listen to the abyss and the veterans who know well how to pronounce the words factory tin and money order my blood you have not understood that you must perform your ablutions like a good muslim my blood i must croak one day i slam the doors of my blood i lose in its doldrums the Ruby of rubies the Blood of bloods and the worst of the worst my blood editor my blood i exile myself with tons of turtle doves and ivory.

Three Poems

Abdelkebir Khatibi

Translated by Lucy R. McNair

the street

expands in my blood
extends its roots
its tombs, its memory
to the body's limits

The street is invincible
irreducible
all revolt is an avalanche of rocks
doors blown off in the whirling night
avalanche of dust winged with lines
piercing geometries

Standing, in the violent street
man is the first to speak

becoming

The trees cast their frail shadows interlocked
they persist like a childhood worry

The twilight dance of a dead leaf
builds a geometry
of time
my act becomes an axe in the night

riot

You must cross the street
Body suspended
That colorful point
Between my throbbing gaze
And a city open to death.

You must cross the street
Body suspended
Before a wall knifed with cries
In the street my back is dying
Straight as a line.

The sidewalk sporadically rushes up
To cross the horizon of my eyes
Then cracks almost ear-splitting
Like a cat's last wail

Palma

Mohammed Ismaïl Abdoun

Translated by Jennifer Moxley

> Tis the times plague when madmen lead the blind.
>
> **—Shakespeare, *King Lear***

… here I am at the end of my secular sleep. I let out a snort and its thrust pulls up from the dwarf palm tree all of my old sap.

I am here. It is chilly. I am here and it is chilly. My long thin fingers stiffen. It's chilly. I am here. I am here and I don't even know if she will show up. It's chilly. It's chilly. It's chilly.

I waited for her. It rained. She showed up. She showed up lost inside her hair. She was picking at her teeth with a wire brush—toothpick, mirror, and comb—It was raining. We drank coffee; smoked; we eyed each other guardedly. Then we ate a tuna salad with tomatoes and some scrambled eggs. Drank coffee; smoked; eyed each other guardedly.

It rained all night. All night long she told me her life story in a voice sometimes monotone sometimes fiery, hoping to *change* me she said. By dawn the rain had stopped. She left brought low by my inability to promise an eternity to her. She left lost inside her hair and tears worrying her cheeks with her wire brush.

Truthfully I knew well what she wanted, what had driven her to speak to me in this way. Women fear frogs. She feared Palma, but above all she was jealous. I tried my best to explain to her that it was absurd but she didn't want to hear any of it. I want you all to myself she said. I tried in vain to make her understand that in this place everyone is for himself alone and God is for no one…

In the morning when the rain had stopped she left in a rage threatening to return with the police, to sue me for having betrayed her… She left. I am here. It is chilly. She showed up for real. Her chilly fingertips let me know. I am in a graveyard of absence.

Eventually I too went out. The rain had stopped but it was foggy. An empty shell of a day. A chamomile day. A deworming day. A one-way day. A day wrapped in barbed, rusted, electric wires. A half-blind day. A pus-filled day. A bald pimp of a day dressed up in a Napoleon hat. A swimming upstream day. An indecent day.

The streets were steep and slippery. People gathered together in groups on the corners. Anyone who lost his footing was dead. It was necessary for people to walk in small groups and cling to each other in order to keep from slipping.

When the rain stopped the silence of long days of bad weather was replaced by a tremendous brouhaha. Impossible to distinguish a clear utterance. People *talked just to talk*. They waded through an uncertain language.

I left my garret. All I had with me was an ash-gray piece of lichen, a pair of moth-eaten socks, black glasses, and an old transistor radio.

In the streets the people grouped face to face. They went spontaneously towards each other as if old friends. Those on their own didn't last long; after an astounding glide they crashed, dead, onto the ground. They were quickly removed so as to not block circulation. Though some groups were more audacious than others. They succeeded in freeing their arms—which were long—to keep their balance, and with their hands cupped in front of their mouths they shouted jackal-like cries through the opaque air and then waited, serious and satisfied, for the returning echo of their voices—which plunged others into ecstasy and fright by turns—. Afterwards they noisily applauded and embraced each other. Unable to applaud, the others let out great incomprehensible and lacerating cries.

As for me, I knew the score. These acrobats were pranksters. Some of them, well hidden, stooped down to catch hold of their feet while they launched their cries and jiggled about.

I went out to join the group festivities. But really I was running away. I was afraid that she might return with the police. Here the price you pay for indifference to love is permanent incarceration.

I shaved the walls walking sideways like a crab. I was careful not to lift my feet, which would have been fatal. I gripped onto the wall's rough surfaces and integrated myself quickly into a group when it passed close by to me. I made rapid progress to my great astonishment and to the surprise also of some groups, who, envious of my equilibrium, tried to give me chase. But because they were so numerous they became lost in disorderly gesticulations and dreadful curses as they watched me move away from them. In the end I have no idea how long this went on nor how I found myself under the full sun amidst the palm trees in the area near where Palma lived.

I turned on the transistor. At the sound of the music Palma leaped out of the water. It was our signal. She croaked with joy. Bright and always cheerful she understood why I was fleeing. What's more she wanted to come with me. Personally I didn't want to weigh myself down, no matter with what, but in the face of so much insistence I gave in. After all she was the sole creature who understood me. She jumped into my outstretched hand and into a red scarf—pilfered from I don't know who as I walked through the streets of the city—; this is how, when a kid, I captured frogs so that I might sell them to Spaniards who love to eat their legs...

And we were off—in the meantime, as a precaution, I unburdened myself of my socks and especially of my glasses, just in case someone had given out my profile; one never knows, I thought.

Vapors of hot air danced on the caramelized asphalt.

We took off, Palma in the left pocket of my shirt, right over my heart, and me, walking, whistling, and amusing myself at the sight of the indents left in the melting hot asphalt by my shoes... No, I wasn't wearing any shoes... The warm soft tar tickled the soles of my feet.

Perhaps I was wearing shoes...

But it's a detail without great importance because the asphalt is MY MEMORY.

I was walking therefore on-in-my memory, with Palma in my shirt pocket and the transistor turned on full blast.

I wanted to listen to the news one last time. It was the news hour. National anthem. Freedom of movement is once again possible. From now on we can move about without the risk of a deadly slip. The mail service has been reinstated and the stores have reopened. It's a day of celebration but also day of mourning because the number of dead and wounded is considerable. A man's voice alternates with a woman's. They do their best to sound aggrieved while reading off the list of victims.

On it I recognized many of my own. There will be a rally at noon in the square in front of the large mosque. There will be an hour of silence to mark the memory of those martyred by these bad times. The evening will be devoted to festivities of all sorts. National anthem.

Memory is cowardly when it comes to evoking the dead.

In this way the newly disappeared are added to my graveyard.

Speak not of ancestors. I've never known what is meant by that word.

It began with my father. At my first birth cry he vanished. His voice was lost in a deadly fog. Many others followed. All I had left was my old blind grandmother whom I drove every Friday, acting as her eyes, to the graveyard—a windswept and sun-beaten graveyard. A miserable graveyard, tired from birth. An undemarcated graveyard, the kind that crops up just any old place. A graveyard barely above ground level. A graveyard to put brakes on your death drive—I was the transitory and itinerant bitterness in the murky ocean of her past. She made the places where I stepped come alive. I guided her through her memory. I was Ariadne's thread in the labyrinth of her darkness. One day she lost what was left of her vision. My eyes took a long time to accustom themselves to the light.

And then I met this woman. I want you all to myself she said. But I was busy counting my graves. And it was a disaster. I didn't know I didn't manage to hold onto her.

I got off the highway. I placed the scarf on top of my head, the lichen on top of the scarf and on top of the lichen Palma.

I walked for a long time. I sold the transistor at a flea market while passing through a small town before getting off the highway. With the money I drank a nice cold beer and bought a pack of American cigarettes. A way to celebrate my leaving, if you will.

I walked under the oppressive heat on the paths of my memory with Palma on my head while smoking Lucky Strikes.

I left the town and the highway without a single regret. I walked under the sun down a dusty incline. I wanted to get as far away as possible. Every departure is a flight. I walked and I told my life story to Palma. I wanted to settle the score with my memories. Tell her my life from A—to—Z. When the sun had reached its zenith Palma began to complain. She was suffering from the heat. She emitted a hoarse plaint. But I wanted to tell her my life story. My childhood beneath laurel and pomegranate trees... elementary school... my first hates and loves... I wanted to tell her about all my tragedies, to describe in detail the life of all of those who had died on me. But she just kept complaining and interrupting me at the most interesting and pathetic moments in my story. Her plaint continued. I explained to her that this act was essential to me, that I was determined to tell her my life's story, to unburden myself once and for all. In vain. I ended up nursing a genuine hatred for her. And in my anger I decided to make her pay very dearly for her lack of understanding. I devised a secret plan to rid myself of her.

And so I set her free. I made a little hammock out of the scarf and lichen, which I then attached to the end of a stick. I put the stick over my shoulder like travelers of old and continued on my way.

At sunset we were following the bed of a dry wadi. A sandstorm that threatened to become violent began to blow. I stopped.

I took Palma out of the scarf. I stared at her for a long time, reluctant to lose her. I tightened my grip. I wanted to strangle her... I tightened... she croaked with joy because she took this as a sign of friendship. I squeezed tighter. I looked at her. She battled back and I saw in her eyes that she understood my murderous plans. I saw it in her eyes... she wasn't angry with me... but seemed to be warning me about something. Her bulging eyes spoke.

This is what will happen to you:
When all has come to pass there will be no more water for your ablutions. You will brandish your sex at the sun and from your blistering sperm sons who will never recognize their father will be born. Children of silence.
When all has come to pass you will ask yourself where you left behind the one—yourself—that followed you more closely and faithfully than your shadow.
Only the sirocco will remember you.
When all has come to pass you will look even more deeply into your solitude.
You will be no more eternal than a language of death.
You will count your fingers your eyes your limbs.
You will experience your voice your gaze from inside and outside of yourself.
You will not overlook your nails they will have their say.
When all has come to pass you will reclaim the right to silence without having ever spoken.

At the tick of your heart you'll have nothing left but to follow the wind.

But perhaps you will prefer to cash in your skin—thoroughly tanned—thoroughly wrinkled—or mortgage your blood.

You will leave with only the rhythm of your rotten nerves.

You will not mark sundials nor ever count hours by the sand pouring through an hourglass.

When all has come to pass you will cut all moorings. You'll be an iceberg.

Sometimes you'll drop anchor in a nightmare.

You will not walk barefoot in the water for fear of drowning your chimeras.

Finally when you will have exhausted everything

> when you have nothing more to lose
>
> when you have only one trick left in your bag
>
> you will gamble your life in the confines of uncertainty…

I squeezed even tighter to silence her. But I didn't have the heart to finish the job. I closed my eyes and threw her away from me with all my force and then I turned and ran. After all she alone had tried to understand me…

I wanted to tell her my life story. She was moaning. I wanted to unburden myself once and for all. She kept on moaning. I tightened my grip around her twitching body. Her protruding eyes bulged even more. She croaked with happiness but I wanted to suffocate her. I wrapped her up in the scarf. I closed my eyes and I threw her far away from me and then I turned and ran.

I followed my path alone with my lichen. It had grown over the only stone at my father's house built all of bronze so hot in summer and so cold in winter right next to the highway under the brilliant sun of an eternal July. The lichen upholstered almost all of the pale grey stone with its spider-like convolutions. Desiccated brain withered over its history.

But Palma's scent kept following me. You will leave with only the rhythm of your rotten nerves. Sometimes you'll drop anchor in a nightmare. It was the lichen that retained her presence. In time I would chuck it as well.

> That's over. It's dark. The sandstorm blows more violently. So I am alone?
>> Really alone?
> My nerves
> my heart
> my neurons
>> deranged

WHAT SHOULD I DO?
where is the center
where is the why of interrogation
must one retreat, fingernails digging into palms
renounce one's skin
remain deaf to the blood's rhythm
attempt a senseless crucifixion
expose oneself to all infernos
trace once and for all a cross
—a real one—over oneself perhaps to be reborn
from one's own ashes
an absurd death
or else
must one like a stray fish allow oneself to be caught in a net
of dead words
amen to all loop-holes
I hate those who know where they are going
as for me an epithet can make me change my path.
A quiver in my scalp warns me of the next disaster.

It is dark. The wind redoubles its force. At the tick of your heart you'll have nothing left but to follow the wind. I will not sleep, I will not sleep anymore. My flight stops here. I'll retrace my steps. I'll go back there. Back there everything is to be done over. I don't know… redo the geometry of the streets, right the sun to predict all eclipses, create a committee for the defense of stray dogs, write a constitution for the birds. In the end, everything is to be done over. I'll retrace my steps. En route I'll mobilize an entire wildlife fraternity. I will teach them the true language. The language of the raid. We will seed a single word into their hearts and minds. The word *essential*. A wildlife fraternity. The grasshoppers, the mites, the rats… There's nothing like it to put a tottering country back on its feet. Not to forget the blacksmith ferriers, their role is crucial. The maladroit acrobats—among others—will be entrusted to them. For some they will be able to rearrange the neurons—in sum to shoe their brains—; for others they will ensure better agility in the toes; and for others still they will strengthen the joints. I don't know, everything is to be done over.

I will turn back filled with a clear and cold violence and already I burst out laughing at the thought of their expression upon seeing me show up with my wildlife.

I will not sleep anymore. Insomnia a terrain of light alone can help me to defeat the obstacle of monsters. Just enough time to take stock, just enough time to walk back over the burning silica to the source of my nutritious prehistory before being born again *completely new*, and I will turn back. Just enough time to put the topography of my *future memory* right...

Untitled

Mostafa Nissaboury

Translated by Guy Bennett

There is one city that conjures the eye, from which the eye cannot defend itself, were it endowed with the greatest of powers.

A city whose devouring is palpable, since we have been gradually reduced to a collection of bones that break up, turn frail, are scattered to the wind. Am I a city rebuilt bone by bone or am I an extinguished city? Or resurrecting fortresses not depicted in school books (kasbahs, foliage, from cave dwelling to small, low-roofed houses their windows askance) to revive the instincts of the deeply enamored ogress-moon and trigger the entire series of hideaways, shelters, cold and hot spells, ensure the eye works properly beginning with reappearances, perfectly detectable traps used to capture blood for some, landslides for others, the jinn.

Grottoes open for my ribs' crawling
as if I were as if the city and grotto in me
were separated into computers each with its own way of calculating pursuing
its own adventure of furrowing destruction and dream
and machines that outstrip time
time in our head buried in a shirt of old cancers of paradise
since you can't cheat fate
since it's a question of eye something alive something tragic in our eye
since Sesame the grotto Sesame the city my entire town crumbled as by electric
reverberations and my prayer to the fowl the grand master buried in Baghdad
the discord of my vapor my lymph bottles bearing the power of ubiquity
sipped
by the vampire
neither geographer nor geometer had an explanation for the disaster
that threw me
into kif
nor these ruin-girdled legends that
I alone will be left
and I
I shall be devoured by a monster
and who will knock up the moons?
who close the book?

It's no big deal, I say, if nearly every day I am forced to swallow the plate of couscous on which death has been laid out all plant-like and if the street is of anxiety. I telescope. I adjust the dreams that shot out my brain in vast but nearly invisible bands—waves—according to them, and my liver, according to me.

It's no big deal if all I can manage to grasp of the void are its symptomatic shocks and if, once localized, my deliria prove perceptible in the guise of fleeting stains—blood puddles. It's no big deal if my anachronism is unlike the electron, the electron and my anachronism forming that scandal of competing compromise whereby I maintain that transistors capture sirens' voices, black and white sirens, to capture the night, the night and every characteristic of the moon. And your teeth have little cracks that open Tanit-torpor lips in my imagination. And in this clairvoyance an old killer who is time and in my dream patterns abruptly reform, enrobed in sand, luxurious, a crowd full of territories where for myself I measure the city the street and me without managing to deal the decisive blow that would put an end to all Tanit-quivering and hurl this dream the city reflects back to me having never shot out as many heads as many fingers as many doors and as many electric poles as many numbers and caravan legacies nor been as convoluted nor as impossibly unattainable due to the placement of houses bordering it low-roofed as far as the gorge and due also to the electric lights that give it a desert air which reminds me that nostalgia is a virtue of the lunar crescent nostalgia crumbles, I was crumbled at having remembered, crumbled too my companions who stop to better sing the nearby relocation of housing debris affirming that Tanit it's about a lost love a consuming passion Sesame as night which calms which comes without my moving without waking a profound moon hardly recognizable in what it has created to spark an appearance of immobile time. I had a moon turned to spongy mass, half purulent half vagrant, gluing half-smashed douars from which I could extract nothing more than a book of calamitous descendants. I had a moon that paralyzed me could not chase it away even pressing my thumbs from my temples to the middle of my forehead to create a red dot between my eyes, and even if it's about the sun, which topples body after body in each articulation in the slightest cell its stench. Which strikes. Which must be chased toward the trees, toward the dunes, and which bears old grudges.

I have stayed behind to probe this slow
                              infernal
                                   swelling
my voice
          muddy
                stuck to death's hoof
                              my brain

with the dimensions of a battlefield where Sif ben Di Yazane might have dug
up hundreds of golden scorpions. I, anemic. I and the rest in books the western
galactic will come and detect to assure me of my Middle Ages, my resurrection,
the beauty of my religion, my youth my primitivism my virility my pitiful sex
organ, that it is a question of time, that man must be declared free, that Berber,
that he Barbarian, that I Jew Hindu fatalist fanatical and Arab, that he Phaeton,
that after all we are not so unlike one another except that he correct, his dog,
his wife, his disciple who has not been able to obtain his passport, Carla,
novel for two, kif, tea, I-rave-I-write-trembling-under-the-weight-of-raving,
and Brahim whose life he knows better than anyone better than me Sicily
Essaouira before the small photogenic Ayrabs dumbfounded as by some young
folly listen up I'm a Roman prophet awaiting the revolution action first action
for the galaxy and the moon in me then the moon where I am my entreaties
he more Muslim than me
the prophet in Rome
with his electronic calculators in the midst of the futurist desert
with a city with only two gates
pyramids totems
people in love with the same cow as me
in this city I know my official number
I too
lived in futurist deserts
I too conquered most of my satrapies
how many sirocco days I can gulp down I the Minotaur
how non-violent I can be
how many fantasies circulating in my blood I have
tombless cadavers facing the city
                              to be destroyed
and of which all that remains will be another city that we shall call

Palmyra

the grotto

five men the sixth a dog and I the Minotaur
and I the Minotaur again the grotto six men and the seventh a dog and I the
Minotaur and the grotto again six dogs six men and the grotto again a dog with
no men and the dog appears
with the effigy of its absence
the grotto especially to populate with surreal visions where other cow heads
can be tracked down laughing in streets piled up open to the very walls of the

age-old lair of the sleeper with the cow the bronze town lacking passports
ropes machines wadis but with caravans

laughing
I the Minotaur and Tanit again the animal done to a turn in my irregular daze
of bookish insomnia
and Tanit again her embryotomies her draughty thighs
and my night apprehending the moon were it
only to photocopy it were it
only to reconnoiter my brain of sea foam only
my night my anachronism my double kif belt round my waist

I contemplate the structures

Planet of the Apes

Tahar Ben Jelloun

Translated by Anna Moschovakis

Go quickly! It's a country that's ripe for the taking
It is there for your pleasure
Ah! What a beautiful country Morocco is!
Ouarzazate! Ah, these benevolent storks tucking their bills in the crook of their
    wings.
Leave your office, your wife and your children
Come quickly, surround yourself with barbed wire in the ghettos where guts lie
    drying in the sun
Come hang your testicles from the ramparts of the Zagora
Go retrieve them from Red Marrakech
                      let your memories hibernate
                      and bring back new neuroses

Point your finger toward the sky
Snatch some sun from our under-development
Your impotence will be multiplied in decapitated memories
                      and your inky night will deploy its fortification walls
                              against sewer streams

Beware of ARABS
        they are rotten thieves
        they can rip out your brains
        scorch them and serve them to you on tablets of mute earth

(listen, instead, to another voice):
The club of my med is your salvation
French ambiance guaranteed, required, reimbursed
Climb up on the dromedaries
        your vertigo will be in the image of your gyrating hunger;
        your mouth will open to apostolate the Fall and tears
In the morning, drink a little Arab blood: just enough to decaffeinate your racism;

To your friends, offer your tattooed memory
                    a postcard of beatitude in aluminum
                    dim resonance of your skull-cemetery;

And then go ahead, take an Arab
                        he is natural, a bit savage
                            but so virile ...

Sex in shreds of deracinated flesh
will remain
            Hanging from the thread of your shameful memory
You will no longer be able to chase him from your fantasies
He'll ejaculate humiliation and rape right in your face
Wounded
            you'll collapse beneath tame trees
            you'll see the stars dissolve in your facile dreams
            a fever will come and you'll spit up blood
            all over your good intentions
            the bastards are going to crucify you dead
            in the shadow of the marvelous sun of the club of my med

FROM **Jebu**

Etel Adnan

Translated by the author

o dead cities of the XXIst century
Beirut and Tel Aviv!

these days you should learn to count
in order to survive count the tortures
of Sarafand

> in the geological cliffs of Western
> Asia vultures thank the sky for the
> abundance of their food: more dead
> Arabs than stone in this desert!

We had learned sorrow in Algiers
lived a happy moment and now
it has to be started again...

Noises...

We shall atomize the mountains so that
there shall be no more Revelations
truth will emerge from a well

Jebu commands the ghosts that are following
him to disappear in the gasoline of
our neighborhood drugstores
the wind is coming...

> Sitting in humid movie houses
> we have seen slummy Christs bless
> electric screens
> we have loved...

> We have now to crucify
> the Crucified
his age-long treason has sickened us

Ra   Shamash   Marduk
the astronauts have invaded the moon
so that in the grandeur of your
loneliness
you come back alone in your boats
o geometric monotheism announced by Jebu

Sun of the Past
        hunger
        shame
            thirst
            fear
            sickness
        isolation
        madness

cargoes of solar boats
in the free zone of Beirut harbor
our ships are armored cars
that our men lead on the roads of the
sky   the sky is an ocean where they
drown   doom is a jazz trumpet
howling on the Place des Canons

On the return (the Moon-Earth trajectory)
in the cosmic railway
Jebu says:

I have seen the earth   magnetic ball
burn at its edges   radioactive   primordial
solar   in a language atomic
electric
magnetic
she said:
I am a cosmic vessel
and my blood-brothers (the primordial bedu)
on the mercurial altars where they are slaughtered
will be born again they are my essence.

Jebu Canaanite   founder of Jerusalem
tells the Crucified:

you have suffered three days
I have suffered for three millennia

(the fedayi is a writing glued to the ground
and pushing ahead   wounded   his saliva
heals the open earth   in his agony he
sees a rain of meteors

in death he forgets that they dried the
cisterns so that we eat worms and
consider happiness to be a funerary oration

                    but we have displaced the sky...

they do not know that the wind
is a bird which flies)

Darkly our children were drowning
in our peaceful rivers   the people
were in a swamp and we called for liberation

now do I announce:

            napalm
            hunger
            the cunning of the enemy
            the slow flying airplanes   the dynamite
            torture
            and more corpses than larvae in a rotten
            pond
            we are guilty of innocence

and also:

            the backward movement of the dead
            the guns carried by ghosts
            plants growing only in winter
            a tank made of jelly which will break the front
            and soldiers of the year two thousand

creative disorder
is our divine stubbornness.

      He will mount an attack on the
      Fifth Ocean   give Venus the investiture
      of his breath   inhabit Uranus

the people will come out of their ratty sewers
and discover the immensity of the world. Let a
single piece of bread feed the tribe. The father
will call his son: his brother...

Jebu has millions of roots innumerable heads
a proliferation of bodies   he is the whole and
each one of us since the first break of Time
he is the People on the space-time equation

I have seen the women-sounding villages
of my generation: Samua   Kuneitra   Kalkilya

      rapacious foreigners   drinkers of
      bitumen you have in abundance but
      hatred and on roads where serpents
      can't feed   you forced the women of
      Jericho to chew diamonds   Arabs are
      but a mirage which persists...

In the beginning Jebu had been killed
but his eyes are the Tigris and the Euphrates
his belly is Syria his penis is the Jordan
his long leg is the Nile Valley
one foot in Marrakech
his bleeding heart encased in Mecca
his hair is still growing on the Sannine

The X-ray of his being on the day of Hiroshima
like a sweat appeared on the Jerusalem Wall.

I know
the total moon
the slow-motion sadness
the poisoned rainbows

betrayed faces filling newstime screens   turned
towards vultures as if there was any other
messiah to wait for than the bomber
the total exile.

I know the coffins walking to the mosque
in a city where roses are watered with
gasoline
the foreign capitals who like dying bees
secrete lies
and the total moon
closing its claws on the tribe.

The torrid heat of the first king of
Jerusalem—astronaut coming back from
the moon that he inhabited and on whose
craters he left his sacred writings—the
heat is still glued upon the face of a
cosmic snow

    drinkers of blood   drinkers
    of petroleum   newcomers to napalm   nouveauxriches
    of torture   Gilgamesh shall plant his sword
    between your eyes

the City covered by the wind   by tears   by ultraviolet
rays   is trembling…

Palestine   mother of nations   is a glorified pestilence
with solar tumors on the face and repeated rapes in the
belly

EDITORS' NOTE

This is an excerpt of Etel Adnan's translation of "Jebu," originally published in *Women of the Fertile Crescent: An Anthology of Modern Poetry by Arab Women* (Three Continents Press, 1978) and most recently published in *To look at the sea is to become what one is: An Etel Adnan Reader* (Nightboat Books, 2014). We have retained the order, elisions, and typographical layout of Adnan's translation, which is based on the complete French poem, published as *Jébu, suivi de l'Express Beyrouth enfer* (P.J. Oswald, 1973). We are grateful to Etel Adnan for allowing us to reprint this excerpt.

we are all palestinian refugees

Abdellatif Laâbi

Translated by Olivia C. Harrison

at last I remerge from my body
I come out of it bearing essential questions   My scream ready   Carried high
cutting through the Scandal   Dismantled mechanisms
                    I am armed from head to toe
my armor is strong to oppose any erosion   my memory is long to force any
embargo   My laughter inextinguishable   I am new   Scars and grafts have
moved toward the plants   They weigh down my step but no longer stop my
expansion
for a long time I had dreams   They were nightmares   Slow motion races of
repetitive executions   Whirling eyes   Opium-burned demonstrations   They
were cannoned temples   Erotic and pagan crowds practicing obsessive rituals
They were nights pregnant with moons   Unlit stars   Glimmering deserts
Swastika-engraved domes   Branded faces   Cataclysmic winds   The Atlas
mountains erupting in a deluge of collective memory
memory you saved me from the deception of books   You dictated to me the
itinerary of violence   You led me to the source of decisive interrogations   ou
plugged me into the pulsations and tremors of my people   From a terrorized
humanity relegated to the hibernation of caves guarded by the Cyclopes
Scientist-Kings of Barbary I carved along their crimes and your signs my arcs
and my arrows   There I made the Weapon and the Word   There I nomadized
across killing fields and illuminations   The taste of freedom projected to the
confines of the future
                    a swell of conquests

at last I remerge from my body
it was neither the ghetto nor hell nor a seawall to flee the world   It was not
the call of the void   education by emptiness   I am not very contemplative
even if this had to be a touchstone of what one might call my "soul"
I no longer respond to obsessive calls   To whatever call
I choose my touchstones my obsessions and my targets
I choose my era my victories and my defeats
I am the Arab man in History set in motion built anew by the vanguard of
Palestinian guerrilla fighters

Arab   Arabs   Arab
a name to be remembered
great voices
                of my seismic deserts
a people marches
over 8000 kilometers raises tents
command bases
how many are we
yes how many gentlemen statisticians of pain
give us a number
and the prophetic masses retort
with infallible equations
today

WE
     ARE
          ALL
               PALESTINIAN
                         REFUGEES
tomorrow
we will create
          TWO...   THREE...   FIFTEEN   PALESTINES

Poetry

Edited by E. Tracy Grinnell, Jen Hofer, Paul Foster Johnson, erica kaufman, Nathanaël, Maryam Parhizkar, Zandra Ruiz & Jamie Townsend

Molly Zuckerman-Hartung, "Petit Four Arp"
2011, acrylic, oil paint palette scrapings, spray paint, collage and found wood an asymmetrical panel, 16 x 14 1/4 inches
Private collection, New York

FROM **BOSCH STUDIES**

Joan Retallack

Another Patriarchal Pastiche

> The historical materialist leaves it to others to be drained
> by the whore called "Once upon a time" in historicism's bordello.
> He remains in control of his powers, man enough
> to blast open the continuum of history.*

The great intellectual patriarch must be no less man-
enough-man among man-enough-men. He, from whom
all generic male pronouns, all great male nouns, all great
greatnesses have for millennia been spawned in service
of the great continuum of the great history of the greatest
natural languages throughout linguistic time, that he is the
he of whom Gertrude Stein wrote, *they were outstanding in
coining words without women.* The patriarchs cannot escape
history nor can history escape them. *They are caught because
they have won the right to be in meaning.* Where the shadow
of the patriarch falls the agency of the others may relax
and withdraw. *I mean,* she said, *I mean,* she said, *was not said
of women.* Just as the great intellectual, the great spiritual
patriarch must by the logic of the praxis of patriarchy
embrace misogyny while reviling the word itself *the colonel
has directed the soldiers to grow nasturtiums.* Meanwhile,
once upon a time, one of many shes responsible for these
salient observations danced all night with her beautiful dog,
danced right out of the patriarchal family romance, right
into a welcoming ambiguous figure.

---

* Walter Benjamin, Theses on the Philosophy of History, xvi. Italicized passages, Gertrude
Stein, *History or Messages from History.*

de *La ópera fantasma*

Mercedes Roffé

The Ford
(O. Redon)

nubes
nubes
resplandor
caballos
caballos
sombras
cuerpos

roca tallada
a punta de plumín

tinta
tinta y luz

y a pesar
del retumbar de los cascos
en la grava

qué silencio
¿no?

qué profundo
e íntimo

silencio

FROM **Ghost Opera**

Mercedes Roffé

Translated from the Spanish by Margaret Carson

La Gué
        (O. Redon)

clouds
clouds
brightness
horses
horses
shadows
trees

rock incised
by dint of needle

ink
ink and light

and despite the hooves
pounding on the gravel

what a silence
                — listen

what a deep
intimate

silence

L'Oeuf
       (O. Redon)

huevo   taza

el horror de los ojos
no es lo peor

:

la boca
        la falta de
boca
la asfixia
esa falta
esa falta
de

L'Oeuf

(O. Redon)

egg   cup

horror in the eyes
that's not the worst

:

that mouth
            that lack of
mouth

asphyxia
that lack
that lack
of

Ostie (Tour du Castello)
(François-Auguste Ravier)

una plancha de metal
azul
un papel azul

una *película*

el crujir de la cinta   —el
aletear del extremo
                    suelto
contra el riel

y el girar del rollo
en vano
en el
vacío

círculo blanco sobre negro en la pantalla
y la sala a oscuras

murmurando

Ostie (Tour du Castello)
    (F-A. Ravier)

a metal plate
blue
blue paper

a *film*

the film whirring   flapping
its end
against the spool

and the reel turns
in vain
in
emptiness

white circle over black
on the screen

and in the dark theater

whispering

Mouthnotes

Oana Avasilichioaei

what if resonance vocally sits in the mouth? or rather
what if you vocally resonate[1] in my mouth?

---

1   we made us wet supine in the pond we tuft
    woodswollen mossheavy with gesture
    margin the bushy aftermath of

    we wet our pines and made us swollen
    often the undergrowth   often piercing through
    here we might insert

    we swell our made and pond us wet
    in the fibrous ligature
    motion joint branch stamen frond

    we slick lapping between the wooded wet
    jugular juncture
    joining of a singular to a singular

does the mouth practise its conclusions? the sonata of
linguistic ruination interrupted, shifting (sprouting) [2]
in the encounter with your word, i.e. your being?

---

2 the simplicity of *a hunger in my mouth*

   or *all night your hand slept on my hipbone*

   to wander in the melee of matter

   how *you* could feel so tender in *my* throat

the thinking house of the mouth (à la Leblanc) dwells
in the angles of its recesses (lexical necessity) as
prepositions commit (dive off) cliff's (mouth's) oblige[3]

---

3 the barbarians are gathering, glutting the streets, the firewires,
   cellular signals, anticipating a gluttonous feast.

   we pack in, a calamity in their wake.
   though we must teem
   we need not mud thin confuse.

how[4] to disarticulate in order to articulate?

---

4   what of truth then?
    what accord to the chords?

    we strew a sentence along a limb's passage
    deceived into believing
    we've accomplished something

inflection crease shade pleat variation tangent
fluctuation hinge[5] deviation

---

5   how a life gets living making i's like furrows (tracks)

    labyrinthine lab of wordmatter

    bending word to fjord (fluctuate) its subject

    animal pleats of oscillating dermis

    vibrating intimacy of (fluid) i to (fluent) eye

    you the boldest pronoun i pronounces

in the body's warren a face (soaring swarm) proposing[6]
what angle?

---

6 in turning, the face faces with its innumerable subjects
   in subjecting the turn with its faces, an i facets

   faceted i slips (slopes)
                     the saying face
                              flips its subjects
   animal facet   i invents a face
   notional facet   a face invents its i
   speculative facet   the invention is subjective

my written mouths[7] the book and follows the book
(à la Jabès)

---

7   before a word a being (an i perhaps)
        intersects naked about
        to distend into disgorging

    after a word naked intersections (possibly interdictions)
        traject outwards
        dispersing and coalescing

    while my own barbarian world
        sticks in the throat
        contorted into inexpression

how a tongue's manner? *you* stands[8] in (lips) the opening

---

8 stance of minding in nature
   stance of meddling in notion

   enveloping (voweling) your consonant
                    my voice timbres

FROM **Nomenclature, Miigaadiwin, a Forked Tongue**

Aja Couchois Duncan

We hold mirrors. Bloody our lip under the rent in the
backdoor. They crow for the quick and the dead and on
the third day they rise and crow again.
Very soon now
we can return to our life of wonder and regret.

— **C.D. Wright**, *Just Whistle*

Bring me the sun. Bear it on the palm of your hand...
Bring me the brains of the sky so I may see how large they are...
...bring me the girl with the watery teeth...
Fragrant shall be her odor when I remove her skirt...

— **Leslie Marmon Silko**, *Almanac of the Dead*

LAMENT:

To be gathered together under one roof, to be staked and
hobbled. We are stabled by the limits of.

To be american is to be gichi-mookomaan, a country of
butcher knives. Such isolate objects. For five hundred years,
there were generations whose sole purpose was to split
and swallow. They broke the continent into states, into
fragments of.

We people, the first people. Our word for ourselves is the
word for our tongue. There is no difference between the
naming and those being named. But americans have been
burdened with the difficult translation from self to other. It
made them dangerous.

We people have become ozhaawashko, adjectival, a bruised
face, an injured mare. It is the only word to approximate
this moment, here in the stall, with little room to move
in any direction. But my ancestors remember and in
this way we work ourselves backward. We were not born
bebezhigooganzhii, hoofed and swoop-backed. Of whatever
state, we were once free.

MOHAWK:

Before the Sex Pistols there were other markers of
resistance. Take the state of Connecticut for instance, all
those nice puritans and their heretical belief in a dour
god. Who can blame them for their fear of extravagantly
shaved heads, of beautifully decorated objects of the
mundane. Of axes. After the skirmishes, there would be
bedroom communities. Long cocktail hours. What woods
remained were like the houses, crops of uniform height
and dimension. Teenagers began shaving their heads in
defiance of the repetition. Few saw the irony. They were
the inheritors of this great promise: freedom to worship a
life unfettered by sacrament. But miigaadiwin is ritual and
death. Beneath the elegant, suburban houses is earth fallow
with human bones.

OPTICS:

The science of sight ignores the spirit of mescaline, of cactus, of natives of the new world. After the earth split, there were two, old and new. The old world was heavy with everything that began it. The new world was fecund, virile.

When the first people came out of the trees they found themselves on a wooded island already crowded with bear and wolf. Stripping bark from the trees, they built canoes and paddled to the other side. When light moves through solid particles it losses pieces of itself. It is altered once it reaches its destination.

Omoodayaabik is shattered, a piece of broken glass. Before it could have been anything, a lantern, window, a bottle of whiskey. The science of sight does not trouble itself with such inquiries. There are only the intricacies of the eye, its mechanics of doing. The eye does not know which side of the earth it is on. The eye cannot see the birthing folds, the suckled nipples beneath the limbs of trees. The nose is far less complicated. There is no discipline dedicated solely to its mysteries. But it is the nose that remembers our disastrous origins. We are sentient. We are this scent of things.

POSSES:

We have tried to codify each calamity in order to present time in equal measure from beginning to end. I have grown tired of this chronology. Reckless, I turn to the depth gauge and the shovel. Archeology requires the absence of unrecorded interventions, a world without mamigaede or theft. With one robust thrust, I have rearranged history, burying plastic robotics beneath centuries of the ubiquitous earthenware. In the presence of such science fiction, what story can the future make?

FROM **Arizona Senate Bill 1070: An Act**

Ryan Clark

1   Be it a naked leg, a slow oar of dust taut over

2   a canyon tent

3   the ledge where fingers map a line at rest in the

4   furtive calf muscle

5   ahead of the shak

6   ing train of a step   of sandal

7   feet gaining Arizona   the rough sun sanded sh

8   ore where a scar in the earth hung law over a young presence of

9   line and economic activity   pressing on fully present in the untied d

10   ust

11   as a wall of fence severs our vein   a bea

12   ten river d

13   rifting forward   In a loss

14   event everyone ends in a forced

15   migration   in wind and sun

16   and no safe water   Skin n

17   ears a division of soil   is IDd as a

18   restricted remainder   All immigrants change

19   as entry touched a body raw

20   Before any law is an act made by an arm   an official one

21   of a state   a subdivision of us

22   as we are   A wrist suspects it hears aliens   is

23   unafraid to say reasonable attempts shall be made t

24   errorist   to say blood determined the immigrant a soft person   The

25   person is migration to us   is all of our ID   Our nomad

26   pursuit unites us   centuries of our us

27   See aliens in love   fully present in the untied status

28   of visit   of voila   tie it here   localize here

29   What is a native if the map said the line shall be

30   transferred immediately to the west   What hunted immigrant

31　cuffs mean　　or the United States Customs and Border Protection

32　Do not stand here　　Law will force again a m

33　arch or　　for an alien　　a ship　　Residents stay

34　and watch as custody of a dry land is tor

35　n　　Others fear　　and fear the outside　　the

36　jurisdiction　　fear seeing agents

37　Alien is made to search where a person

38　has probable cause to believe that fear is a home　　It

39　pulls a fence that makes the fear a song of buffer around us

40　Fix us　　river　　Wash off this

41　stain in the sand　　dry as a fish in a d

42　esert　　dry and restricted from sun

43　River　　remain in formation our linked migration　　a state of

44　vital exchange of form　　a wide feral state

45　a river meant to flow across

FROM **Contracorriente**

Tedi López Mills

s

Que estuvo en Utopía, presume, periódico bajo el brazo, mi hermano
viajero, horas de espera, recalca, la mente en blanco, la duda inscrita
como método, dos islas, dos ciudades, repetido el pasmo, dos atalayas
entre puerta y puerta, norte invadido por la fila de anhelantes, sur desviado
hacia una hondonada, agua en brotes por cada brecha; que estuvo en secreto,
disimulando el tedio: tanto lema espiritual entre pórticos, peristilos, el retiro
de los claustros, no condujo más que a sustitutos, hermano caviloso, pulcras
metafísicas donde nunca contaría el cerebro que las sostuvo, y tú y yo
y ellos, hartos del giro impecable, la horma del universo en la cabeza
igual a la dimensión de los ritos empleados para convocarla, no seríamos
ni siquiera uno, ni siquiera tú, Utopía o isla en luna creciente, mutilando
la llanura exquisita cuando recitabas, guiño en vez de gesto, hermano refinado,
lo indemostrable: la república de seres perfectos, pensados, primero, descritos,
en seguida, cuando iban por la calle, humanamente sencillos, sin asomo
entre ceja y ceja, rala paradoja, de algún dilema ético, aunque malos hoy,
leyendo entre líneas al prójimo, sabiéndolo todo, cómo miente cuando afirma
la verdad; barroca Utopía la que van imaginando, barroca isla aunque tenue
tan pronto recurre a las trampas de una claridad que nadie agradece,
para qué entender, oscuro el oficio de la bondad, niña tente en pie, amaga
Utopía su propio escondite, has visto cuando llegan los seres perfectos
a este lodazal de lluvia, su elocuencia, limo en la boca, la has notado,
cuánto articulan las palabras destino, grandeza, valentía, que labrando
futuro se gastará mejor cualquier trunca conjetura del mundo, lo que sea
en esencia, repítelo, maestro o mimo, Utopía tuvo su centro pertinaz
en un revuelo de teorías, su íntima agua en borrador por los costados,
corriendo el tiempo con esa aptitud para prolongarse más allá
de las predicciones, mañana serás bueno, hermano inconstante,
en Utopía no hay lugar para los ilusos, nadie se lo explica, tras cabaña,
tras choza que linda con la cueva, primavera en principio lasciva
con sus injertos, su flor multitudinaria, su río adulterado por las luces,

FROM **Against the Current**

Tedi López Mills

Translated from the Spanish by Wendy Burk

s

He's come from Utopia, gloating, newspaper tucked under his arm, my brother
the traveler, hours spent waiting, he insists, mind a blank, doubt inscribed
as a method, two islands, two cities, repeated shock, two watchtowers
between the entrances, north invaded by the line of supplicants, south diverted
into a gully, water gushing through every gap; he was there in secret,
hiding his boredom: so many spiritual maxims between porticos, peristyles, the calm
of cloisters, leading to nothing more than substitutes, neurotic brother, tidy
metaphysics in which the brain that sustained them never mattered, and you and I
and them, fed up with the impeccable turning, the form of the universe in our heads
equal in dimension to the rites used to summon it, there we would be
not even me, not even you, Utopia or island below a waxing moon, mutilating
the exquisite plain while you recited, with a wink instead of a wave, refined brother,
the indemonstrable: a republic of perfect beings, imagined first, described
next, as they made their way down the street, humanly simple, no hint
between their brows, scanty paradox, of any ethical quandary, though they are evil today,
reading each other between the lines, knowing it all, how one lies while insisting on
the truth; it's a baroque Utopia they imagine, baroque island that nonetheless weakens
when resorting to the traps of a clarity that no one is thankful for,
why try to understand, kindness is a dark profession, daughter get on your feet, Utopia
counterfeits its own hiding place, have you seen when the perfect beings come
to this rainy slough, their eloquence, muddy mouthed, have you noticed,
how frequently they articulate the words destiny, grandeur, valor, by forging
a future they'll end up wasting some maimed conjecture of the world, whatever it is
in essence, repeat it, maestro or mime, Utopia found its pertinacious center
in a whirl of theory, its intimate water a rough draft sketched along the edges,
time running with that ability to prolong itself beyond
all predictions, tomorrow you'll be good, inconstant brother,
Utopia has no place for dreamers, no one explains why not, behind the shack,
behind the hut bordering on the cave, a springtime lecherous in principle
with its grafted trunks, its manifold flower, its river adulterated by lights,

calla hermano, qué premura para opinar civilizadamente, hoy
no es lo que parece, prensa transcribe toda semejanza con la realidad,
he visto que ayer siempre ocurre al día siguiente, hermano perogrullo,
tinta no soporta tu letanía de virtudes en retroceso hasta un origen inmaculado,
donde mundo es un jueves, augura, triple dado, y si se dispersa el azul
que empuñas como si fuera posible arrebatarlo, una atmósfera menos
liviana, áspera al tacto, intervendría con su brote provisional quizá
de cielo vagamente más viejo.

keep quiet brother, what's your rush to venture a civilized opinion, today
is not what it seems, the press transcribes every likeness to reality,
I've seen how yesterday always takes place tomorrow, platitudinous brother,
ink will not bear your litany of virtues retreating into its immaculate origins,
where world is a Thursday, foretelling, triple dice, and if the blue
you clutch as if it were possible to pull down should disperse, a less light
atmosphere, rough to the touch, would perhaps intervene with its provisional gush
of an indistinctly older sky.

U

Me elucida cara en discordia, diablo babeando hasta en la leche, afuera
la lluvia, adentro la sardónica evidencia de las paradojas, pan duro, mojigata
la señora me cuenta, yo mirando su escote hundido en la grasa del cuello,
pan suave entre los dientes, pica de nuevo, hocico, dos o tres epigramas,
muñón de concha, como si nada una ventisca que remeda en los manteles
la sutileza de la gasa, me describe, paloma y polvo, lo *genuinamente mexicano*,
y oigo pensando, ese apelativo que se me pega con un laberinto adicional
en la oreja, solariego entre mis bastidores, ese rito de cascos y coronas,
será la nación, mi señora de tiza, de borla, de esquila, lo será esa resolana
entre tabiques, esa racha de mala política, ese difuso grafiti de alguna idea
de país camino a la tiesura de una pancarta, *¿genuinamente mexicano?*, señora
lírica, por mi parque de arboledas divulga una rata la misma historia, allende
el monte, ¿hortelano en un jubileo de arroyos o égloga distraída por el saqueo
de sus habitantes?, la pregunta afirma su contrario, he visto, señora coqueta,
cómo una estructura, discursiva en su descenso, se inmiscuye en mi colonia
y acaba haciendo patria, bocacalle, vecindario, melodía breve, rancio musgo,
cómo la rata de hoy, deambulando entre troncos antes de evolucionar
hasta la ardilla, se extiende hasta mañana, escarba cuánta leyenda diminuta
en su pesquisa, señora de estopa, y resuelve: sobra el futuro, ¡tanto y luego
tanto!, por quién toca, a la puerta, y qué puerta, de aldabones, qué inmensa
puerta la que se abre hacia fuera, mundo por fin, mexicanamente,
aunque yo no genuina, amortiguo la caída, voy, ya voy, anda, tiéntame,
diablo de marras, dime qué mitad de mí corresponde a este paraje nacional,
pues vivo de su cauda y mi resquemor en la sortija de su lumbre se parece
a un tributo que le rinde un instante geométrico al resto de una sombra,
padre o madre, me comentan que hay fronteras internas y externas,
un destino de la línea, buena, mala, cuánto daría por saberlo, adoquín
bajo la ansia, ¿licenciado o poeta?, declárase que hay híbridas multitudes
que conciben su espíritu variopinto de modo unitario, siempre cuchicheando
por la estrofa y más vivo que nunca, afirman zarpa en mano,
ésos que lo regatean.

U

Poised to enlighten me is the dissonant face, devil slobbering even in the milk, outside
the rain, within the sardonic evidence of paradox, stale bread, priggish
lady who tells me, as I gaze at the cleavage submerged in her fatty neck,
soft bread between her teeth, another sliver, snout, two or three epigrams,
stumpy sweet roll, just like that a tremendous gust on the tablecloths mimicking
the delicacy of chiffon, she describes to me, dove and dust, the *genuine Mexican*,
and I hear her, thinking: that sobriquet sticking to me like another labyrinth
in my ear, an ancestral seat waiting in my wings, that rite of crests and crowns,
is that the nation, my lady of chalk, of tassels, shards, is it that swelter
between thin walls, that spell of bad politics, that diffuse graffiti of some idea
of a country on its way to becoming as rigid as a placard, *the genuine Mexican?*, lyric
lady, within my wooded park a rat divulges the same story, over the mountain,
orchard keeper in a jubilee of streams or eclogue distracted by the massacre
of its inhabitants?, the question affirms its opposite, I've seen, coy lady,
the way that a structure, discursive in its descent, encroaches on my suburban turf
and ends up making a fatherland, side street, neighborhood, brief melody, musty moss,
the way that today's rat, sauntering among tree trunks before evolving
into a squirrel, extends until tomorrow, digs up each and every miniscule legend in its
investigations, my lady of burlap, and resolves: there's too much future, much too much!,
knock knock, who's there, at the door, and what a door, with a big brass knocker, what an
immense door opening outwards, the world at last, how very Mexican, although
I'm not genuine, I cushion the fall, I'm going, I'm really going, come on, tempt me,
dreary devil, tell me which of my two halves corresponds to this expanse of nation,
as I live in its train and my resentment under its diamond light seems like
a tribute lending a geometric instant to the remnants of a shadow,
father or mother, telling me there are borders internal and external,
fate along the line, good, bad, what would I give to know for sure, cobblestone
beneath the anguish, scholar or poet?, let it be said that there are hybrid multitudes
who conceive of their multifarious spirit in unison, always whispering secrets
with every stanza and alive as ever, clamoring claw in hand,
those hagglers.

V

Es la V de vado, de vagancia, de venganza, de varada, de vahído, de valla,
de vente, de vino, de va, de nuevo: mi instinto, por el amor de los otros,
mi calle en el mundo, por las manos entreveradas con la noción de un tiempo
y el peso de una pena, ¿verdad tangible?, me burlo, veinte días avisté
la línea tenue entre mi casa y la región ajena, grandilocuente, veinte días
de vuelta me dije, esto hiede a ganga, melodrama y tragedia en un solo
vuelco de ruedas, hermano veloz, cuéntame tu vida, es demasiado tarde,
ya comienza el episodio mudo, recalcas, leyendo hasta que termine,
en ese mullido sillón se retrae cualquier personaje, el quién de ayer,
pegado a la tele, canal por canal, sujeto a un actor de reparto, bigote
postizo, qué peluca sin rango luminoso, qué beso en los labios de un espejo,
qué guiño entre neón y cigarro, humo manso por la corriente, mi pensativo,
mi taimado, asesina mujeres en un baldío, mi amigo, hermano, mira
decapitaciones en videos clandestinos, de aquí me voy, de aquí paso
a la página, al quién de ahora, lince perspicaz, le repito a sus letras,
gato obligatorio y lúcido, garra en ristre, lemur o mantra, según desee
bienestar el alma, recítale como si estuviera sola: *tanta mente que el cuerpo*
nimio es apenas teatro de pesquisa moral, alma la panza de un dios de todos,
la adulo, tripa sin tesituras, le propongo, y a cada actitud un gruñido,
voy, vengo de cínica por la carne ahíta, romántico responso, voy
de hambre, de mística vengo, de noche por el cuarto, escala al cielo,
mi peldaño tendrá el mármol de otra nieve, la posterior, cuánto
cuesta esculpir suficientes arcaísmos para inquietar al ejecutante
moderno, fortalezas luidas por la bruma, basta de mofas, pido pausa,
por buscar lo más simple di contigo, siendo un silencio, ya no va.

V

V is for vessel, for vassal, for vengeance, for vast, is for vertigo, verge,
is for veer, is for venture, for voyage, *de novo*: my instinct, my love for others,
my place in the world, my hands clasping a vague sense of time
and the weight of sorrow, a tangible truth?, I'm only joking, twenty days I divined
the fine line joining my house to everything outside, grandiloquent, twenty days
in reverse I muttered, this stinks like a bargain, melodrama and tragedy in a single
turn of the wheels, vanishing brother, how have you lived, it's too late for that tale,
it's time for the silent film, you insist, reading until the final credits,
any character would get swallowed up in that easy chair, any has-been,
glued to the TV, changing channels, subject to a character actor, paste-on
mustache, lusterless toupee, kiss-kiss on the mirrored lips,
wink-wink with the neon and the cigar, slow smoke on the water, my pensive one,
my sly one, chopping up women on a lonely hill, my friend, my brother, watching
beheadings on blurry videotape, here's where I veer away, revert
to the page, to the here and now, observant lynx, I join my voice to the letters,
omnipresent and clearsighted cat, paw at the ready, lemur or mantra, however the soul
desires its peace, tell its tale as if all alone: *so much mind that the body
is barely a trivial theater for moral investigations*, soul the belly of a universal god,
I adore it, gut untouched by nuance, I propose it, and a grunt for every change of stance,
I voyage, I veer like a cynic into sated flesh, romantic prayer for the dead, I voyage
into hunger, I veer into mysticism, at night in the room, a ladder to heaven,
my step as alabaster as a different snow, a future snow, how much
will it cost to sculpt a sufficient number of archaisms to trouble the modern
performer, bulwarks brushed by mist, joking aside, I pray you, pause,
seeking the simplest solution I saw you, a silence, once removed.

Caminos del espejo

Alejandra Pizarnik

I

Y sobre todo mirar con inocencia. Como si no pasara nada, lo cual es cierto.

II

Pero a ti quiero mirarte hasta que tu rostro se aleje de mi miedo como un pájaro del borde filoso de la noche.

III

Como una niña de tiza rosada en un muro muy viejo súbitamente borrada por la lluvia.

IV

Como cuando se abre una flor y revela el corazón que no tiene.

V

Todos los gestos de mi cuerpo y de mi voz para hacer de mí la ofrenda, el ramo que abandona el viento en el umbral.

VI

Cubre la memoria de tu cara con la máscara de la que serás y asusta a la niña que fuiste.

VII

La noche de los dos se dispersó con la niebla. Es la estación de los alimentos fríos.

Paths of the Mirror

Alejandra Pizarnik

Translated from the Spanish by Yvette Siegert

I.

And, above all, to look on innocently. As if nothing were happening, which is true.

II.

But you I want to look at until your face fades from my fear, like a bird stepping away from the sharp edges of night.

III.

Like a girl drawn in pink chalk on a very old wall, suddenly wiped away by the rain.

IV.

As when a flower opens and you see the heart it does not have.

V.

All these gestures of my body and my voice just to turn me into the offering. The bouquet the wind has left behind in the door.

VI.

Cover the memory of your face with the mask of who you'll become, and frighten the girl you used to be.

VII.

The night for the two of them has thinned with the fog. It is the season of food gone cold.

VIII

Y la sed, mi memoria es de la sed, yo abajo, en el fondo, en el pozo, yo bebía, recuerdo.

IX

Caer como un animal herido en el lugar que iba a ser de revelaciones.

X

Como quien no quiere la cosa. Ninguna cosa. Boca cosida. Párpados cosidos. Me olvidé. Adentro el viento. Todo cerrado y el viento adentro.

XI

Al negro sol del silencio las palabras se doraban.

XII

Pero el silencio es cierto. Por eso escribo. Estoy sola y escribo. No, no estoy sola. Hay alguien aquí que tiembla.

XIII

Aun si digo sol y luna y estrella me refiero a cosas que me suceden. ¿Y qué deseaba yo?
Deseaba un silencio perfecto.
Por eso hablo.

XIV

La noche tiene la forma de un grito de lobo.

XV

Delicia de perderse en la imagen presentida. Yo me levanté de mi cadáver, yo fui en busca de quien soy. Peregrina de mí, he ido hacia la que duerme en un país al viento.

VIII.

And thirst. My memory is of the thirst— of me below, in the depths, in the well—and that I drank from it, I remember.

IX.

To fall like a wounded animal into a place that was meant for revelation.

X.

Like someone not wanting something. Not anything. Mouth sewn shut. Eyelids sewn shut. I forgot myself. The wind inside. Everything shut, and the wind inside.

XI.

Words burnished in the black sun of silence.

XII.

But the silence is not certain. This is why I write. I am alone and I write. No, I am not alone. There is someone here who is trembling.

XIII.

Even if I say *sun* or *moon* or *star,* this is still about things that happen to me. And what was it I wanted?
I wanted a perfect silence.
This is why I speak.

XIV.

The night is shaped like a howling wolf.

XV.

The pleasure of losing yourself in the image foreseen. I rose from my body and went out in search of who I am. A pilgrim of my self, I have gone to the one who sleeps in the winds of her country.

XVI

Mi caída sin fin a mi caída sin fin en donde nadie me aguardó pues al mirar quién me aguardaba no vi otra cosa que a mí misma.

XVII

Algo caía en el silencio. Mi **última** palabra fue yo pero me refería al alba luminosa.

XVIII

Flores amarillas constelan un círculo de tierra azul. El agua tiembla llena de viento.

XIX

Deslumbramiento del día, pájaros amarillos en la mañana. Una mano desata tinieblas, una mano arrastra **la** cabellera de una ahogada que no cesa de pasar por el espejo. Volver a la memoria del cuerpo, he de volver a mis huesos en duelo, he de comprender lo que dice mi voz.

XVI.

My fall that is endless into my fall that is endless, where no one expected me, since when I looked to see who expected me, I saw no thing other than my self.

XVII.

Something falling in the silence. My final word was I, but by this I meant the luminous dawn.

XVIII.

A constellation of yellow flowers makes a circle in the blue earth. The water is rippling, busy with the winds.

XIX.

Dazzle of the new day, the yellow birds in the morning. A hand releases the dark; another drags the hair of a drowned woman who is crossing endlessly through the mirror. To return to the body's memory is to return to my mourning bones, and to grasp what it is my voice says.

Equivalents

Jessica Baran

It was all based on a paisley motif. Getting started, running along, scent was never questioned as particulate matter. Particles filled the air, and you took them in. A minute moth swirl. Exhalation from a million grinding machines.

What you know now is the dampness of caves, how yellow light tarnishes a memorable movement. If you hit your head on a low-hanging entryway, someone—someone you may not know—may take your head in their hands and rub away the bruise. Wondering over contact is the tragedy of oversight. So many nets, meanwhile, keep dragging in the ocean's barrage.

Flocked. The uneven texture of broken stone under foot. Trains wail over crossroads so far from where you are that the thought of them feels thick. The need to toggle that thickness to this thin air is a symptom of febrile memory. How can one travel into strangeness and end up at the plainest sense? Napsacks and milkshakes; wall-to-wall carpeting. Without speaking, coloring piles of papers through the night.

Spinning around the real estate development. Your bike was an imaginary taxi. Your taxi carried phantom passengers. At sunset, your fees and tips were tallied on a broken punch-card machine. This was the way time passed—in the absence of others or witnessed once and never explained.

Always wanting to ask the big dumb questions. But here, where streets and sidewalks for several miles are hollowed of people, what seems smart is very small. A way of licking stamps, stapling down rough edges. How unsealed brick sifts daily to the floor—a wan garbage pile of pale pink pigment. Where did all the sugar go? Why is the ringing phone so colorless?

You'd like to lie on blue carpet again, dance the Christmas dance with your father. A pain in the joints signals the need for higher market prices—browner drinks, clearer stones, purer metals. Get the whole motley group together again, and have them meet differently than they originally did: fast and with wit, checking each other's credentials. You met in India, then Africa, then somewhere near the Illinois state line.

Whole biases can turn against you, as drones slice the night and uncertain forces establish shadowy bases. This news is happening at this point on the map. Tear off a notebook page. Remember all the pain you felt, stitching up moccasins from a kit. That sense of clarity in the small city square—fountain bubbling crystalline, men lunching in suits, large flowers blooming and unchanged since prehistory—it was a bargain. It was a way of imagining something for yourself, like a glossy frame around trivial memorabilia.

There can certainly be trouble with rising temperaments. The ssss sound of certain speeches makes a powerful impact—it links together such things as snakes and civic strife and sand. A growing menace is this jumble of days, their diminishing girth. Remember the rough crack in the canvas, the inner layers of blue to gray to red. That was something to see.

Dire consequences befall these little irritants. Crumbs in a borrowed book, the glaring streak of poorly wiped windows, the next Senate race. It's a law of unforgiveness—the rapid flush of intentions gone to the clinic. You made that mark—swerving, unerasable. Everything sees through it.

Rubble intended for posterity. Arch your back while you paw through the classifieds. An arch like a cat's back. Animals are banned from this metaphor, despite your seeing in them so much reasonable behavior. Growing impatience is a powerful institution. It cracks even a traditionalist's ardor, forging new allies when desperation calls.

What you saw in that performance was sincere—limned of performance-enhancers of the childhood variety. Fear, exoticism, one's first sip of coffee. It was damp then, too, in all those far-away ways. You cannot stuff your guilt down deep enough. The nomination was approved, 3 to 1.

You're talking about the snapshot subscriptions, the way someone might throw out a word like "Cartesian" and the whole conversation comes to a dumb halt. Retire that battle, sell your collectable car. Modern restoration is rich with amenities, but do you really need more amenities? Isn't "bright and clear" room enough?

Everyone's bidding on Twinkies, which is a triumph for a certain kind of cultural musketeer. A paved, wet circle of gravel is what's ringing in your mind, lacing together the orange and yellow rope of marigolds and everything in Winesburg, Ohio. You wouldn't turn down the opportunity to repent, in the old-fashioned way. You wouldn't mind coming across something that involved moonlight, dishevelment, Renaissance pink. That kind of glitter isn't made-to-order. It comes of sitting there, at the TV-dinner table, sorting other people's overlooked trash.

Swimming in a large hole. Drinking from a cup full of sliced lemon, granules of sugar, a thin coat of wax. This wasn't your county fair. You forgot you'd been there, as it was never your blue ribbon to claim.

Every chair looked like origami: folded together from a single sheet. Every flower was crisp-clipped and fit with a crystal vase. A jagged haze of blue static gargled from a distant booth, while something about silence was printed large on a wall in front of you. This is the American Flag. This is a Brillo box. This is something you can take with you, for free, because you paid the admission fee.

Flame orange with a crisp black row of prison bars. A massive set of eyes behind which a washy face forms. The ocean laps forever at a specific height, regardless of how close you are. And you are close. There are fifty men before you. There are many questions. Trade this installment of mint-colored linoleum for the one half across the country, and you have yourself a problem.

Reading the name "Kevin" across an apron forms an uncanny sense of continuity. Try to peel the stitched label from its fixed place along your collar. Denude yourself of identity. You're a clever conversationalist when on the clock. Every preference feels like the absolute one, even though they infinitely overlap—a haphazard stack of recyclables. An artificial blending.

Safety information includes directions for managing blankets. "Bridge Over Troubled Water" may be your theme song. The roommate collected knick-knacks. This meant she had an interest in small objects. Further analysis reveals a pattern: this newspaper is free. This owl is a decoy. Every slumped figure in a waiting room awaits their respective charge while failing to heed the pile of revelatory *Horizons* piled at their side.

Journey into the woods. This gray day is like March, every March, even though real estate prices tell you otherwise. Find the fine grid that nets window glass; find the horizontal lines that plot out certain rear windows. Familiar facts, points of exchange. Ethnic meant exotic. Poor meant forgoing the casual lover's spat.

Consider yourself comfortable. Consider yourself fit for an airplane seat. Far away a blanket is taken from castaway bins and placed in an animal's box. Weighing this exchange with ones more immediate—potted plant for socket, cardboard for bookshelf—a moral pain antagonizes your spine. The cushion is a flotation device. You must remain seated.

The last bit of floss linked the old place to the new—the nauseating feeling that this set of toiletries is illicit. Soon to be regretted. You will never earn your time. Your place is not among the necklaced and charmed. His charm was his tumor. You can't tell if that's poignant or not. It is blood, you know—this curdling suspicion, this moisture flooding your sleeve.

The theater of a Christmas tree requires your participation. Lie down, look up. The branch is gilt with dime-store lights. Without you, there is little stock in this wan branch; there are no retirement plans to long for. Wishing for wishes is a better way to explain it—get something in your portfolio, and it falls to the floor.

Slick street, a flat disco ball of fugitive light. Rush in from whatever temperature, and you're still hot. You crouch in a bathroom stall to rub it out, rub out the hiss, flatten the high notes. It is key not to think about what has been on the floor. It is key not to consider observers. This happens for at least ten years—the power of invisibility, gluttonous stretches of time that vanish like a dried-out puddle.

A mashed chunk of rusted iron looks heart-shaped. Tipped in gold, it has all the potential of a black-and-white reproduction of a great Renaissance painting. You never questioned the order of that narrative, how that heart didn't make it onto the page. How many hearts were likely stamped out. How many melted into, say, a kettle.

It was the longest interview. You had to relive a moment of otherwise unrecorded intimacy by running the track once again. The tarmac track that garnered many awards for the more civic-minded youth is cracked and grown-over. Wasn't she something? Wasn't that an innocent time?

So-and-so is cuddly. On another coach, a chasm yawns wide between two listless co-eds. Gravitate toward isolation and your dreams will come true: the alarming but silent mob of characters in an awkward dream, the endless chatter on a page, the look of yourself gazing back from the hand-crafted thing on your wall.

Give thanks for having a house rather than an installation. Give more thanks for radical opulence over refined restraint. Excess can be of the spirit, and that's honorable. Translate it into form, and its just another load of junk.

Make no mistake: the megaphone belongs to you alone. An environment created for interaction does not necessarily guarantee a result. Don headphones, look at objects, watch videos—pretty much the same as any other day. You look and take nothing with you.

Paper clips, candy wrappers, your lost childhood tooth: small objects tell a story when placed in more or less orderly fashion. Tennis balls, light bulbs, congealed toilet paper; nickels, dimes and pennies; nails, screws and metal washers. You needn't explain to anyone what it means, as this alphabet is universal. Every ocean washes it ashore.

Packing to leave, you find only bow ties in your everything drawer. Look at this collection of string. A wind passes, and somehow the tune you were whistling does, too. It's no longer a love song but something more like Taps, played on a boombox via cassette tape. Cover yourself in a flag. Lay down like a veteran.

The universal forms of minimalism are as such: cube, ball, plank. Find them anywhere—strung onto chains at a children's park, lodged into the vast deserts of the Sahara, stacked like miniature cities in a rail yard. See it all again in a white-painted room, and nothing's familiar: your hands are a threat, your mind's ill-informed. It's a top-down narrative, that of simple shapes. Place them once and then better next time, and their value soars sky-high.

Somewhat lazily, this is your occupation: a place dotted by certain public confusion. Soapbox rants, romantic diatribes—the difference between private and public space is to what degree you gravitate toward it. A riddle-like text scrawled on torn-out wide-ruled paper is a note only you can understand. Double-sided, you flip it back and forth, fingering it in moments of distress, imagining it as an exotic visa.

Absorb your decade, but from a critical distance. It's a cris de coeur that's impossible to heed but easy on the ears. A pile of garage-sale items attracts a not-so-intrepid audience—everyone's desperate for a good bargain. Admire the stagecraft: what holds you and anyone else together is desire, desire for that one special ceramic animal, cast in dust and missing a hoof.

The proof is in the sticker: you voted. Political references are always complicated by emotion—you liked the way one candidate looked. You identified with the outsider, even though, by their measure, you're deep inside convention's fold. Only cardboard separates you from the next person. Experiment with preference. Brush up against a stranger in a bristling line.

Knowing that everything else has failed is an excellent counterpoint. It preserves the mystery of headquarters, tree forts, trespassed lofts where confessions to the self go forever unheard. Depending on the utterance, a clue can be extracted. Take a walk. Records can be mixed and matched to form new histories.

$970

John Myers

$15

There could be another of me here, broken credit, sweet and gentle with myself because I know where to be. At the boba place the sealing machine is broken again. I have a lot of shame around finances. I'd love to change my own mind but it hasn't happened yet. I had my own face cut open is how finances felt. The problem of the hero is going to meet the father. I can ask myself why I feel so shredded. Is it because I have a gorgeous obsession. The lotus of finances but what are they other than a human invention. I open my face to the horrors of the public. Finances have given me bad service. He was on the ottoman, half-dressed for dinner, and pressed for time. How would I handle myself if my credit card were declined. A cow is a name for a heavy woman or a woman with sloe eyes. You have many ideas that all give me money. I have five eyes full of dollar signs, honestly.

$45

I ask myself to be sweet and I ask myself to be the best candidate for all or many things. We planned to play tennis again. The plant was growing at the bottom of the cosmic sea. Whom the father prefers. I limit myself if I am a piece of money to be a representation of the things one needs and wants broken, and therewith like a bubble vanishing. My funds do not mean I am a human being. My being means nothing broke. My credit card has been snipped into two pieces. Yes it is a tough convention. Conversationally, I am hurt. You didn't do it. I won't be ashamed but I will work. My money spilling onto my shoulders, where, from my eyes. My laughing eyes are filled all five. And desiring peace beyond victory. I could wait the eleven seconds it takes to get a new life here in Wall Street. The angle of my tears shows me exactly who I am, my credit score doesn't. Are you interested in me or in my eyes of gold. Green and gold.

$5

This is the redeeming insight. Never documented no matter how quickly we all chose to congregate. These simple and unresolved bills. The check did not bounce but that was not my question. Brown and undone bows of intestines steaming like coins. And so it must be known that no matter how often the ogre breaks us. You need a better—more expensive—pair of shoes. I need a rainbow. The tight circle of a sleeping rattlesnake. Everyone talks on couches and my teeth flash out at them. I want love and I want a dollar for the AA meeting and I've never been able to pick myself up out of dependence not ever. If I didn't have the chance to be. Two halves of a split pea. The beauty of each dollar pulls me on as though I'm a string. This is exactly how popular we are. That even, three eyes later, we have a nice sectarian vision of the future. Of the poem that first made us so broke, then paid us.

$5

I let the faucet go and go. I was pretending to be in the past. I wasn't pretending to be a crowd any longer. I was bored and rich of it. I had had enough. Money for years. Broke, representation, a poor vocabulary despite years of dreaming and walking the neighbors down. I had a minor league. I had abstract cruelties, luck. I had three things for myself as gifts. One was my sense of humanity, of being a member of a monied race. Of letting the faucet go and go well that is two now. And my third gift was listening to the group of bonds chuckle among themselves, drunk as fingers. Which of the three meant I could never go home. Money too was a good. The ultimate ember. To be blown either on or out. Some noun! I can be said about like anyone else. Stars, darkness, a lamp, a phantom, dew, a bubble, a dream, a flash of lightning, and a cloud. And pieces of me all over pieces of money. Plus whatever else I've ingested over the decades.

$20

The best thing about boba is that it doesn't give big flavor. It can be happily the background. I sit all day in a cup of gumdrop. Trying to boba like how I wanted. Music, boba, light: Here in the clouds of being rich these three are the sky. If I could be said to have maximum flavor. Denomination and money? A quickset aspic pleasure.

FROM **NOISE, a novel**

Abigail Child

Novels built of stance seem to interchange their effects
Novels built of chance affect seams exchange, lengthening
Novels built of class crisscross places, rising and lowering, arriving
      and leaving, maintaining hierarchies
Novels built of seams are looking closely in between, searching spaces geo-
      physically
Novels built of fun are playing tricks and minute minuets, pubescent and
      flowery
Novels built of sun are full of views that decompose into fractured settings
      and sensations of spaciousness looking differently
Novels built of plots migrate intensely
Novels built of looks stand still in stalled insomnias solipsism
Novels built of letters address the lover and the mom, the family and the
      loop we are attached to
Novels built of fiction drift

2.

I've condensed this
Framed by time
Taking apart the present

To belong to the shadow
And shine group
Stuffed with roundels of live light

Fried with point of surface
Scooped out of earth
Boiled with beaten flame

5.
Ungratefully,
                        semi stiff at the end of his remote
a voice, a line or voice versa
            (unprecedented teleology   *Dear Valued Customer*

signaling
the minty whiff of delicately illuminating
            Envy

                                                streets' world
at the near century

                                    reticulated in sun sprawl

blotching sleep
            Venus rose
....

11.
I could have said memory
a dactylic contusion

drawn on swimming trunks
and other things formed:

Motorola sperm rearview error
broken sticky glistening

bosoming
between beside

beyond knobs
wobbling (narration-ally

ambiguity presents itself
as a face of complicated release

15.

Teen swimmers buddy lightly
practically a Lesbian in Blue
(lovely neutral well-chilled braced

A plain American ambivert
what's-her-name?
under-covers pricking him

Girls
at the melting peak bright
mirror the feel

A homosexual female
an act, or conversely
they add in

Tropical moonlight
comforting black foliage
for his favorite buzz blond hair

Or somebody goofed
there and then when
she metamorphosed, transposed

If nothing was to come of it
(after all) and in the ecstasy
shouting a dada-ist message

A fecal black, blue morose
sarcastic and captious stunt
in the dark of volume

A girls' existence
reveals sub-harmonic command codes
ears sheathed in assembled research

The second artifact is aboard
up to their ears
pax on the misprint

In the micro dusk
caramelized buds occupy the command
The rest of the picture

Buy one. Get one free
catches its own reflection
sad suspiration *(shiver-y)*

13.
(See the message
ads related to
the posture of pictures
Why Should it be Illegal to Let a Horse Sodomize You?
that little graphic poetry jammed
midst face-Lifting and prisoner abuse

INTERLUDE

I seem to see something
the little, the whole
corrupt, so unprepared
more of a nucleus

Small
as the picture of a turn
and tune and turn
to yearn situations' wants

One is "letting one self" now
the absence of their each
other
ineffably unconsciously

Anti-climatic with male
part for female condense
a polyglot possibility
a kind of continuum

Confetti of poppies and bluets
many times!
the day up against inertia
butting in retinals

Self delusion
sinkholes (new each day)
market maxed mortgages
with an epidemic

Person eaten up by humidity
tries to de bureaucratize
formalism
tugging apart audible yields in the now

As elusive as fundamental
honesty, which I doubt
in front of my tiara (yuck)
LIVING IN SELLS

You vibrate, respond to suggestion and
precipitate easily
A thing catches us up
coincident to our funk

I can't gouge out.
The waste of present
is the real economy.
The picture somehow moving

against the background
out of which their obsession
comedy (little fantastication basis)
seemed nice to me (to work with them)

The rapid landscape with a sudden ravine
recorded impersonally
slapped by both sides
overhanging clouds unfold

This quick fix
which she supported
The business practices of that niche—
This future: when you receive this

A fissure
a charm
a loin
happiness

Experiencing wind
an empty lot
between fumes
disorganized (mildewed)

cartoons on pink paper
A bundle of 'thereafters'
half open
torso messy

blue jeans
authorless
pointing antiphonally
in sun-dusted dyad

holding disfigured denominations
minus the panties
not so much remedy comedy prosody
a la mode

blotch botch
but bluff
interrupt
lustrously

17.

Anachronistically
mnemonic reason
metamorphosed into
jumpy Assemblage

possibly self-inflected
Gob
with black scrota
of sweet creeds cacophony

spawned from dark
to shining seas
O everywhere
in the workshop kitchen

in red-shirted stunned continents
in proportion to the
the gradual shred
(and was allowed

to float away.
Or words to that effect.

23.

I wanna ask: reproduction of
fist
the steady squeeze circumscribing
lamps become blast become burst

knocking indecent prisoners
into displaced cosmetic get-well envelopes
exacted by a demented
word

chop-licking polka-dotted squeamish
and then tinted
pimply)
oversexed possession groove

feted in red ink
on call —bits of pink, dust, snow
feigned, gauzy, cloned
gamey

discomfort
shaping remembrance
The window of attention
renovating the tableau.

FROM *The Gulf*
(between Rigwreck & Dis/aster)

Pierre Joris

3- Dis/aster

DISASTER: NOT THOUGHT GONE AWRY
when all this first started
    my body broke out into real bad rashes
        my eyes my face my neck my chest my back my shoulders
big giant holes on the back of my legs,
    holes the size of a #2 pencil
        looked just like the holes
            in the fish
                in the lab
                on the slab
GULF: FROM GREEK κόλπος (kólpos) m. [masculine], A BOSOM, FROM PROTO-EUROPEAN
*BHEU-ə- :"TO SWELL, BEND, CURVE"

WHAT HAVE YOU DONE TO KNOW DISASTER?
    we went to detox —December 11 to January 12
        the children feel much better now
            Alina still has bad days
                she may never be 100%
my little boy is doing fantastic,
        my husband's better &
            I'm feeling better too…
    I've shelled out $40.000
GULF: A HOLLOW PLACE IN THE EARTH

DISASTER IS ON THE SIDE OF FORGETTING
we did blue crab before BP
        but since BP
            we don't blue crab anymore

GULF: An abyss, a bottomless or unfathomed depth

DISASTER: care for the minuscule
        all of a sudden we had shrimp
              with what they call black gill disease
                  if they were blue would it be blue gill disease?
we've had shrimp
        with growth on them
              we've had fish with growths on them
GULF: A deep Chasm, a steep-sided rift, gap or fissure, a large difference of opinion

DISASTER: sovereignty of the accident
the Vietnamese & Cambodian communities had
        a really tough time getting hired on
            to help in the cleanup because of
                the great language barrier:
                    90% of the information put out
                    in the first 60 days was English only
GULF: A basin, from Latin "bacca" wine jug, Welch "baich," load, burden, Irish "bac," hindrance

In relation to disaster, one dies too late
        the herring came in to mature
            dropped on the seafloor dead
compromised immune system couldn't
        fight off a parasite, a natural bacteria
GULF: A rock formation scooped out by water erosion

Disaster disorients the absolute
        grey amberjack, king mackerel, red snapper, mangrove snapper,
caught offshore when gutted
           had black sludge in their stomachs
        crossed stomach walls
           made holes in the flesh
              you could see it with the naked eye
GULF: (obsolete) That which swallows, the gullet

DISASTER COMES AND GOES

the blue runners will hit the oil

off the top of the water, the droplets,

eat it, get sick

larger fish get it inside of them eating

the blue runners

their normal food source and now

that's gone,

it's gone

it's not there anymore,

it no longer exists

GULF: THAT WHICH SWALLOWS IRRETRIEVABLY

DISASTER: NOMAD DISARRAY

the whole circle of life

in the Gulf things too that we don't eat

whales dolphins turtles all this if the disaster

if it kills everything

then what do we do?

GULF: A WHIRLPOOL, A SUCKING EDDY

DISASTER LIES ON THE OTHER SIDE OF DANGER

an overflow, people flooding

the area all the way from Arkansas & all over the US and they

were able to come down here with boats

because they weren't from here,

they took some of our fishermen & put them over in Alabama

& took some Alabama fishermen & put them over here.

And what it was all about was

controlling the images!

GULF: A LARGE DEPOSIT OF ORE (ROCK CONTAINING METAL OR GEMS) IN A LODE (A VEIN OF ORE IN BOUNDARIES, A RICH SUPPLY, ALSO SEE WATER-COURSE, LODESTONE, LODESTAR)

DISASTER MEANS TO BE SEPARATED FORM ONE'S STAR
                —if everybody got up and said "enough is enough"
                        —there is power in numbers—
                                then we may be able to move
                                        & really get it cleaned up—
—*it is still leaking*
                —mine said they ran through oil all day yesterday
                        oil & dispersant
                                in the water the dispersant
when they first put it out looked
        like sand from the Sahara desert
                into contact with the oil it gets foamy slimy nasty
on top of the water
GULF: FROM GREEK κόλπος (kólpos) m. [masculine], anatomically, vagina and/
or atrium of the heart.

                        DARK DISASTER CARRIES THE LIGHT

                        TAKES CARE OF EVERYTHING

NOTE

The spoken words in italics are taken from an interview I did with Kindra Arnesen in New Orleans, February 2012. The texts of the bold-faced "frames" use disaster definitions/phrasings from Maurice Blanchot's book *L'écriture du désastre*, & etymological definitions of the word "gulf" from various dictionaries.

FROM **cuori di testo**

Bibiana Padilla Maltos

L'IMPORTANZA DELLA CULTURA [*]

---

[*] The Importance of Culture

IL PROBLEMA DI GENOVA (II)*

[redacted] nostra [redacted]
costernazione, [redacted] dovrebbe [redacted] sufficiente [redacted]
coscienze [redacted] per
[redacted] desiderare.

* The Problem of Genova

LA CULTURA È IL PRINCIPIO DELL'EVOLUZIONE [*]

* The Culture and Principle of Evolution

La Casa de Lo Curro

Carlos Soto-Román

1.

A house without a face is a map
A house without a body is merely a puzzle

The rooms may look like small pieces
shaped by the absence of residents
molded by the accidental transit
of unfortunate passengers

Our house for instance is a cradle
Our house is a nest

In our children's imagination
we often cut this house in two
From ground floor to the attic
from port to starboard

So all the space can be simultaneously visible
And all the rooms circumstantially tangible

Mother reads Borges in the living room
Father works like a watchmaker
assembling explosive devices

2.

There's a blindfolded guy in the garage
He's been beaten to the point of exhaustion

It seems most likely he's not gonna make it

We read a house
We read a room

In our perfect understanding
that this space builds to a map
that'll helps us to comprehend intimacy

So together we dwell in the hiding place:
these dead zones of fake morality

Although in this fortress, in this stone keep castle
there is no formal space for intimacy

Just dead rats and rabbits overflowing the basement
Just bits of sulfur & cyanide in the gusts of wind

3.

Dry, stiff and popeyed bodies on the grass
smelling like rotten eggs and almonds

The gardener patiently removes the corpses
day after day
none of them has a single scratch or a wound though

Death is such a riddle
Death is such a joke

This is how a whiff of inhumanity should be
This is how time is compressed

The being and the well-being
dissociated, dismantled by force
in order to follow a certain order
in order to elaborate a partial truth

This is what space is for

A weak alibi
so all misrepresentations
of the ethic & the aesthetic of the so-called
reconstruction, can take place

An anechoic chamber full of ghosts
A place where only grief & silence can exist

Four Poems

Samuel Ace

Begin message:

From: S
Subject: It's driving around the mountain down the rushy place down the
hello hand down the furnace round the mountain here she comes so watch
the flint it could be treasured so watch the cry it could be parsed so consider
the trouble the course so consider what comes the trap the pump the me I
had that dream but you weren't so pretty and it was behind the warehouse
whole lifetimes of culture in how my hand fits around your arm that I would
hide behind an arm is more interesting that I would feel so little at your lips
that it was like a block of wood a travel piece an experiment but clearly not
to you because you came so fast you really came so fast so here I am free and
unfree here I am so tied into an account of something a wood floor a wall a
trial of turns

Date: July 15 10:33:11 AM MST

To: L

> The rush down the hello hand   we must keep the flirt down the
>
> cribby pie   surely it's not you who holds me   surely not so fast

Begin message:

From: S
Subject: The blue shirt the bread in the glass the trend of purple legs anchored in the subject instantly pouring an abject slew of words a performance every time we sit to write a packer the syringe in the back leg I had it down that it was your birthday I had it down that it was your consideration we had between us barking

Date: July 19 10:29:34 AM MST

To: L

> I flushed the blue bacto bread in case your hand thought it was a
>
> herd   the instant we walk down the sidewalk to pour out the
>
> remains of our checkbook we find a trail a gurgle hanging with
>
> money

Begin message:

From: S
Subject: That's not the most correct the most correct is the humble rum of voices a chew a blanket of simmers the revenue of not knowing the vault that's growing beyond itself in the dawn where the hour at 4 then 4:01 expands to fit the tremors and the stale corners of steel the summertime crescent never gets to 5

Date: July 22 2:01:14 PM MST

To: L

A grey henley and a slightly hidden neck tattoo   it's   salt   a cradle

for my chin   can't you stay a little longer?   send a little more

sweat of trains?   a little more breath or a little cross of rushes in

the marsh?

Begin message:

From: S
Subject: It's been a crisis around here too (besides the flame that mixed up so much crucial information) come barreling through the volleyballs come brandishing sticks and partial goons trailing the storm drains the vagaries of work shorts an evaporative wind a vacant story

Date: July 28 6:04:18 PM MST

To: L

Told to me by swimming   by news   by a dirty flannel shirt   work shorts and lips   a nostril   a balding   dream   it's been a current that we had a future   a freedom we had finalized   it's been a pretense that volleyed from one to the other   mixed then furied it's been a bird inserted into the twenty beards   it's been a tripwire for us to travel   to sever the locked cases   the neon green bottles in the dark wood of the table-top   discussions taking place so often across the face of the clanging   the bowls

Ten Broeck Street / At Fayoum

Kimberly Lyons

In the margin of the earliest capitol
Encaustic sticks piled into bricks.
A library of burning colors
Behind the wall.
At Fayoum,
A curtain of bricks keeps us.
A curtain of wax is the imprinted faith.

To go back is to look for its limits.
Starting out, register the implacacable blue.
The storm road imprinted
In the mud behind the factory.
What kind of factory produces
A folded book of mushroom shadows
Saffron colored wax bricks
The ledger of a life.

At Fayoum, the portraits of the dead
Are more alive than anyone.
Each report I write
The limits of this road.
At the edges of, a little girl.
Offers her books, her discarded magic.

When I go back there it's like I have nothing,
No vestige of what I thought I had.
The air carries its reports, cools the wet
Hand over pages.
In a stone underneath the papyrus leaves
Eyes turned inside
Witness fireballs.

Each report that I wrote fell apart.
Each time I went there
I realized I had nothing. The little girl
Who sells mushroom is witness to a storm,
The discarded wax.
The hand folds
The map of nothing.
The key was loving
My fayoum is at the edge
Of the air's folded shadows.
Bereft of wax
The dead in the river
Behind the factory.
Whose eyes, turned inward
Carry a portrait
Imprinted on the brain
A fireball.

At the edges of the road a folded shadow.
In the factory, a hand cools the wax.
A report, ledger of magic
Came from the limits of nothing.
A little girl was the key
Witness to a portrait on air.
When I go back to the angel
It's like he's more alive than anyone.
Eyes turned to the storm, saffron
Colored River Road.

Blue shadow, a hand
The key to a book is its edge.
 Leaves imprinted in the mud behind the factory.
Each time I go back to Fayoum, I realize
The portraits are the reports of a life
Turned inside out.
The brain
A fireball
Storming its rivers.

Writing what I thought
Witness to an angel.
The cooling hand of the storm.
Eyes turned inward
The implacable
Book is the road.
The key to Fayoum is in the papyruses
Imprinted reports.
Witness to the brain
Magic writes
On folded leaves.
Factory of
Saffron mushrooms behind the road.
The air carries
Its fireball.

I write
I have nothing.
Each time I return there.
The ledger registers
Portraits of
The mud of a life's
Imprinted bricks.
Fayoum, its tributaries
Its edges.

The book of life is the key.
A wax implacable wall
A saffron shadow of a road
The cooling hand.
At the edge
Eyes turned to the blue
Factory of the brain.
Magic storms
Folded books
I write reports in the mud.

A little girl
At the edge of the river
Offers reports of blue mushrooms.
Her discarded hand, the key.
Writes: I have eyes
Witness to.
In wax tributaries, the folded
Wax bricks
The saffron book.
The factory produces papyrus portraits.

At Fayoum, implacable mud bricks
Of nothing. I realized
My life was a ledger.
Imprinted by a storm
The key was magic.

The factory
Produces books
Folded in the hand
Of an angel
Who cools the fireball
The saffron leaves of this factory.

Two Poems

Ana Ristović

ЛЕП ПОГЛЕД
(страх од рутине)

То је један трг и на њему никог.
Никога, чак ни трга нема, рекао би песник
само наше ципеле, две спремне барке
и поред ципела, две кашике
за лакше назување:

У твоје се слива слана
у моје слатка вода
из истог облака, давно
нам повереног на чување

И тако свакодневно, редом

Свуда унаоколо сасвим је суво
ниједне једине капи

И нигде никог, чак ни нас

Само у кашикама нечији леп,
изврнути поглед, прикован
за већ уходано небо.

Two Poems

Ana Ristović

Translated from the Serbian by Steven and Maja Teref

Beautiful Reflection
(fear of routine)

An empty square.
Encloses no one, not even itself, a poet claims;
only our shoes, two eager boats,
and beside them, two shoehorns
to slip out of with ease:

Salty water drips into yours
and sweet water into mine
from the same cloud given us
long ago for safekeeping

The dripping endures without end

Arid all around

No one around
not even us

Only metal shoehorns
and someone's beautiful
reflection fixed
against the heavily trafficked sky.

ПАДАЊЕ У НАСЕЉЕНИ ПРЕДЕО

да дуго падамо са врха
листа траве
и никада се не посечемо о њихов руб,
да то буде лет у насељени предео
и да треперимо, опипавамо,
ширимо се преко својих граница,
да буде нешто нас у сваком тесном
осмеху који бисмо могли срести,
чекању бицикла крај зида,
сненим очима возача, ширењу зеница,
да не пречујемо тишину у шуму
причања, да се не догоди да
не приметимо руке, спуштене усред кретања
два тела која заједно са лишћем клизе кроз неки парк,
да не заборавимо на додир
коже и дугог звецкања,
када камен разбија стакло и тихог шуштања
спреја што пише по бетону, да осећамо
како талас лови талас
лови талас и коначно чини кретање,
како се речи подижу, пене и глатке,
а ућутале ствари проговоре,
да прсти на ногама пронађу ослонац на зиду,
да будемо заједно
и сами,
и да на крају не превидимо онај тренутак,
када се у јутарњем мраку
погасе улична светла

Falling into a Residential Area

To fall from the top
of a blade of grass
without cutting ourselves along its edges;
to fall into a residential area,
to flicker, to feel our way,
beyond our limits, into a tight smile,
onto the bicycle leaning against a wall,
into sleepy drivers' eyes, into dilated pupils;
to not overlook the pauses in the murmur
of speech; to not ignore
hands swinging at the sides
of two bodies gliding over foliage in a park;
to not forget the touch
of skin, the resounding crack
of a rock smashing a window, and the quiet rustle
of spraying paint on the pavement; to feel
a wave hunt a wave
hunt a wave and at last
lift words, foamy and slick,
so silenced objects can speak up,
so toes can press against a wall,
together
alone;
to not overlook
the darkened street lamps
in the predawn.

Four Poems

Peter Neufeld

Je Promene Mes Yeux

For L.M.N.

From the very
First line come

The very
Last words

Shipped,
Shivered,
Or Slipped in

"Dear Blaschka, What a lovely
Young glass Octopus
You make," techniques,

Once used,
Can often be

Lost across only
A single generation

Something of value
And then here

Something in Latin
For common weed

Fitting in like
Four casement

Windows short and
Bunched between bricks

Or the Moon
Popped up

Above the terraced
House chimney pipe

Turn the corner
You're close to

Home; the last
Of the words

Like jets bound
To whatever sort
Of landing admire

The entry an exit
Of the couplet

That here
Then ends

After Callimachus

I too refuse to drink
from the public fountain

I hope you sleep
you are handsome

as handsome—April
is digging in

these planes these others
have built

cause the sky to be crossed
in the book it is written:

you are no man

inside any head
traveling towards

the where
of anything

for D.L.

this essay is about
an impossible male body

giving birth—a body
seems to recede

before the rhetoric
of alterity

an exchange is something
other people do

his star witness
working among the Basques

(an athletic type—loved
dancing and going out)

was quoted declaring categorically
and in French—"cette coutume

n'est pas connue
chez nous."

there is no invert like a man
no, this hero is a poster child

for J.N.

will you search
for the miraculous
or drive a bicycle
straight into a canal?

in any event
I like you
and keep my wardrobe
on the roof

"The sea, the land,
the artist has with
great sadness known
they too will be no more."

a quote

from Bas Jan Ader

on a loose sheet
of notebook paper

no date

First Works (1-8)

Dan Thomas-Glass

First work within
the world. Premium
coverage for pajamas
toddling wakely from
new rooms. First
dead black man in
America. Costs to
bleed. That I could end
this featureless bounty
with my pen. Alma's
bright O each morning
at the bells. That tenderness
this. That tenderness
wins. Intimate air at
first work in the bowels
beside books. Call
the work of your dreams
to your dreams. Wretched
Earth below trees. Songs
where they question
after termination. The day
ceases. One last disclaimer:
the information provided.
Great granite walls for
histories. Open season.

First work within
the world. Imminent
teeters—tomorrow
& tomorrow. What
withers low income
land, one point about
industry. What I know
what I been through.
Splice figures: bhangra
feels pain to get rich. Sonia,
moved, keeps whispering
her hurts—*stupid, stupid.*
Sun daughters once &
then again—how empty
fists where diamonds
were. Hmm. Alma takes
a header at the market
& bears new braille
on her growing skin.
Forward lisps standing
at the window small
shoulders at morning
branching to smaller
trees smaller still. We
rockin stilettos ho. So
so so.

First work within
the world. Body of
clouds pressuring
moisture to thinning
skin. Humming power
lines streets & blonde
as my girls the wishes
effervesce toward
imagined brunches. So
little wilts. Humming
coastal tunes morning
& what I love. What I
love. Sonia explains
that her sleeveless nightie
has long sleeves & these
words leave me sleepless
in LA like a movie set
with the labor gone home
& the morning cawing
like hungry painted crows.
O tomorrow & again
Alma curls her head against
my groin where Kate jokes
she can't go home
she can't go home
when it's her body &
the body she grew.

First work within
the world. Etch coverage
in freeway clovers:
signal tower to life
guard reds between
shutters & humid
beach. Sonia digs &
preens, new outfits
for each season
of the AM. Language
where we start
in the night: retching
sounds in the tin
of monitored air.
The slag of vomit
like a city on the sheets,
with peaks of what's
hip oozing over scars.
How the stars love cars.
How the clouds repent,
washing asphalt for us
so the smell of tomorrow—
while Alma wags her finger
no, owright—will
twinkle twinkle newly
as our songs.

First work within
the world. Godblack
the stars shine
our ends. Ender
before the box
office receipts,
as in heaven. Hallowed
there? Wait, umm—
Sonia stirring sheets
to bones of dreams
with mixer limbs—
wait. Sidewalk
home stretches to touch
city like astrodust
littering our balcony,
butterfly wings or
branches I guess,
whatever it is we are
when we slip that march.

First work within
the world. Morning
snaps to skin like spandex
—the labor of it—or
the fog? It gets harder
to speak the precision
of moisturizers. Morning
& its needs, Sonia still
sleeping, Alma says *up*
& then *walk* & gets mad
when I say I need to
work. In the abstraction
of yesterday—Sonia
keeps asking what it
means—or before? Sonia
learns songs from TV
about keeping her cool
& she whispers stupid
this or that less which
is shorthand for settling.
How home becomes
a buoy only if time is
the sea & we are drifting,
buying. Low income
tomorrow we walk in
widening gyres, circling
centuries that turned
once & so we know too
can these.

First work within
the world. Language
settles like wireless
static from buzzing
poles upon Alma's
tongue. *Owright.* Then
turns, running ahead.
Alone in vastness
like tolled air
we loll feelers,
unfurling feathers, *owright.*
Sonia slips fingers
filled with plastic
across my shins,
massaging or exfoliating
or something. Morning
comes again. De
La Soul prologues:
I know I
love you better.

First work within
the world. She blooms
plenty, arms linked
to neighbors gone
distant as stars when
we turn to blink
afterimages of August—
mom in her black
sackdress, Sonia's white
frock a negative blur
as she falls to sleep
& misses her swim lesson,
or Alma's clinging legs
like a koala & curls
against my neck sore
with a summer cold—
from our bloggy eyes.
Blear is a painting
technique says LA AM
green, lurching down
the long hill below
stiffly crackling lines,
nearly out of time.

Late Spring Journal [2012]

Stacy Szymaszek

her work is done
no more chicken bones
in this park

●

man with friend
"I'm ready to leave New York"
day after I told Y
New York feels like
a regime
and I keep hearing
my name
or names that rhyme
in the wind

●

default outfit
what Al Pacino
wears in *Cruising*
as his off-duty
cop self

●

guy reading: *Rings of
Saturn* on the F

4-30-12

gray shirt
from farm bin
de-ranked

souvenir draped
over gate

regret it now
that I have
right pants

and that T
sent me that letter
way past 10 years

"at least we have our memories"
(after losing her youngest child
youngest sister and turning 90)

obsessed with
who will get
their clothes

•

she trots
over to the rattle
of pills

these are
my pills

5-1-12

serial jogging
dreams enjoying
something I dislike

while getting bored
with weights

losing weight
calls attention
to dark circles

[undated]

find K's earring
eye-balling rain

•

Golden Gate Bridge
anniversary poem
turned out good
met that deadline
screwing up next

•

thievery at panel
on community
decide not to call
the police

•

public radio stream re-buffering
every 5 minutes

dog sings with siren
on her back easy
return to nap

•

watched *Sea of Love* again
but Pacino best
in the 70s

•

so many spring
visitors

what to do

5-9-12

there will be
a fireworks display
near Liberty Island
tomorrow

•

"you have a dog
I have a bird

see him in the corner
he fell out of a tree

I'm going to take him
home and try
to make him live"

•

nose started to run
while reading fuck it
who has a napkin?

5-12-12

start to enjoy
housekeeping
when I realize
it's my house

•

masochistic filthy
mother's day

•

type instructions
for Brett
how to
love Cass

•

napping on the
wood floor and
it's only May

5-13-12

call Gail
for pronunciation
of "vulve"

•

"Je suis la"

    5-24-12

rain fills
apt. with
smell of
briquette

    6-3-12

FROM ***North American Zoos Worldwide***

Peter Valente and Cole Heinowitz

1975

If the avoidances of probability are so sonorous
start a punk band with every newspaper clipping there was
never caught anything—it's the thought that counts
spent a glorious March weekend with the Swedish girl I was
obsessed with figuring she would stay in my apartment
forever but on Monday she left wearing my overcoat
diving into what? oh nothing, just diving
nobody had a nose ring in those days
winter's here. make some calls. do errands. more later.
I decided to play the guitar as if I existed in a pure state of
mind and could attack it
read your own life and see.
I only live up the street.

Port Authority

The homeless hold the door for people
coming in and out of the bank
it's hard to look up at the sun
when I can only think of these streets
and walk along with the dead
Billy, Tommy's brother, became a cop
the mistakes that can't be undone with charity
inside the station, heading—with all the others—
for an exit
and then she was out of doors, needle tracks
down both arms, lacing onto his hands
looking for something
late again
Margerie sat down at the bar and ordered
a ham sandwich
I paraded my guesses, unconvinced.
Tommy had seen her too and grinned
in the old way so she'd know
then nodded out
a cigarette between his lips
as she stood before the subway doors

The Hindrances of the Householder

Jennifer Bartlett

Today was James 31st
birthday so she would write the poem,

the poem of today, James' 31st birthday.
The following Saturday, the day of James' wedding,

would be Mark's birthday. Mark was 22 years
older than James, nearly to the day.

This would mean that the day James was
born, Mark was married (or nearly married)

to Jeanne and Mark owned (or nearly owned)
a house and had surely finished college

though not graduate school.
Mark's mother wanted him to

"do something useful" and by this
she did not mean paint.

This all occurred in Minnesota
naturally, which was also where Bob lived.

The day James was born was also
the day that Jean-Michel Basquiat

died. However, this was in 1988
so it was (in reality) James' fourth birthday.

Connie knew Jean-Michel because
she worked, at the time, at the Great

Jones Diner and Jean used to often
come in and trade things for food.

By "things" I mean art.

Sometimes it was a green cap.
Sometimes it was a two year-old blond baby boy.
Sometimes it was a bicycle.
Sometimes it was the pink and black textured wallpaper at Sweetleaf Coffee shop.
Sometimes it was the coffee itself.
Sometimes it was a watch.
Sometimes it was a wedding ring.
Sometimes it was a beautiful, intense woman with long, salt and pepper hair.
Sometimes it was the children's park.
Sometimes it was the homeless cats at the river.
Sometimes it was the number 104.
Sometimes it was a pair of shorts.
Sometimes it was abstract painting.
Sometimes it was a pencil factory.
Sometimes it was a beer.
Sometimes it was a name.
Sometimes it was Montauk.
Sometimes it was the ocean.

Jennifer imagined herself
much to be like her paternal

grandmother. Marion, a Minnesotan
in every sense of the word, passed

away when Jennifer was six years old.
Marion was a true lady. A cocktail

drinker, a neat freak, Jennifer's
father was not allowed to have animals

as animals were dirty. Perhaps
that is why he had so many animals

as an adult. And Jennifer had
many animals as an adult, as well.

How many things could she do at
once? She raised a boy, she cared

for four animals, she cleaned,
she did errands, she loved,

she hated. She carved a path
from Andrea's house to her

house and back again. She did
this despite the hole in her shoe.

She did magical things and
she did mundane things.

She studied birds and trees.
She flirted with boys and drank liquor.

She read books and slept. She wondered
who would win the essay contest

at the Ukrainian Institute. She wondered
about the men who worked at the Iraqi

Consulate. Despite the wars, the Iraqis
always seem relatively cheery, although

they often had trouble keeping their parking space.

Every few weeks she met Saint Jim in the park.
She just wanted to get on Saint Jim's bed and float

away; the bed which happened to be on the same
street as her beloved Mark. But, Saint Jim was

difficult and recalcitrant as is often the
case with saints. So, for now she had to be

happy with their short walks and discussions
of New York October light, tiny animals, and politics.

Saint Jim told her *don't you dare put me in a poem.*

Three Poems

Douglas Piccinnini

Bowery

to freeze and lift why alone
abandoned stream
in season—se vende

fundamentally who you are
verbed until you are
a dead system— a debt

of uncut forest—a head
parts of a street
scene behind a building

gas of interior cinema
in a burning time
a smoking time

in a want unsaid
wish you never —
the note seeded

pinning extremity
washed and well
beyond recognition.

As in Every Ism

spread by runners—
poor creeping
for one day hate is

pure stimulation
preceding kink
"simulation"

one way of grieving
a dethroned self
one mouthful of being—

an aeon of inert ideas
like negative streets
the suffocating pill

softening the body
through touch-
less immobility.

Old Weather

pressure in the skull
I'm told to end—might
my boat fold

a presage I guess
to slowly winter?
to light where you are?

a habit thinking of you
when it's not now—
that radar becoming

this windowless feel that
nosunnorshaddow
panic of everything

FROM *La Torre*

Camilo Roldán

there can be a
brick in a brick

wall the eye picks
whereafter he

sat wailing on
sidewalk for all

the world we've seen
we made and broke

upon our selves
cardboard plastic

gum chewed and spat
pavement laid or

motionless wings
that are the not-

music the dead
things at the plinth

where in peals we
heard this lament

we fucked up we
fucked up and I

want to go home
I want to go

home but you know
et cetera

all a hot wind
et cetera

strangers shaking
hands in words home

hands shaking deaf
with tears mucus

run down it all
there found I held

brushes mixing
an orange with white

visage my friend
half obscured by

himself center
turning pink streaks

or vermillion
understood as

a fist of worms
in the brain a

worm in the brain
inverse image

of green drop it
the human hood

spread orange in time
teeth dead in soil

unwound to re-
corded bird song

to recorded
flute concerto

I listening
twenty years late

FROM 31 Stations: Morning Hours

Eléna Rivera

17.

Right along the edge of thought "I"
run counter to the motion of the general
direction—sirens in the distance interject
sound inside the Muse's words, untethered

That's a beginning, how we form our mouth—
confused by another "I"—I forget the effect
of the alphabet—We "move our arms so much"
said the poet "if we could do nothing for once"

Stop, the bells have stopped ringing, tongue
attempts to pull the words out, trembling
A series of images come forward the size
of whales not gold fish, ruby bits of youth

that disintegrate in the bright sun—cut
to a home with a red room, a rusted ceramic pot,
a long wood table to sit and eat at,
cold tile floors and the stain of something

Thoughts change, memories fight in court,
children fight over who will sit in the middle,
that and tying up loose ends in the epic view,
that and the fact that the whole will never be captured

18.

This morning the thorn bush
no more
thirsty than yesterday

listening for an omen
the waterfall
held in suspension

This morning half-open shutters,
where entrance ends,
that edge, the resistance

a gate
of conflicting responses
grates on all possible language

This morning nothing symmetrical
can't say "come in"
The wind full of rain, & setbacks

knocked me down
A folio suspended
There are these patterns

19.

Into hours as into a city in fragments

We all have to get through customs,
cram into a suitcase as much as
we can in this custom made
drizzle made by a tailor

Don't look now
How many boxes will you have?
You'll reach the end and
How many masks? costumes?

Established and full of duties
Smiles and layers of How Do You Do
—a problem of noise—
arriving into hours as into a city

Fragmented by all the noise,
the mouth is a line stitched according to
specifications—Our suitcase—
Are you suitably packed?

The poems go in the opposite direction

Mystes

Matthieu Baumier

Elle peint le soleil en cendres de pierre
et sur le corps de la terre
éparpille les traces polaires,
scande le deuil des charrues
des spirales esseulées
et des salines sauvages

Le sang suinte des étourneaux.

La chevauchée des nuées est à l'heure.

Pourtant, au creux des larmes végétales
certains portent le lointain du chant
dans le silence des terres.

• • •

Sur la terre noire des dolmens
Épuisés par la rumeur des voûtes silencieuses
Dans le ciel des landes ruinées
Vêtues de la rouille des étoiles

Sous le fracas oublié des tertres perdus
Étouffés aux silences des univers
Dans les viscères de cercueils pâles
Et les sépultures masquées d'arbres éreintés

J'entends l'ancêtre lointain du saule
Et la voix brisée des oliviers.

• • •

Mystes

Matthieu Baumier

Translated from the French by Nathanaël

She paints the sun in stone cinders
and on the body of the earth
scatters the polar traces,
scans the grief of plows
of solitary spirals
and the wild salt marshes

The blood of starlings seeps.

The cloud coach is on time.

Yet, in the hollow of vegetal tears
some carry the distance of song
into the silence of the lands.

· · ·

On the black earth of the dolmens
Exhausted by the murmur of silent vaults
In the sky of ruined moors
Vested in the rust of stars

Beneath the forgotten din of lost mounds
Smothered in the silences of the universes
In the viscera of pale coffins
And the masked sepulchres of spent trees

I hear the distant ancestor of the willow
And the broken voices of the olive trees.

· · ·

Il y a eu le silence primordial
Le vacarme minéral des lunes premières
Le déferlement d'univers
En vagues indicibles
Et l'eau racine des temps
Il y a eu le chant des océans
Le labour intime des graines de la matière
Les incantations de l'éternité
Et le vagabondage mesuré des nébuleuses
Une voix s'est attardée en nous
Et nous n'entendons rien.

· · ·

L'oiseau rouge jetait des poignées
de sel dans les entailles de la terre
et tu épelais en toi les couleurs du silence
Il y avait ce sel en lui—et
il parlait aux écailles bleuies de l'univers
aux courroux des écluses,
et des arbres meurtris.

Il disait :

« Plutôt le vent
que la geste sombrée de ce temps ».

Et tandis que tu en appelais encore
aux socs muets des regards
L'oiseau rouge se fondait dans la minceur
du saule aux lettres arrondies,
emmurait nos sons, le silence d'argile,
la matière du potier, l'âme du Poème.

· · ·

Rôdent les yeux des arbres
à la lisière, l'épaisseur des décombres
la plaie de vents éteints.

There was the primordial silence
The mineral din of first moons
The unfurling of universes
In unspeakable waves
And water the root of time
There was the song of the oceans
The intimate labor of the grains of matter
The incantations of eternity
And the measured vagabondage of the nebulae
A voice has lingered in us
And we hear nothing.

• • •

The red bird threw fistfuls
of salt into the earth's gashes
and in yourself you spelled the colors of silence
That salt was in him—and
he spoke to the blued scales of the universe
to the wrath of the sluice gates,
and the bruised trees.

He said :

"Rather the wind
than the sombered gesture of this time."

And while you were still calling
at the mute stumps of gazes
The red bird was dissolving into the thinness
of the round-lettered willow,
immuring our sounds, the silence of clay,
the matter of the potter, the soul of the Poem.

• • •

The trees' eyes do wander
at the verge, the thickness of wreckage
the wound of extinguished winds.

Une faille secrète du ciel cède
quand l'aulne transmue des piles
de galets en chemins d'hommes.

Résonne alors la cantate, le refrain
des êtres aux mille visages,
le chant qui se tait au creux de la parole.

Les temps sont nés.
Il y a un bestiaire discret
À l'heure des frondaisons de ce monde.

● ● ●

La voix déchirée des lunes
dérive sur les continents
face aux mémoires englouties
et s'éteint dans la nuit des pierres

Tout est silence.

Elle regarde les oiseaux aux mains coupées
leurs fissures déshéritées, le sol gris
la cendre du sens.

Il ne se passe rien
Quand un monde se meurt.

Tout est dans le chant absent.

A secret fault of the sky yields
when the alder transmutes piles
of shingle into paths of men.

Then does the cantata resonate, the refrain
of beings with a thousand faces,
the song that quiets in the hollow of speaking.

The times are born.
There is a discreet bestiary
At the hour of the foliations of this world.

•   •   •

The torn voice of moons
drifts over the continents
before the smothered memories
and extinguishes in the night of stones

Everything is silence.

She watches the birds with cut hands
their disinherited fissures, the grey ground
the cinders of sense.

Nothing happens
When a world dies.

Everything is in the absent song.

FROM **Firn**

Kevin Holden

•

made an orchestra made
of glass, foam flotsam

supple crystal the ice
flashes outside logics of

forms, we hope child
knows the bluer blank

aporia staring fast at
the coming colored lights

•

bank of clouds he
loves him splintered reflected
fourfold in the double
glass, lake effect, swan

turning into pixilated flower
at the edge of
the reflecting waters, too
beautiful music chasing flows

•

static, snow, sun, egg
complex voice muted muffled

they twins bearing wool
logical eightfold eightfold telepaths

piano frothing at the
sea the void starry

ova and foam at
night the glacier flashes

•

boy moves among aspen
groves, rhizomatic root music
silver foil variations up
in his mind while
he desires the boy:
poised at the edge
of the pool, outlined
in rose colored air

•

you there looking in
snow a mirror fractalline
form of the human
figure edge tracing hive
flung striated situation you
say you love him
and we shiver here
never been happier

•

ordinary lattice ordinary salt
caked on the screendoor
perched at the sheer
edge of the sea

so cold the brine
threaded rime layers architectonic
could cut your hand
in a measured flow

•

heaped around clearness the

points ringed you can

never get to, trying

to construct the lattice

out of which would

flower the vegetal folds

or bright stone breaking

open into black birds

•

solheim is a glacier
home of the sun melting

far too quickly the
farthest in a field

single magnetic geodesic sheet
breaking open, we would

build a chromatic scale
to be washed away

FROM *Amulet Sonnets*

Laynie Browne

Phantom Amulet

for Alice Notley

When I was alive in a faux city adamant
And unknown to myself, waxen
When I ordered a tulip to carry my mail
When you said you hadn't livid fur spectacles

When I was burned, pallid as a witch
When we returned and took each other
Verdant—when the midwife asked me to rise
From the cognizance of an unknown stream

When a shell-hinged desk became possible
When you were no longer dying, disrobed
Voice of navy coal—I became an endless hollow
More emptying of maps than I could fathom

I was removed from a train of privatized
Constellations and lifted snow was no longer cold

Occipital Amulet

Problem—arctic ice melt
Phytoplancton blooms
Salinity and temperature fluctuations
Experiments carried out in the dark

The back of her head looks like yours
Melting rapidly
I can almost see at the nape, her hand
Physiological behind morphological and behavioral

In the first hour it is not uncommon that the
Back of one head will resemble another
A handful of apricot clasped in elastic
Naturally, it starts with your brain

Take observable light, convert
Chemical to electrical stars

FROM **Some Worlds for Dr. Vogt**

Matvei Yankelevich

Outside

outside myself

there is a world,
— **William Carlos Williams,** *Patterson*

... so, posing a line
in repose, passing the time
instead of time passing, you
may contemplate some
meaningful coherence even
now fragmented into segments

as a shoulder jutting from
behind a garden urn on which
it leans, hair attached backwards
as spider legs to be a section
of a head, a face turned away
never to be more than image

imagined in expectation, i.e.
a contemplated form, the more
seductive thereby promise of
meaning; its beautiful
constructs, or "a way of putting it"
doesn't in the end matter—line

wrestles with words and means
in the glade or shade of cool
grotto until worn out where
it breaks at a point over the hills
with tradition, as the surveyor
folds the tripod of his scope

over a bee in the grasp
of an ant in the dirt, as "as" points
to a simultaneous resemblance
unfilled, unconsummated, yet
reciprocal, all-consuming in
its decor—a drowsing line

in lieu of a revised totality in
sunlight's daytime sense, a
line, then, at leisure to
describe (as in *un-write*)
the shape of a day off—
a patter not for sake of art

to celebrate a sabbath
that is useless to this world
of labor relations, useless to
you, too, now, following the line
with a working finger, that is
a finger that has been made

by time to represent your work,
entire occupation, nimble, severe,
its rings of skin, etched crosshatch
and frayed horizon under
a half moon tell of the wash
of waste. Outside

where nothing cuts, nothing
joins, someone is calling on
the phone as if a line tethers
to the world, whereas in fact
it circumscribes another: *It's
for you, Dr.*

● ● ●

A lush taxonomy breathes deep in the blue wood.
Mowers, harvesters along the perimeter. A park
or no place, which is the same. A crack
in the pavement from one side of the road to the other
in the shape of lightning. A post, lightened by holes in the metal
lifts a rectangular sign above human heads, slanted
in relation to the two yellow lines. Numbers and arrows
and letters—twigs of wood. Splotches of green grass
amid dirt and pebbles. Squat iron hydrant,
its flattened spouts. The water running free beyond it
in the shadow of dark limbs, things that stay
uncarryable away, and the unmistakable
preciousness of a theory of artifice.

● ● ●

The path of a snake on water—a line
that is natural to the word. With time
the line abstracts itself from the branch,
from lightning, from the path of the bug
coming for the corpse. The bug in your
starched shirt: a phantom
touching a nerve. A world in a flash
of contours, but without shape.
The contour of a wave or of wind,
but not its path—a shape you can
somehow signify in a straight line.
The margin tightens, the touch
of pain grows dull. The swimmer
wades into the water
consuming air, or flight.

• • •

     ... the cadaver climbs
toward other astronomies, beyond
the bed and the bath. Wine like blood
from a rock, Courbet's Jura in the mind.

     ... a call for papers
in White Plains. Serifs advertise
fast food at the rest stop. Hands
over mouths as over the lens.

     ... there is a world different
from any other that is happening now
occurring in order to push this world
into the past.

     ... the changes play
to skipping, a record of your failure
to meet the world. An infinite refrain
pours over the writing hand.

• • •

Pose a world as a tautology, or an equilibrium —
a state of balance, or static. Something like
"the river flows"—already redundant. What
in fact is its shape? For instance, someone
gave you this beer, so you can't do anything
about it. You can drink it as long as you stand
relatively still, describing to yourself the view
or the way the tree trunks lay in the northern
woods, leafless then, save for the ground cover
so that vision is not a noun, but
the unachievable form of the verb "to read":
legere. (Greeks choose to speak while Romans
pick through the ruins.) All this is well known
but bears repeating. Cherry blossoms in the rain—
the season's emotional efficacy. To chew the crust
is another way to bite down. Even
the shapes of Eros, you know, are finite.

On Solar Physiology

Will Alexander

"I of the electrocuted hamlets
of the transfigured remnant
of inclement nostrums
subsumed by swirling electron soils

I work by means of solar isolation
by means of solar isolation
by means of cryptic soma & bird

trying to yield by figments a world beyond eras a world with inter-magnetic
hydroxyl commingling with outer suns with the electrical motion of distance
through alterity

& it is because of this distance that I've been claimed by the ambiguous by
dynamic hesitations being kinetic & counter-kinetic by a cathartics which
rises through sub-fervour & vacuum

true
I've hovered within uncountable disorder
yet I've flown like a bird
from stunning iguana transposures
by blood type channelling through strange charisma & error

I've never been able to reason from induction
or hold my mind
point by point
according to mechanics
accrued from traumatic incendiary counting

my difference
understanding the equator as absence of mass
outside the realm of fecundity as abstraction
as if
absorbing by means of supra-physical infusion

because
I am not of the conscious body
I am focused by the osmotic planes
by levels known in certain parts of the world as Aesopian issue

by mingling in private
I've come to know certain aspects of being
through trans-rooted fields
through roots & wharves of vertigo
through imploded species of deer
& the political subsets
& the random holograms of speaking
is where the Sun oneirically swims
where the Galaxy intrinsically lights & suggests
this being my Shaman's biographic
the oneiric glass in its genes
sometimes stumbling in a shaken vitreous house
peering through a porthole of integers
as if the numbers were formed by an unbalanced wheat
or an interior chart burning with a folio of diamonds

the rhetoric of the Sun
associational gulfs
empowering my soma
as a charged uranian power
not a warren predictable as ideology or mist
but as resonance
as a relay of bells

over vast projection beyond limit

& this limit
being nothing other than the consciousness of limit
of thinking of itself
within prediction of that limit

therefore
phantoms
being limit as being
& projected limit as being

therefore I exist
as numerology as circle
as a combined 4 suns
being a great astrology of rivers

& these suns & rivers
by breathing
by gnomic scattering & burning
create by magnification
momentums of tension
fractals
a-positional soils
summoning codes beyond cellular inculcation

because I have only been judged by limit
by culminate fragmentation
I remain obscure
pillaged
by exterior determination
by untoward utility
practiced
as imprisoning mode
no longer of the overtone
of the Galaxy as living obscurity
I'm thinking
of the common obscurity of eras
as figment
the monological steam of the Permian ... Sent on the Sprint®
Now Network from my BlackBerry®

Sopa de Ajo y Mezcal

Florencia Walfisch

En dos cuerpos blandos dos pares de senos húmedos como el agua
que inventa su

recorrido de siesta y espejo en dos cuerpos blancos tibios su
gesto y su gesto.

• • •

No tengo ausencia sino en la región más apagada de la noche.
eso dijiste. lo segundo no lo primero.
mientras me decías también que yo debo dar el salto
porque es mío y porque me pertenece.

no tengo otra región más que mi propia casa ausente de toda
otra permanencia entonces despierto y estoy sola
y tengo por toda construcción un lápiz.

• • •

Mi rostro no tiene más voz que mi rostro
a veces en las ojeras mediocres un colibrí mediatiza las penas.

a veces mis piernas tiemblan hasta encenderse.

en el otro lado del bosque alguien me espera con mi verdadero rostro

que no es único sino desconocido y múltiple

Garlic Soup and Mezcal

Florencia Walfisch

Translated from the Spanish by Alexis Almeida

In two soft bodies two pairs of dampened breasts like the
   water that invents

its way through sleep and a mirror in two warm white bodies
   her face and her face.

· · ·

I don't have emptiness except in the most turned-off region
   of the night.
you said that. the second part not the first.
while you also told me that I should take the risk
because it's mine and it belongs to me.

I don't have another region other than my own house empty
   of every other permanence so I'm awake and alone
and have for all purposes a pencil

· · ·

My face doesn't have any more voice than my face
sometimes in the plain circles under my eyes, a hummingbird
   mediates sadness.

sometimes my legs tremble until they catch fire.

on the other side of these woods someone is waiting for me
   with my true face.

which isn't special but rather unknown and multiple.

. . .

¿hay suficiente oxígeno en tu caja? tu corazón como una caja
llena de cosas inquietas,

¿lo recuerdas?
¿hay suficiente oxígeno en tu caja-corazón? preguntó su
amiga eslovena.

. . .

Mi estar quebrado en la fragante ausencia de lo próximo
cuando el corázon es un objeto lleno de otros objetos
como un cofre rojo y los zapatos
valijas, sombreros o todo lo que es posible recorder

siempre una azalea colorada
o un campo de batalla entre magnolias

es inútil componer otra clase de cosas
todos los objetos por los que has pasado me seducen
como si tu presencia pudiera traducirse cuando
el corazón.

. . .

Cuerpo que quiebro en el orden elemental de mi nombre.
madrugada deshace su traje de oscuridad. sus dos ojos
preguntan. buenos aires es un mapa rodeado con su nombre.
también pañuelos blancos. también una ciudad que tiembla
cuando se derrama la noche.

●　●　●

is there enough oxygen in your box? your heart like a box
　　full of fidgety things,

do you remember?
is there enough oxygen in your heart-box? asked her
　　slovenian friend.

●　●　●

My being broken in the fragrant absence of what's next
when the heart is an object full of other objects
like a red trunk and shoes
suitcases, hats, and everything I can possibly remember

always a colorful azalea
or a battlefield among magnolias

it's useless to compose another class of things
all the objects you have passed by seduce me
like your presence could translate as
the heart.

●　●　●

The body I break in the elemental order of my name. the
morning undoes its dark suit. its two eyes ask. buenos aires
is a map surrounded by her name.
also white handkerchiefs. also a city that trembles when the
　　night spills out

• • •

En mi noche sagrada sobre la tela teje el espacio su lenta garganta

de dicha. los buitres esperan encontrar un traje a su medida.
en la mano alguien recoge la sangre con un grito.

no quiero gritar y sin embargo mi corazón afila su existencia hasta

extenderse y llagarme la boca.

• • •

Después repite su gesto
último
íntimo como quien mira el cielo, un cuerpo querido;
la memoria de su ciudad natal, el olor
de su infancia
la humedad que viaja donde lo de
nosotros es húmedo

íntimo como el dibujo de tu rostro en
mi memoria
repite su gesto como el
último

y comienza

• • •

(nosotros, la madera inesperada de nosotros.
ser el tiempo que abriga la memoria.
ser el costado agujereado del ángel.
ser la sed que decora sin espera, sin otro mundo posible.
sin ausencia.
ser el miedo cuando acuesta su cuerpo doble
sobre las sábanas hambrientas de nosotros.)

. . .

In my sacred night on the cloth she weaves a space her slow throat

joyous. the vultures wait to find a suit in their size.
in their hand someone collects blood with a scream.

I don't want to scream and anyway my heart sharpens its
　　existence until

extending and wounding my mouth.

. . .

After she repeats her gesture
the last
intimate like whoever looks up at the sky, a loved body;
the memory of the place she was born, the smell
of her upbringing
the wetness that travels to where each
of us is wet.

intimate like a drawing of your face in
my memory
she repeats the gesture like
the last

and begins.

. . .

(us, the unexpected wood of us.
to be the time that covers memory.
to be the pierced side of an angel.
to be the thirst that adorns without waiting, without another
　　possible world.
without absence.
to be the fear when resting her double-body
on our hungry sheets.)

Y saber que cruzar una frontera no es gratuito.

cuando la máquina eleva su cuerpo el aire cambia su propia
    duración.

respiro en el costado del día. la cara que se va apagando tras
    las montañas. es un cuerpo presente de otros colores.
    no hay retorno. pero el

sonido tiene su propio destello. los márgenes de
una montaña se aproximan a mis dos pies
sobre tu cuerpo.

el otoño es próximo cuando las hojas cantan por los cuatro
costados.

· · ·

And to know that crossing a border is never free.

when the machine elevates her body the air changes its own
    duration.

I breathe on the side of the day. the face that keeps turning off
    behind the mountains. a body is present in other colors.
    there is no return. but the

sound has its own sheen. the edges of
a mountain approach my two feet
on your body.

autumn is coming when the leaves are singing from all four
sides.

Three Poems

Nadia Anjuman

ثبع

من اوخب هچ زا منک زاب نابز هک یقوش تسین
من اوخن هچ من اوخب هچ من امز روفنم هک نم

مماک هب تسا رهز هک دهش زا نخس میوگب هچ
من اهد هدیبوکب هک رگمتس تشم زا یاو

مزان هک هب این دنی همه رد ارم راوخمغ تسین
من امب هچ ،مریمب هچ ،مدنخب هچ ،میرگب هچ

ترسح و یماکان مغ ،تراسا جنک نیا و نم
من ابز هب دیابب رهم ام هداز ثبع هک

ترشع مسوم و دوب ناراهب هک لد یا من اد
من اوتن ندیرپ هک مزاس هچ هتسبرپ نم

مدای ز همغن دورن مشوخ تسیرید هچرگ
من اهرب لد زا نخس اوجن هب هظحل ره هک ناز

مفاگشب ار سفق هک یمارگ زور نآ ادای
من اوخب هناتسم و تلزع نیزا مرآ نورب رس

مزرل بل داب ره ز هک مفیعض دیب نآ هن نم
من اغف هب میاد هک تساج رب و من اغفا تخد

1378 ولد

Three Poems

Nadia Anjuman

Translated from the Persian-Dari by Diana Arterian and Marina Omar

In Vain

I want to open my mouth, but of what can I sing?
I am despised these days—so what if I sing or do not sing?

What can I say of honey when it tastes like poison on my tongue?
I curse the oppressive fist that smashed my mouth

There is no one in the world who is sympathetic to me—whom
    should I praise?
So what if I cry, I laugh, I die, I live?

Alone in this corner, with defeat and regret for company
I was born in vain—my tongue is sealed

I know, my heart, it is spring—a time of celebration
but my wings are clipped—what can I do without flight?

Although I have been quiet for sometime, I won't forget the song
for every moment I pull the words from my heart in a whisper

Celebrate that day when I escape from this miserable cage
and fly, drunkenly singing

I am not that weak willow tree that trembles with the wind
I am an Afghan girl, and so I wail*

— *Dalw 1378 / Early winter 2000*
رشته های پولادین

---

* The word for "wail" or "alas" is "feghan"—Anjuman is playing with the
  similarity between "Afghan" and "feghan" here.

رشته‌های پولادین

ز بسکه رانده شد از جام لب ترانه من
شکست زمزمه در روح شاعرانه من

مجوی در سخنم معنی نشاط و سرور
که مرد در تب غم طبع شادمانه من

به چه چشم دفتر من گر ستاره میخوانی
فسانه‌ای است ز رویای بیکرانه من

مپرس عشق که الهام‌بخش چامه توست
به یاد مرگ بود حرف عاشقانه من

به پای بلبل امید رود خواهم گشت
که کار ساز نشد اشک دانه دانه من

اگر چه دختر شهر قصیده و غزلم
خراب و خام بود شعر ناشیانه من

نهال خودسرم دست باغبان نشناخت
خم خواهد لوله بسیار از جوانه من

به دست و پا و زبان رشته‌های پولادین
به روی لوح زمان این بود نشانه من

عقرب 1380

Steel Strings

They pushed my song away from my mouth's cup over and over
finally breaking the humming thing in my poetic spirit

Don't look for joy in my words—
fever rent lyricism from me

If you find a star in my book's empty eye
it is my fantasy

Love, don't ask for an ode—
I sing tender words only in celebration of death

I will be the river at the feet of the rosebush of hope
for my tears helped no one

Though I am the daughter of the city of elegy and lyric
my poem is flawed and broken

My stubborn sprig did not heed the gardener's hand
don't ask for much from my sapling

Steel strings bind my hands, feet, tongue—
so on the book of time I leave this token

—*Sarataan 1380 / Summer 2001*

گل دودی

من از احساس تهی بودن لبریزم
لبریز
و این فراوانی حقطی است کم گهگاه مرا
در تب آتشیی مرزعه جان
میجوشاند
واژین جوشش بی آب عجیب
چه مره کاغذی دفتر شعرم، ان گه
جان میگرید
گل میاندزد
گل بیمانندی است
ولی افسوس تنش را
رگه های از دود
رنگ و بو میبخشند

جدی 1381

Dark Flower

I am filled with emptiness
        Filled
And it is often this burden of nothing
in the burning field of my body
        that smolders within
From this strange seething
my poems suddenly
come alive, papery features
        unfold
        It is a rare flower
Yet
these wisps of smoke
        give the body
        its smell and color

—*Jaddi 1381 / Late winter 2002*

Bridge of the World

Roberto Harrison

this morning I went to the doctor
and talked to him about this move

on New Year's Eve I had trouble connecting
my thoughts on Sade and reason

we rang in the New Year
with Miriam Makeba's *Africa*

I'd noticed that my inner life
had expanded, and that I was having trouble

thinking through it. The doctor said that Geodon
would loosen my thinking—I noticed

that I'd been moving through life for 10 years
in a Zyprexa mold. thought control, at its best,

like a sonnet. I do not feel invaded
by the television that I never see. Brenda made me

feel more loved than ever this morning, as my thoughts
expanded. Last night, in the slow cooker, I made

Lamb and Goat curry—amazingly good. I'd thought
to send Joel, and Peter, and Michael an email

letting them know of my transition, but did not. The consequences
of this transition could be catastrophic. I feel more loving toward Brenda

than ever. I could die, or worse. As I meditated today
my books to the left of me seemed packed and dense

against the wall. Soon, Chuck will be here
to play chess upstairs. I told the doctor this morning

that the philosophy and religion of the cyborg
have not yet been written. My

poetry
has just begun. I am

a Fourth Form,
though not as Dodie saw it. Together,

we can belong in this world. Artaud
arrived at the double

as I have. We share more in common
than I'd known before last night. I need less sleep

than before, and I sleep better
and am more rested. I feel sad and cheated

that I need to rely on drugs
so completely. I wonder about Paul Bowles' stories.

I need to reach out
to others

through this. The doctor, this morning, said
that I was enlightened, but not

quite there—somehow—I can't remember
how. I doubt he knows

what he means by "enlightenment." I felt far away
from my sister yesterday, when she called. Michael

talked to me of Christ's
tenderness. I feel tender in this moment. Over

and over I feel that words
do not represent me. I am not

sure what that implies of my intentions
in using them. Yesterday, Brenda and I saw

the Warhol show of the last ten years
of his life. There seemed to have been hope

to live meaningfully in capitalism then. ~~~~~~~ The waves
of this beginning, the new life of my mind

is settling. It's been a while since I've written. I've decided
to mark my continuing with the seven tildes above. And I added

a title tonight, *Muerto Vecino*, after Zizek's dubious interpretation
of Kierkegaard's neighbor, and because of the funeral home

across the street. My thinking has changed, my being has changed,
I am more alert and more engaged in thinking through the world.

And I am able to speak better. I don't know what this means
about who I am. I try not to feel let down that for so much of my life

I've been restrained by psychotropic drugs. Before Zyprexa it was even
worse, with up to 6 meds, as I've said over and over to friends. I feel

the need to make clear what my obstacles have been. Not for pity,
a little for pride, but also for hope. If I can do that, then maybe I can help

someone not suffer so much, like Brenda. I replaced the kitchen faucet
this past weekend. It makes me very happy that I was able to do it

successfully, without ever having been handy before in my life, and after
spending most of my life disdainful of being practical in that way. What a joy

to make Brenda so happy. I don't know how much longer I will live,
and have often thought, recently, that it would be tragic if I died anytime

soon, but that it's imperative that I accept death when it arrives, after
affirming life as fully as I can. It's too easy, and stupid, to be simplistically

oppositional. And to not know that people can ruin anything, but
that the substantial things have value of themselves, is foolish. I don't want to stop

at my own ignorance and lack of forbearance. I don't believe in the West
on its own. As Michael says, the only thing that makes sense here

is love. I have everything I could possibly ever want or need for now. More books
will come, more music too. And love is immeasurable

when it's real. I am so grateful to have more waking time
on the weekends. I plan on making breakfast for Brenda

every Saturday and Sunday that I can
from now on. Early. I see gardens in the future of our household.

And I wonder about a Great Spirit. What does the name matter? I see the
  stones that live
without water. I see the smoke that cleanses my vision, and a network of
  consciousness,

with each node another, on and on that way to the depths. My thinking will never
grasp it all

because of that recursively created network of interior life. My thinking stops
then, barely able to contain the spherical and vast darkness

from which all light arises. That's why what I see is dark. It is brilliant
in its darkness. Like onyx and flint. I can only talk around what I've seen

the past couple of weeks. It reframes, completely, the rest of my creative
life and the rest of my days. All I aim to do now is to focus my attention,

so that I can see it all again in retrospect. So that I can read
and gather more tools for understanding it. So that I understand myself,

and something of the world, and love, and so that I help others. Geodon
will not erase it. I've seen it already, many times. It is my natural state.

I no longer see it as only hallucination. It is a way of being. A way that I can flesh
out, here. Slowly. Carefully. And as I do, its destructive powers,

which are massive and righteous, will subside. As it will know that it is being
given to the world. Because it belongs to all. And all will be there soon.

There are signs already. Because to see it is to break, unless one knows something
of love. It makes LSD

small. It is God and the Universe as One.
I am not the first to see it. But I am a person

given a chance
to write it, letter by letter, slowly, in terms of the light of my ignorance

to see more fully
what I do not know. I do not offer anything

but poems. But it breaks through
my mouth to arrive at the hearts of the world, at the hearts of the horses

of the world, to allow us all to speak in silence. It is not God or the Universe.
It is One as All in you. Because I cannot see through myself

without it. I see clearly
that the sun will not arrive

in this new weather. But that the moon
will take its place. I see clearly that the sun is there

to bring meaning to the sky, and that the earth is more full
with the light of the world

extinguished for a brilliant view of wilderness. This is a view
that extends through opposites

and arrives at a single body
to witness this song. And this song is not the answer

that you believe in, because one day
I will speak to you again

in the rain
and show you

that I do not know. Because knowledge
belongs to the earth. And the earth makes everything

I know. And now that there is less and less freedom
from coercion in a moneyed world, and now that Claire,

a friend, is moving on to be Christ in her own way, now
that Guénon continues to call me to understand

my ignorance, to depart again
from the friends at Kuna Yala, where I helped with the water,

with Brenda watching over me
from a hammock between palms, now that Panamá

calls again to give me a union
of the world, in more than two ways,

and to distinguish from the surface of these times, I
receive

a call to awaken in the snow. I receive a call to acknowledge
that Geodon has planted itself

with capital
in my consciousness, but that the world

is stronger than to balance itself
from the ozone and people alone. We are not erased, and we

do not control the earth. Geodon
is an act of kindness, an agreement

to live this life
in a way that arrives

with the weather. It may continue
for the rest of my life, or it may not. I will not be afraid again

to see things as I do, and I will not
seek out the truth, intentionally, without some kind of agreement

with this custom. Because that is a way, for now,
that I speak. And it is useful, though better left

invisible. And the name, Geodon, brings trouble, I can see
through it enough, with enough love in my life, to believe

in the end of the reign of the Anti-Christ (not Obama). I need to learn again
to be and to write. But to deliver

what I saw
I must return

to the explosion of my inner life. To start with, otherwise and generally, I see
only outlines. Creation manifests

from every direction, in an infinity
of dimensions. Most of us

spend most of our energy
conscious of a very few of these dimensions. Imagine

more than the greatest works of art
manifesting endlessly

from more directions than one can possibly count
every micro second, timelessly. It's glorious.

And the only way to see it with any balance
is impeccably, ethically, compassionately, and with at least an aim

toward the Divine. It IS the Divine. God and the Universe
spoke to me. It is all, always, speaking to us. And what it says

is endless
it brings wholeness

to the precious moment. It goes away
when one tries to pin it down, as I do. I say less and less

as I try to describe it. It is endlessly
generative. It is good

but pitiless and merciful. It demands of us
that we arrive. And now that the thinking manifests

in a way that allows
for union and a bridge, in a way that avoids

easy condemnation, a thinking that reveals
the links toward light

in motion, a primordial
form of being

in a new world that needs no one
to believe in it, a vast chasm

in what a bureaucracy of thought
tries to pin us down with, the hole in time

that allows us to be free
is here, we know it. All of us

can see through delusion. There is no road
in the aftermath of earthquakes, no need for the time

to extinguish the elements, no person
locked to your heart

in the morning, no water to drink
without thirst, no air is necessary to breathe

under the water of seeing, no
need for the earth to do anything

other than revolve, in this
new light. Space

undoes our links
to the immovable. We deliver

the undone to the plains
and see what the harvest

will fill with seed. The whole
does not exist

within outlines. All we can do
is move to it. The music

is unheard of
in this world. It exists

without origin. It is otherworldly,
primordial, and gentle. It vibrates,

equally, in the Lamb, in
the Lotus, in

the stones—there is no place
unknown to it. It is

music, and nothing more,
and nothing less. It is that

everywhere possible. It is harmonious
infinitely, and allows for any sound. To some

it might seem like noise, but that
is only the part. To achieve it

one need only listen. I cannot always
hear it, but I have

heard it. And now
in my new mind, I listen for it

undaunted and silent. I feel it filling
my body with love. Sometimes

I have horrific thoughts. But I am learning
that these are but strong notes

in the fullness
of the music

of my new mind. I can't always hear the song,
but I feel it now. It makes all context

vast. I will receive it
as long as it is here. I will not push

one way or the other with it. It is a fullness
and does not want to be made

into a force. It is a force
without me, and only to the degree

to which this is true. No longer being able
to receive it

will imply a failure
of my imagination, of my ethics,

and my spirit. There is no way
to hold on to it. It serves

no one. And it includes us all. To continue to receive it
more fully

I grow. This implies
the world. It implies clarity. It implies

motion. But it rests motionlessly. If I have a softness in my voice
it is caused by this music. When I don't

I feel less. My voice can be loud
to receive it, but this loudness

cannot be yoked
in outlines. There is nothing I can do.

There is nothing to expect. I can only
let it go. And I can only be afraid

of the horror of my thoughts
without this music. But now that I know

a taste of it, I have
hope. Good people

feed it. I haven't always known
what to do with it and others. But now

I am a little less confused
about this. This is due

to Buddhism, the little that I know
of its practice. And to love. But it does not stop

at my experience. I am ignorant
and cannot offer knowledge. Except this

music
does not require knowledge. I'm not sure

what it requires. It requires
to be received, but does not need us. Is there a pact

between humanity
and God? I don't know. Is there a God?

I don't know. I'm not sure the question
is enough on its own. Or maybe it is, if God

is not limited by concept. And concept
seems to be only a note in this song. Problems

feed it. "Love
is the absence of fear." And "love

believes all things,
yet is never deceived." I aim

to see through my delusions. I aim
to be one of many, a small voice

in the song of the world. I rest
in silence

as I always have. "To have a view
as vast as the sky

and as fine
as a grain of sand." All beings

want to be loved
and to be free

from suffering. We strive
diligently

to learn the vast expanse
and the laser pointed focus

of this gift. Remember that light
makes us. And that in this

new world, more and more
is made of light. And if that is the case,

we move to move
the light of the world. Someday,

perhaps, we will move
the light

of the computer world. Only the compassionate
and true

will be able to do so. Because only they
can be selfless enough

to let it move through them. I am not there
to move it

but I saw this. Long ago. Briefly. I was offered
a glimpse. It is utterly simple and beyond

thought. There is hope. Intention
is a thought. So one

sees. I cannot tangle
myself

in the line. But only to bridge. That is part of why
it will all move. But I cannot wait

until that is possible
to become. I can wait

eternally and actively in the world
to remain

still. With the calm and expansive
link

that allows us to live, so preciously
together, I see through

the trouble that startles me, every moment
and allow the seeing

of my inner eye
to burn through it. I do not remember

what Zyprexa was like any longer. Except that it seems
I have more to work with now, with my mind. And these

words are plain, so as to be careful in this new place. I see
that they do not break open my heart, as I read. And for that

I relinquish this poem, and allow it to be only
a mark on the road to further inquiry. I allow it to see

as I have made a vow to bridge, that my life
aims to be whole, even in the face of potential

catastrophes, I grow more and more
to accept death as it arrives, to allow it to soften me,

and to transform me as I have been transformed through Geodon, only
to know that there is an isthmus, and that it is eternal. Only that there is one

heart to allow myself to speak
in the storms of tribulation, as one speaks

to allow the teamwork of the fabric of need
of the bird malingerer to see this

in the aftermath of one who has died. Like a bicycle never once
together enough to ride, I see this word here, again, to the removal

of a people, to the homeland of union and peace, to the isthmus
of a double link, one ocean to another, one continent

to another, to the only union (even as it may be erased in my history), the place
of one heart to allow the song to continue through conflict

as she saw it then, one time, far away, when I hadn't known yet, that this
would be timeless. And there is one to it there to see it there, to allow

it there to become and to see there as one is there to see
and to allow one to arrive with it there and to see, and to be one with it

there as one is there to be with it. And to see there as one is there to believe
as it is one to believe it there

and to see it there as one with the soil and the air and the light and rain
and to be there with one to be there one with it there once again, and to see it there

and to believe as there is one there to believe it there again and to see. And to see
there as one is there to believe as it is there again

and to see there as one is there to arrive and to be with it
there and to see it there once again and to see it there again

and to believe as there is one to it again and to see and to hold
and to see it there and to hold

being that nothing holds
dissolving

NOTE

written in transition from Zyprexa 10 mg/night to Geodon 160 mg/night—December 23, 2009
(transition started), January 2, 2010 (poem started)

Essays, notes, reviews

Edited by E. Tracy Grinnell, erica kaufman,
Jamie Townsend, and Zandra Ruiz

Molly Zuckerman-Hartung, "To the Detriment of the User (Finally)"
2013, eyelet doiley, L brackets, graphite, oil paint, and brushes on canvas, 14 1/4 x 16 1/2 x 1 inches

On Translation, with Pleasure

Jennifer Kronovet

I.

In a review of the poetry collection *Alphabet* by Inger Christensen, translated by Susanna Nied, Wyatt Mason says this:

> The curse of translation is that at its best it can only be adequate—and yet my dependence on translators for much of the literature that I love has made me not merely grateful for adequacy but convinced that adequacy in translation is itself a kind of beauty, a worthy target for the striving.

As a translator and as a lover of translations, this quote irks me not only because of its condescension and dismissal of the heights translations can reach, not only because of its apathy in not seeing beyond the surface adequacy of translated texts, but also because I am so familiar with it. I find I am regularly alerted to the impossibility of translation, what is "lost in translation," the trials of the translator. These are the clichés of translation that haunt the practice, always suggesting the ghost of a better text lies beneath any book in translation one might truly love, as I truly love Nied's translation of *Alphabet*.

Luckily, there are so many beautifully made arguments about why translations can be more than adequate, why are they are downright necessary politically and culturally, and how they often reach the same "kind of beauty" one might hope for from a poem or novel in one's native tongue. Eliot Weinberger's essays on this topic are especially powerful. But, on a personal level, I sometimes ask: why undergo something that needs so much defending? Why do something that many people believe is destined for failure? (Poets might be especially good at asking themselves such questions.) Here, I want to look at what, on a personal level, can come out of the process of translation for the self. Take the final product out of the equation for a minute and see what the process can do for us, selfishly perhaps, decadently perhaps, to make this endeavor worthwhile at three in morning, in front of several dictionaries, when the audience for the translation is itself a kind of ghost one might not even believe in. I am going to begin this exploration by looking at what some translators have confessed about the translation process and then briefly discuss my own joys.

In *Dissonance (if you are interested)*, translator and poet Rosmarie Waldrop overtly asks herself the question, why translate:

> I have often asked myself why I go on translating instead of concentrating exclusively on writing my own poetry. The woes of the translator are all too well known: little thanks, poor pay, and plenty of abuse. To this traditional triad we may add that American publishers at present seem even less eager for translations than for original poetry—if this is possible. (137)

Waldrop thinks that the reason she goes on translating "must lie in [her] relationship to the original work." She writes:

> As I read the original work, I admire it. I am overwhelmed. I would like to have written it. Clearly, I am envious—envious enough to make it mine at all cost, at the cost of destroying it. Worse, I take pleasure in destroying the work exactly because it means making it mine. And I assuage what guilt I might feel by promising that I will make reparation, that I will labor to restore the destroyed beauty in my language—also, of course, by the knowledge that I do not actually touch the original within its own language. (138)

The utter pleasure Waldrop takes in the translation process is apparent here. It is not the joy of success or of skill, but the joy of ownership and the joy of destruction. It stems not from a sense of duty, but from the more base feeling of jealousy. Yet, it is the very pleasure in destruction that initiates the labor of translation. Pleasure and guilt conspire to force Waldrop to make amends, to make beauty. Here, the public and political arguments for translation fall away, and Waldrop is bound by a different kind of duty that only a work of art one is passionate about can require.

•

For Anne Carson, the process of translation can carve a third way out of the dire dichotomy she sees as entrapping all of us who think in language. Here, the process of translation is not one of devious pleasure, but a pilgrimage to a new place in the mind. In "MOLY: Variations on the Right to Remain Silent," Carson discusses her belief that in writing and in life, we have a choice between cliché or catastrophe, a choice between naming and chaos. Carson demonstrates this in her discussion of Joan of Arc, who did not simplify her experience of god, though her inquisitors required it. Carson writes, "And one day when the judges were pressing her to define the voices as singular or plural, she most wonderfully said: 'The light comes in the name of the voice'" (177). There is a silence there—a sentence that is untranslatable into a kind of logical parsing. Joan of Arc refused to simplify, refused the cliché of the god of her time and what followed was catastrophic, she was killed. The choice is between cliché or catastrophe—this is clearly a devastating way of looking at the world though many of us who write have felt these poles as the available options—and yet, there is a process out of this duality according to Carson:

> Most of us, given a choice between chaos and naming, between catastrophe and cliché, would choose naming... And here is where we can discern the benevolence of translation. Translation is a practice, a strategy, or what Hölderlin calls "a salutary gymnastics of the mind," that does seem to give us a third place to be. In the presence of a word that stops itself, in that silence, one has the feeling that something has passed us and kept going, that some possibility has got free. (186)

The labor of translation, the work of the mind in that act, allows for new kinds of thinking, allows for speech that moves beyond cliché without falling into the cavern of catastrophe. For Carson, translation is a process that brings meaning without sacrificing meaning. Translation can literally save your life as you try to chase down the possibility it unleashes. Again, it is the doing that matters, the thinking the process demands of us, not the resulting product.

•

Poet and translator Pierre Joris has a mechanical model of how translation can propel the translator into a new language. In his introduction to 4X1, he writes:

> I read to write. The closest reading I have yet discovered is translation. Which is a writing. And thus a circle or, hopefully, a spiral is set in motion. The pleasure of reading combines with the desire to write to engender a third, the work of translation. A sort of energy-recycling Wankel-engine with its eccentric shaft and its peritrochoid curve from which also at (the best of) times shoot the tangents that are the writing of new poems, the latter feeding on and growing out of the energy generated by the reading/writing translation-engine mixed with what they can adduce from the ambient air, i.e. Her Dailyness. (5)

The process of translation is an imaginary, sophisticated machine that can lead us, among other places, to writing. The energy one puts into translation, according to Joris, is recyclable and regenerative. This explains why so many American poets are translators—many poets learn to write through translation, which is the teacher, the instigator, the way of living in language so language generates more language, a way to break away from canned speech, from the too known. Now translation is starting to seem less like a doomed and thankless art, and more like an art the translator thanks for all its work it does on the mind.

•

Waldrop celebrates Brazilian poet Haroldo de Campos's assertion that Lucifer is the angel of translation. Through her we get at the devilishness and irreverence of the art, but another thread through translation theory is that translating can elevate one to heavenly heights. Walter Benjamin, in his famous essay on "The Task of the Translator" writes:

> If there is such a thing as a language of truth which all thought strives for, then this language of truth is—the true language. And this very language, whose divination and description is the only perfection a philosopher can hope for, is concealed in concentrated fashion in translations. (77)

The idea of a language above the languages of the world in which the distance between language and thing is closed, in which communication is a one to one process is one that I think most poets dream about. For Benjamin, when a translator reaches out of one language toward another, language can reach out of itself and give the translator a sense of this pure language of meaning. Here, Benjamin might as well be the leader of a new cult: the cult of translation. Sign me up. For those of us who love books, it does seem right that by serving them, we may gain some heavenly, or really, metaphysical reward.

All of the essays I have discussed, if you go on to read them, also imply specific translation processes. They are guidebooks, mind maps toward a kind of devilish nirvana of language, of impish piety, a process that leads to the pleasure of one's sense of language opening up and fastening down. Translation allows us to live in and own and expand a text with awe, while feeling, in a tactile way, the relationship between language and meaning, feeling and form, and all the while breaking into new ways of making meaning happen on the page. In their light, "adequacy" becomes irrelevant.

III.

My own pleasure in translation is not quite as devilish as Waldrop or dire as Carson; it is rooted in my love of the rough and tumble, of bodies wrangling. Learning to find pleasure in the act of translation has allowed me to translate poems in a way that serves them. This process starts in my home as a child. In our family, there was a culture of mishearing. We often misheard each other, songs on the radio, requests, and recriminations. And so, when young, I thought that the common folk song that goes, "My Bonnie lies over the ocean. My Bonnie lies over the sea. My Bonnie lies over the ocean so bring back my Bonnie to me," was actually, "My *body* lies over the ocean" and so on. This version made perfect sense to me—that a soul would be separated from the body, would belong to or reside in a different place. I can trace this feeling, in part, back to growing up in a Jewish culture in the Jewish diaspora. Our ghosts were that of immigration, of escape, of the other life that could have been led if all that had led up to World War II had not happened.

The ache for my soul and body to feel of one place led me to learn Yiddish. I thought, maybe this would be the language that could unify a dividedness within me, or help me to fill that desire to belong to a place. It was not. No language can solve that kind of rift, but I did learn to love Yiddish, a fascinating language, and in my studies I came across the poet Celia Dropkin. Celia Dropkin was born Zipporah Levine in Belarus in 1888. She began writing as an adolescent in Russian, and in 1912, she moved to New York and began writing in Yiddish. She had six children, five of whom survived, and died in 1956. In her lifetime, she published many poems and stories in Yiddish journals, and one collection of poems, *In Heysn Vint* [*In the Hot Wind*]. She was a well-regarded member of the vibrant Yiddish literary community in New York in the first half of the 20th century. She was known for her experimental approach to lyric verse, her secular and sexual focus, and her searing imagery. She was also recognized for writing with complex and frank ambivalence about being a mother. In 2000, two Yiddishist friends, Faith Jones and Samuel Solomon, and I began translating her work. We divided up her poems and were tasked with creating "literal" translations from which to work.

Back then, the pleasure I found in the translation process was social. Meeting every other week to talk about these poems was a joy. I had the chance to meet Dropkin's son who was in his 90s, and his pride in his mother gave my work more urgency. Yet, beyond this, I got little out of translating. (Around that time I co-founded and co-edited *Circumference*, the journal of poetry in translation; doing that work was extremely rewarding because I was able to read and present fantastic new translations by others from around the world.) When I started translating Dropkin, I was a young poet just discovering my own relationship to English, just trying to get a sense of my own concerns and aesthetic drive. Dropkin's work remains so different from mine, and at that point hers felt threatening. I was worried she would take me into her writing. That I would lose my own voice. I was also very insecure about my Yiddish competency and compensated for that by making my translations as "literal" as I could, without trying to carry across how her voice or radical formal choices might have been heard by her contemporaries. We finished a draft of the book and put it aside.

Then, ten years after discovering her, I returned to Dropkin. So much had changed for me that allowed the translation process to be different. I had been writing poetry for a decade and teaching it for years and felt sturdier in my compass as a writer. It was this sturdiness that allowed me to take risks in my own writing and in these translations. I also returned to the poems as a mother. One need not be one to understand Dropkin's work, but becoming a mother gave me immense respect for her stark honesty about that role and the time she must have stolen to write—her drive to write and speak out of her time fueled mine to translate. During these ten years, I had read enough translation theory to no longer singularly value the literal as a marker of a good translation. Rather, my goals had shifted to that of reenacting the potency and meaning of the original in our own time.

Yet, the process only became truly pleasurable and potent and mind-altering once I had a metaphor with which to think about it. This metaphor stemmed from, of all things, my study of kung fu. I have studied a style of kung fu called Wing Chun on and off for eight years. There is a training exercise in this style called "sticky hands." Two people stand facing each other with their arms always touching but rolling through a series of positions. The exercise trains your sensitivity: you learn to feel your own strengths and weaknesses, to feel how attacks happen—what kind of openings might allow a strike to come through—to feel how a small shift in structure changes your relationship to your partner. You learn your own body through another's in an exercise in which there is both an element of trust and an element of danger. Sticky hands became the metaphor through which I could explain to myself a process of translation that allowed for a new multi-directional relationship with the text.

I returned to the literal translations. I changed them. I stuck close to Dropkin but nothing about that sticking was static. I moved with her, and she moved with me. In this, I felt the pleasure of getting to know her strengths, her force, but also felt my own poetic body—I felt my own grasp on the tools of the poet, my own grip on English and how I might wield this to draw her into our time and ear. I could feel her body teaching me how to be more honest and radical, and I could feel her shifting from a past she was often at odds with. There was a physicality to the process that made the time between us, all the distances between us, both malleable and traversable as long as we stayed connected. Through a fighting art, I learned not to fight with Dropkin's poems, rather the process trained me how to move with her in language, sensitive to us both—and it was as much of a thrill as training in kung fu can be, or training with a ghost might be. And while it was the process that I grew to love, not the product, this process allowed the new translations to be more subtly attuned to both the original Yiddish versions and to the English lyric. Here are some examples of how the translation changed. These are co-translations with Faith Jones and Samuel Solomon:

My Hands (final translation)

My hands, two little bits
of my body I'm never
ashamed to show. With fingers—
the branches of coral,
fingers—two nests
of white serpents,
fingers—the thoughts
of a nymphomaniac.

My Hands (original translation)

My hands,
two little bits of my body
that I'm not ashamed to show,
with fingers, like the branches
of coral.
With fingers, like two nests of
white serpents.
Or ... like the thoughts
of a nymphomaniac.

You Plowed (final translation)

You plowed deep
into me—fertile earth—
and sowed there.
Tall stalks grew—love-stalks—
with roots down deep in the ground

and golden heads to the sky.
Surrounding your stalks, red poppies
amazingly bloomed.
You stood, suspicious,
and thought: Who planted poppies?
A wind passed through;
you had an impulse
to show it the way.
A bird flew through;
you followed him
away with your eyes.

You Plowed (original translation)

You plowed deep into my fertile earth
and sowed it.
Tall stalks grew up—love-stalks
with roots deep in the earth
and golden heads to the sky.
Over your stalks, red poppies blossomed splendidly.
You stood, suspicious,
and thought: Who planted the poppies?
A wind passed through;
you had an inclination
to show it the way.
A bird flew through;
you followed him far away with your eyes.

IV.

I have a young daughter and often I sing to her, "My body lies over the ocean.
My body lies over the sea." I like singing it this way. It is wrong the way every
translation is wrong. But I imagine how this mistake will proliferate meaning.
I imagine my little girl someday realizing the mistake, and all the ways she
might make sense of that slip, and that there are ways I cannot imagine. I
know the song will mean more to her, will be part of the culture of us. I wonder
if someday she will sing our version to someone she loves, sharing a secret
that only happens when you bounce between two versions, when you take
pleasure in the space in between.

Works Cited

Benjamin, Walter. Ed. Hannah Arendt, trans. Harry Zohn. "The Task of the Translator," *Illuminations*. New York: Schocken Books, 1968. 69-82.

Carson, Anne. "MOLY: Variations on the Right to Remain Silent." *A Public Space*, Issue 7, 2008: 175-87.

Dropkin, Celia. trans. Faith Jones, Jennifer Kronovet, and Samuel Solomon. *The Acrobat: Selected Poems of Celia Dropkin*. Huntington Beach: Tebot Bach, 2014.

Joris, Pierre, ed., trans. "Introduction," *4X1: Works by Tristan Tzara, Rainer Maria Rilke, Jean-Pierre Duprey, and Habib Tengour*. Albany: Inconundrum Press, 2003. 5-10.

Mason, Wyatt. "Love Exists, Love Exists." *Harper's Magazine*, January 2009. Online.

Waldrop, Rosmarie. "The Joy of the Demiurge," *Dissonance (if you are interested)*. Tuscaloosa: The University of Alabama Press, 2005. 137-43.

My Dinner with Bernard Frechtman

Shonni Enelow

Act One: My Dinner with Bernard Frechtman

Scene: A meeting room, gallery, or lecture hall. A lectern. A water glass. A white projector screen. A spotlight. A young woman with papers.

1

When I was asked to speak about Jean Genet's American translator Bernard Frechtman, I was thrilled but admittedly somewhat overwhelmed; indeed, despite Frechtman's crucial contribution, he is little known even in the academy, little more than a footnote to the American ex-patriot scene of 1950s Paris. So let us begin with the facts. Frechtman was tall and handsome. He was a champion fencer at college, as well as an avid croquet player and pipe-smoker, and very charming; he knew interesting people, like Kenneth Burke and William Carlos Williams, and could recite pages of Dickens from memory. After the war, like many other underemployed literary aspirants, he went to Paris, where he heard about Jean Genet and began to read him. Frechtman had great taste. He began by translating Jean-Paul Sartre and André Gide, and soon set up a literary agency and started translating Genet. It was around this time that he met Annette Michelson, another American writer, and moved in with her. Frechtman became more than Genet's translator; he was also his agent, banker, and friend. Neither Genet nor his texts, it should be pointed out, were easy to work with. But Frechtman lived and breathed Genet for the next ten odd years. During those years, however, Frechtman also had a series of severe nervous breakdowns. Tensions between Frechtman and Genet mounted, and Genet finally dropped Frechtman around 1965. Shocked and hurt at this betrayal, Frechtman wrote a series of raving, panic-stricken letters to publisher Faber and Faber. He spent time institutionalized. And in 1967, Frechtman hanged himself, in the garden of a friend's country home.[1]

---

1 Edmund White quotes from these letters, sent to both Faber and Faber and Grove Press, in his biography of Genet, *Genet: A Biography*. The biographical information in this paragraph is also taken from White. See Edmund White, Genet: A Biography (London: Vintage Books, 1993), 399–401, 551–552.

Annette Michelson went on to become a well-known film scholar, found the revolutionary journal *October* with Rosalind Krauss and others, and write many books with long impressive titles. She is currently Professor Emeritus at New York University, where she taught for over 15 years.

On February 27th, 2009, I wrote to Annette Michelson the following:

Dear Annette Michelson,

My name is Shonni Enelow and I am a doctoral student in Comparative Literature at the University of Pennsylvania. I am also a playwright and erstwhile performance artist. Occasionally I write other things, which are occasionally published. I tell you this in lieu of listing my credentials, which are anyways more impressive in the abstract. I understand that you are a very famous scholar and furthermore that the way in which you are a famous scholar means you also possess, as a scholar, an enviable hipster cachet: first because you write about film, and second because you belong to that generation of visual culture deconstructionists that grad students like to name-drop at cocktail parties. By which I do not mean to imply that your work is not of superior intelligence or historical importance, which I am more than ready to believe. But the fact is I have not read any of it and I write to you today not as a grasping graduate student but as the playwright and erstwhile performance artist to whom I briefly alluded. I am in fact, not interested in you, per se, but rather interested in the romantic relationship you had in the late 1950s with the translator Bernard Frechtman. To be blunt, I have become interested in the little-known life of Bernard Frechtman to the point of obsession. I am in love with the idea of Frechtman and want to inhabit it fully. This love dates to my coming upon a photograph of Frechtman leaning against a doorway holding a cat in Edmund White's 1993 biography of Genet, *Genet: A Biography*. Frechtman, as you are undoubtedly well aware, was very attractive. I love attractive men and I love them even more when they display both flashes of brilliance and signs of extreme emotional instability. Luckily these three things very often go hand in hand and so I have had many lovers. I think of Frechtman, however, as the summation of them all.

There is, of course, a good deal of precedent for critics and scholars to fall in love with their subjects but that is not an accurate description of my position, you see, because Frechtman is not my subject as a critic or a scholar. Frechtman could not be my subject as a critic or a scholar because Frechtman had no original artistic output. His only role was that of translator. There is therefore no possible object of inquiry.

But since I cannot study Frechtman, I am going to canonize him another way. I am going to write a play about Frechtman's death and life. It will be called "The Life and Death of Bernard Frechtman" and I will get an extremely attractive actor to play the lead role. And it is for this work that I need you. I want to know everything about your life with Frechtman. There is no detail too miniscule. In my play, *everything* about Frechtman's life will have *great* significance. I would therefore like to request an interview. I am available Mondays, Wednesdays, and Fridays, and would be more than happy to meet you wherever you would like in the New York metropolitan area. Please let me know if this request can be granted. I would be very grateful.

Yours sincerely,
Shonni Enelow

2

I heard back from Annette Michelson immediately.

Dear Shonni Enelow (she wrote), "it [is] framing as the quintessential composition strategy which challenged [...] pictoral purity. The frame, empty and infinitely mobile, proved an implacable generator of forms."[2]

Annette then asked me to meet her the next day at 8:25 am, on the observation deck of the New York Stock Exchange.

I arrived the next morning punctual and well-dressed. Annette was standing close to the window glass overlooking the floor of the Stock Exchange in a large black coat. I approached her and we shook hands.

Forgoing formalities, Annette Michelson and I spoke of our lovers. Bernard was very charming, Annette said. He was also kind of an asshole. Very passionate but also very remote. Very idealistic. When someone annoyed him, he could be very censorious, but he was really a very vulnerable person. He bared his soul constantly, sometimes in very inappropriate situations. One time, we were in line at the post office, and he struck up a conversation with the woman behind us, and immediately started telling her about his private life in the

---

2 Annette Michelson, "About Snow, " *October*, vol. 8 (1979), 112.

most excruciating detail, things about his mother, things I'd never even heard myself. I kept trying to extract him from the conversation but he—perversely refused and—brushed me off and—I became hysterical, completely hysterical. I started hissing and pulling his arm and finally I pulled him outside and started walking, thinking he would follow me if he knew what was good for him. But he didn't follow me. And there I was.

Go away. Leave me alone, he said.

And I did. I walked around the Luxembourg gardens until it got dark. And then I went home and found Bernard in bed. I went into the other room.

I remember once I had a drunk conversation with Simone de Beauvoir in which we both confessed that sometimes we had fantasies about being Victorians, bourgeois Victorian housewives, with melancholy little private lives we could never share with anyone. Bernard liked Dickens, Annette concluded, irrelevantly.

A silence followed, and in my anxiety produced by that silence, I ran through all my shameful fantasies, and picked a few to tell her. Then I realized that I was talking to Annette Michelson, more than familiar with the common tropes of psychosexual perversion. So instead I started talking about my trip to Paris between college and graduate school. My relationship to Paris up to that point could only be described in candy-colored cliché: I'd been an exchange student in high school, learned the language, decided it made me glamorous, and proceeded to use the experience throughout post-adolescence both as a metonym for my superior sophistication and as a kind of talisman to ward off any latent feelings of upper middle class mediocrity, while privately unable to destroy the suspicion that, however excellent my accent and well-honed my sense of subtlety in dressing, I was just another American girl with a French fetish, a middle class cliché if ever there was one. That trip after college, however, somehow I digested the cliché. I became both more cynical and also more aware of the cataclysmic sincerity that characterizes even our most banal delusions. And part of what prompted that latter realization was the walk I took, one cloudy late afternoon, to the apartment of a photographer named Sébastien.

The sky was dark, it was going to rain, and it was muggy, and everyone looked sort of disagreeable as they came up from the metro. I was listening with headphones, while I walked to an apartment of a person I barely knew, to a song about walking to the apartment of a person the singer barely knows. She's the kind of girl who makes me feel at home wherever I am, he sang. About Sébastien, I felt exactly the reverse. He didn't make me feel at home, but in outer space, practically, so completely away from home and into the realm of the merely possible. I have never felt so complete—by which I mean, so completely in the realm of the purely possible—as I felt on that walk down Rue Diderot, through Place de la Nation, to Sebastien's apartment. As purely possible, which is to say, as evaporation, as pure lightness—as if hardly there at all.

3

I looked at Annette Michelson. She looked back. And how glamorous she looked there, in her square glasses, glamorous and remote. I wanted her to take me by the hand. I wanted her to call me "my dear," and pluck me from the sea of toil of thousands of invisible graduate students, locked in their studio apartments with Judith Butler and a box of Raisin Bran. If she puts her hand on my shoulder in this instant, I said to myself, I will be forever exalted.

But Annette Michelson did not put her hand on my shoulder. Instead the conversation took a turn, and Annette started talking about her recently developed obsession with bird watching, an obsession she, with her relentless scholarly activity, was often too busy to indulge. That's why I like to come up here, she said. Here I can practice. I count the brokers and identify them by shape and kind. Then I count the tiny little pieces of paper they throw on the ground as they work. Thousands of slips of white paper, fluttering from the brokers' busy hands to the marble floor.

Look —

Look —

They're about to ring the bell.

The bell rang and the floor burst into action. Amid the melancholy clamor of the stock brokers, I imagined myself in a garden, my hands burrowed in the dirt.

There is a way of being that relies only on the present instant. I have the most disturbing feeling that I've missed my chance. Frechtman, too, was "haunted by an unrealizable intuition." The terror that by some subtle movement, some tiny gesture, he would forever miss his mark. I understand this about Frechtman. "He [was] an empty palace. The tables are set, the torches lit, footsteps resound in the corridors…but no one ever appears."[3]

4

When we parted, after watching the activity for several hours, Annette handed me a stack of file folders all the colors of the rainbow. They were Bernard's hysterical letters to Faber and Faber. They gave them to her after he died and she filed them away in a towering file cabinet, in the left hand corner of her windowless office at New York University.

5

Dear Faber and Faber,

> Aristocrats have made gold useless by applying it to the walls of churches. The saint makes the world useless, symbolically and in his person, because he refuses to use it. He dies of hunger amidst riches. It is necessary that these riches exist: divers must seek pearls in the ocean beds, miners must extract gold from the bowels of the earth… slaves must build palaces…so that the saint, rejecting [everything], may lie at death's door, barren and disdainful…Then the world, abandoned, empty, rises up like a useless cathedral.[4]

---

3   Jean-Paul Sartre, *Saint Genet*, translated by Bernard Frechtman (New York: Pantheon Books, 1963), 84.
4   Ibid., 201.

Act Two: Les Dessous Chics

Scene: the stage becomes the elegant stage of a mid-century concert hall. The spotlight becomes brighter. A microphone. The lectern disappears. The woman sings unaccompanied. The song is translated on a video screen.

> Les dessous chics / C'est ne rien dévoiler du tout / se dire que lorsqu'on est à bout / c'est tabou / les dessous chics / C'est une jarretelle qui claque / Dans la tête comme une paire de claques / les dessous chics / ce sont des contrats résiliés / qui comme des bas résillés / ont filé / les dessous chics / c'est la pudeur des sentiments / maquillés outrageusement / rouge sang / les dessous chics / c'est se garder au fond de soi / fragile comme un bas de soie / les dessous chics / c'est des dentelles et des rubans / d'amertume sur un paravent / désolant / les dessous chics / ce serait comme un talon d' aiguille / qui transpercerait le cœur des filles[1]

On video:

Chic underwear
It's nothing at all to reveal it
But by the time we're done
It's taboo
Chic underwear
It's a garter strap that snaps
Against your head like a pair of slaps
Chic underwear
It's a cancelled contract
Like a fishnet stocking
With a run
Chic underwear
It's decent sentiments
Made up outrageously
Red blood
Chic underwear
It's your inner self

---

1   "Les Dessous Chics," by Serge Gainsbourg, translated by Shonni Enelow.

Fragile as a silk stocking
Chic underwear
It's lace and ribbons
Of bitterness behind a folding screen
Afflicting
Chic underwear
Like the point of a needle
Piercing girls' hearts

Act Three: The Task of the Translator

Scene: the meeting room, gallery, or lecture hall returns.

1

On May 21st, 2009, I wrote to Annette Michelson what I knew was a rather odd email. I described how I had come to be interested in her former lover, Bernard Frechtman, and attached a working script of the performance piece I had written in his honor. I described my imagined interview with her, on the observation deck of the New York Stock Exchange, and asked, somewhat sheepishly, if she would be interested in actually meeting me to discuss Frechtman and his work.

After about a month, I heard back.

> Dear Ms. Enelow,
>
> I regret not having answered your message more promptly, but a pile of e-mail accumulated during a recent absence from New York prevented this.
>
> This said, your message is puzzling. The neglect of Frechtman's gifts, of the quality of his work and of his steadfast moral integrity have indeed gone without the recognition they so strongly deserve; here indeed "lies one whose name is writ in water," but your fantasies about him appear unlikely to clarify matters, and I am unable to offer assistance for your project.
>
> Sincerely,
> Annette Michelson.[5]

---

5   Annette Michelson, email correspondence to Shonni Enelow, July 8, 2009.

2

Because upon writing Annette Michelson I had gone out and bought a complex and expensive cellular telephone with the ability to receive email, I received this reply while sitting on a bench in the Brooklyn Botanic Garden.

I was next to the roses. I have not pleased this creature, I said to myself.

Maybe I'll sit here forever.

But pretty soon I got up and left.

3

In Edmund White's biography of Genet, Annette Michelson is quoted saying, "Frechtman invented Genet for the English-speaking world…[But] Genet was determined to remain completely isolated. He once said, 'Sartre has done a lot for me. You, Frechtman, you have done a very, very great deal for me. But if either of you were to die tomorrow, I wouldn't think about you twice.'"[6]

In contrast, in White's biography, Annette comes across as a long-suffering but deeply empathetic lover, who stayed by Frechtman through so many of his breakdowns, until she finally couldn't take it anymore. Even after she'd broken it off, when he fell apart again, she was the one who took care of him. Until he fell in love with someone else. I wish he hadn't, because his new girlfriend was not as kind as Annette Michelson, and when he got depressed, she threw him out. Instead of leaving, he killed himself. That's what happened.

4

Walter Benjamin, another translator of French modernism who killed himself in the wake of bureaucratic hysteria, writes, in the preface to his translation of Baudelaire, "unlike a work of literature, translation does not find itself in the center of the language forest but on the outside facing the wooded ridge; it calls into it without entering."[7]

---

6   White, *Genet: A Biography*, 401.
7   Walter Benjamin, "The Task of the Translator," translated by Harry Zohn, *Illuminations* (New York: Schoken Books, 1969), 74-5.

On video: Die Uebersetzung aber sieht sich nicht wie die Dichtung gleichsam im innern Bergwalde der Sprache selbst, sondern ausserhalb desselben, ihm gegenueber und ohne ihn zu betreten, ruft sie das Original hinein ...

5

When I arrived at Sébastian's apartment, he was making us dinner. But he'd forgotten an ingredient, and had to run down to the street to get something from the grocery. I was left alone in his apartment for about ten minutes. I wrote down a selection of quick impressions, as if I sensed that in the present I couldn't fully digest the experience. This "writing as an aid to memory"[8] seems to me evidence that it is not only traumatic events that we are unable to process in the present, but all kinds of emotion. This furthermore suggests to me that much emotional experience is based on a skewed temporality, a time-collage of sensation: sensory data is transformed outside of the present into, for instance, a feeling of sadness based on the anticipation of what it will feel like to remember.

On video: Small, high ceilings, yellow pillow, red couch. Film posters, fresh flowers, a large white desk. A bathtub with a window. A laundry basket. A woman's negligee. A green lamp. He returns!

Sébastien was in the habit of attaching off-the-cuff pictures of himself to emails. Pictures of himself writing the email. Pictures of himself looking through the email. When I got the email from his father, I was sitting in my squalid shared office at the University of Pennsylvania, the offices they lend grad students as the most transparent kind of charity, with broken chairs and monstrous metal desks from the '70s. One of my more enterprising officemates had tried to spruce the place up, as he put it, with a lone houseplant, but the effect was simply pathetic. It had been maybe six months since I'd heard from Sébastien, which was unusual, because after I left Paris we kept in regular touch, especially once his photography work started picking up and he needed help with English translations. The last time he asked for help, he was picking a title for his latest collection. "Ma chère Shonni," he wrote, "J'ai encore besoin de tes précieux conseils. Voilà je travaille en ce moment sur les années 50 pour un magazine en ligne New-Yorkais. La semaine je dois préparer un teaser, j'ai besoin pour cela de valider le titre de la série au plus vite."

---

8   Lyn Hejinian, *Writing as an Aid to Memory* (Berkeley, CA: The Figures, 1978).

Voici quelques pistes:
Seven Women
Seven Ladies
Smoke gets in your eyes
Come go with me
Please, turn around Honey !
The good old time
The fifties look
A fifties fashion story

On video: My dear Shonni, once again I need your precious advice. Right now I'm working on the 1950s for an online magazine in New York. This week I have to prepare a teaser, and I need to pick a title for the series really quick. Here are some options.

I told him if he changed "The good old time" to "The good old times," or better yet, "A good old time," that could work, but if he changed "Come go with me" to "Come along with me," that could work too. I liked "Smoke Gets In Your Eyes" the best, actually, but in the end he chose "The Rendez-vous."

When, six months later, I read the email from his father, with its strange syntax and awkward diction, I stared for a long time out of the small window to the left diagonal of my desk. And I thought of the last time I was supposed to see Sébastien, right before I left Paris. We had made a plan to see each other. But I canceled it. It doesn't matter why. I missed it.

6

Dear Faber and Faber,

> Many writers have complained of being lonely, often in agreeable fashion...But this proud and melancholy loneliness is of no interest, except to students of comparative literature. Spiritual solitude in the great Romantics, the solitude of the mystics, solitude in the eastern provinces between 1798 and 1832: these are fine subjects for dissertations. Those people were not alone, or else one must believe in the solitude of adolescents, whom "nobody loves, nobody understands." Stendhal was not alone: he lived ...with "the happy few"; Keats was more alone: "here lies one whose name was writ in water"; but this despairing epitaph which he wrote for himself

was addressed *to the Others*. You are not really alone as long as your thoughts are communicable, even if bad luck prevents you from communicating them.[9]

7

Frechtman's favorite Dickens novel was *Our Mutual Friend*, the author's last completed work of fiction, which ostensibly centers on the story of a young man named John Harmon, who fakes his own drowning in order to see the effect of his fortune on those who inadvertently inherit it, including his promised bride, Bella Wilfer, whom he had never met. The real center of the novel, however, is the river Thames, and its denizens, like Gaffer Hexam and his daughter Lizzie, who make their living by fishing corpses out of the river and taking their money. The fantastically complex plot of *Our Mutual Friend* unfolds over a series of doublings: mistaken identities, disguises, parallel histories, parallel episodes, repetitions. One of these doublings concerns the novel's villain, Rogue Riderhood, who, halfway through the novel, almost, by accident, dies in the river himself. It is an oddly climactic scene. Riderhood, unrecognized, is pulled half-dead out of the river, and resurrected in an interlude famously theorized by Gilles Deleuze. According to Deleuze, for the people who pull Riderhood out of the river and try to save him, Riderhood is no longer an individual, with an identity, but only a singular—'a' person. This emerges out of the possibility of his living or dying—he exists in that moment only as pure possibility, as pure potential—nothing less or more.[10]

> If you are not gone for good, Mr. Riderhood, it would be something to know where you are hiding at present. This flabby lump of mortality that we work so hard at with such patient perseverance yields no sign of you. If you are gone for good, Rogue, it is very solemn, if you are coming back, it is hardly less so. Nay, in the suspense and mystery of the latter question, involving that of where you may be now, there is a solemnity even added to that of death, making us who are in attendance alike afraid to look on you and to look off you, and making those below start at the least sound of a creaking plank in the floor.[11]

---

9   Sartre, *Saint Genet*, trans. Bernard Frechtman, 589-90.
10 See Gilles Deleuze, *Pure Immanence: Essays on A Life*, translated by Anne Boyman (New York: Zone Books, 2001).
11 Charles Dickens, *Our Mutual Friend* (London: Penguin Books, 1997), 439.

8

I had a dream about Frechtman. We were having dinner in his apartment. He was wearing a fedora and I was wearing a blue blouse. When you have a lover, you don't want to understand him or her completely. You want there to be a centimeter of the unknowable. In that empty space you draw portraits of the two of you together. These portraits are not collages. You are not you plus the other person but rather this third, strange thing. Without the empty centimeter, that third thing would be impossible. This is also the reason that no translation should attempt perfect fidelity to the original. And why studying things does not mean unmasking them as if to lay them bare, but rather opening a space for the revelation of that centimeter of inscrutable emptiness, which is the possibility of love.

End play.

Epilogue

When I performed "My Dinner with Bernard Frechtman" in New York in 2010, it so happened a close friend of mine was working as an assistant to George Braziller, the famous independent publisher, who had lived in Paris during the same time as Frechtman. She told him about my performance, and when he expressed interest, I sent him the text. A few days later, he emailed me and asked me out to lunch.

I met George Braziller at his apartment on the Upper East Side and we walked very slowly to a diner. Because he was very old, and the walk was so slow, and because I felt very honored to have warranted his attention, it had a dream-like and theatrical quality, almost like a Noh play. At one point he remarked, in a casually significant way, that he had heard the rumors—the rumors about Genet and Frechtman. This idea that there had been a sexual relationship between them had seemed possible to me, and its suggestion is in the background of what I'd written, at least in my mind; even literarily speaking, Frechtman's devotion to Genet seems to display a certain masochism that in Genet's writing is ubiquitously sexual. Still, coming from a person who had known them, I was taken aback by George Braziller's comment; even Edmund White, whose biography is rigorously direct about Genet's sex life, never implies it.[1]

But the "truth" of a sexual relationship, if such a thing exists, is immaterial. It is the repeated triangulation—Genet, Frechtman, Michelson; Frechtman, Michelson, me (or is it "Michelson, Frechtman, me?")—that strikes me now, several years later, as well as the guilty sense that Genet is the truly absent figure in what I've written. This is related to my discomfort that the piece, on the surface at least, is so heterosexual, but here I should point out that I wrote "My Dinner with Bernard Frechtman" while writing my dissertation, which included a long chapter about Genet, who was a central part of my research. It was out of frustrated desire for Genet, a desire that was also a desire *to be* Genet (who, whatever the usual form of their desires, can study Genet and not feel one or the other, or both—masochistically?) that I approached Frechtman. Add another to the list: Genet, Frechtman, me.

---

1   "Although Frechtman was heterosexual, American, and Jewish, Genet liked him, at least at first, and thoroughly trusted him" (White, *Genet: A Biography*, 400).

This is why I want to give Genet–Frechtman, or Frechtman–Genet, the last word.

> The reader is informed that this report on my inner life or what it suggests will be only a song of love. To be exact, my life was the preparation for erotic adventures (not play) whose meaning I now wish to discover. [...] Was what I wrote true? False? Only this book of love will be real. What of the facts which served as its pretext? I must be their repository. It is not they that I am restoring.
> — Jean Genet, A *Thief's Journal*, translated by Bernard Frechtman.[2]

---

2 Jean Genet, A *Thief's Journal*, translated by Bernard Frechtman (New York: Grove Press, 1964), 100.

Third Arm

Jess Arndt

All fall I'd been carrying around something that wasn't mine. But I'd made it mine and now I owned it more than its original owner or owners. It excited me and kept me company. I often dragged it out from where it cowered and tried to look at it. When that didn't work I fed it alcohol.

It's not like I had a lot of time. I was busy with a new job as vice vice something at Queens College—it was a job they were making up and so none of us really knew what I was doing. Plus I was bartending down the block from my Bedstuy apartment and then there was "the writing," that ongoing scarcity feast.

The thing was more important than all of that, it must have been.

Sometimes it made me shout until my voice went hazy and erased. I liked being without a voice, it was a complete relief. On days without sound I would lie around imagining that, my voice deftly abrogated, what was speaking was my meat: the vital part of me that didn't have to first enter and exit my brain but just sat there, a bunch of systems and nerves, opening and closing with my oxygen gulps.

This went directly against what my healers at the Authentic Process Healing Institute told me: that I had a blockage in my throat chakra and had to talk. It was after one of these particularly long sessions that I got into my mostly crumpled Datsun 510, lunged on the engine and began to drive. It was November so the poor air quality that swiped my windshield felt not only atmospheric but in its opacity, right.

I had a 5 o'clock meeting with an Assistant Dean. We were planning a suicide prevention week that was supposed to pre-empt the inevitable depression of the season. In our meetings thus far he'd been sprinting past gung ho and I was invariably hung over, a combo that caused the team of us to skip forward many logical steps and had me in my small basement office calling companies like: Maxi Adult Bouncing Castles, inquiring after the price.

Traffic was bad. Something in my session had made me ancy, my Corps Leader, as they—refusing actual names and the inevitable attachment that came with them—liked calling themselves, had been in a provocative mood. What if everything you think is authentic about yourself is nothing more than affective glare? she'd said. For instance, that "thing" you carry around. It's bullshit right? And when the winter line comes out you realize Uniqlo's selling them too?

Not if H & M gets it first! I'd whooped. Then had spent the rest of the session in the long hallway, cycling between the vending machine and the bathroom, back in my haze.

In the car the news station droned: stocks belly flopping, a shooting, but there was nothing I could catch onto. I unbuttoned my jeans, dug my hand under the band of my boxers. I only liked to jerk off while driving otherwise the sincerity was gag-worthy.

I surveyed the choke of cars on the BQE. How many other commuters were fishing for pocket trout? Waxing the carrot? The terminology drove me nuts. Ok, so what do you call sitting against a steering wheel with all that freeway filth below you, imagining you have a cock in your hand? And about the cock: it's yours, you made it, but you don't care about it too much either. You aren't that dumb.

But I was too restless. Plus a thingy in the catalytic converter had broken off and in the review mirror I could see a deathcloud spewing out from my exhaust pipe. Other drivers were glaring and pointing. Now not only was I the so-and-so practicing self-abuse on the freeway but I was single-handedly causing the oceans to bulge, the atmosphere to wimp out, deforestation of forests so virgin they should have been pre-teen but instead they were irreplaceably ancient, all of it: me. I turned up the radio, mashed my face against the glass. Instead of feeling cool on my cheek it seemed brick hot.

"This is Bubba the Love Sponge on Cox FM." The speakers gasping back to life. "...ok hunters, LISTEN UP." Great, I thought. Following the squalling trail of a Zeppelin song had stranded me on a tea party bandwidth.

"Do YOU know what YOU were doing in 1840?" Bubba coaxed in baritone.

Easy one, it was my favorite era.

Oregon trail! I shouted. The wagon broke an axle and Sissy's got the cholera!

Lime green pixelations on a field of black descended over my windshield.

Date: June 30, 1848
Weather: hot
Health: poor
Food: 242 lbs.
Next landmark: beer?

"Well if I know you like I THINK I do," Bubba drawled, interrupting my near mortal position, "you were probably shooting bear." But he said it *bahr*, I knew that word, I'd been there last night and part of this morning; my clothes spread between the bed and the toilet when I woke up.

I listened absently as I drove down 495. It had been all over the airwaves, one of those stories announcers couldn't put down. For the first time in 2 centuries, and only for this weekend, we were free to spray bullets at Connecticut's black bears. I wasn't an animal lover, they're probably dangerous, I thought. Besides my antipathy to Bubba's voice, I didn't much care.

When I got to Queens College, a pudgy dark had descended and the big beech trees rattled above the PTL parking lot. My phone was cluttered with a series of texts from the Assistant Dean. "You're late," he said. "Now you're really late." "I find it a big bummer that you don't care more about what we're trying to do here," went text #3. "Honestly it makes me worried about you." And finally "Call me when you get it together?" He couldn't help himself. "Whenever that is," smirked text #6.

As I walked to the lounge, I wondered where it had gone wrong with us. There was a night a few weeks ago where we had been the last two at a post-reading wine reception. Both single, both ambivalent cooks, we crouched over the fig puffs and mini quiche that I fervently wished contained chunks of ham. Had I tried to tell him about...? It was likely. September and October had been so bad I'd been practically hibernating but the sea of Fisheye merlot had done its thing and woken me up.

The problem's the women I'm into, I'd managed, massaging the hollow above my clavicular head like my healers had instructed. Confessing to my habits made me feel wide open, part of the universe's radiant core. Talk, I thought, TALK.

I shuffled my feet around meaningfully, waiting. But something was sticky. When I looked under my shoe there'd been a bit of gore.

Oh god, I'd said. Look, gore.

Gore? he'd said. He dived down towards my shoe and re-emerged. It's an edamame potsticker from that platter. He pointed. It's not *gore*.

Salman Rushdie, the season's big ticket reader, had just exited the room and to be honest there'd been a kind of stampede. It was possible that food had been crushed. But as I'd inspected the fleshy blob, I became more and more adamant: gore. The department always looked down on us creative types anyway. Thought we were liars and hacks.

Now I flicked on the florescent lounge light and stared over the scene. Microwave, mismatched chairs, multi-weave carpet with a mid-90s pattern made from some impenetrable armor-like fabric so it seemed barely worn. No Assistant Dean. It was a Friday night and Queens College being a commuter school, I was alone. I didn't want to be here but couldn't stomach getting back into the Datsun, rolling home.

Maybe I should go to the library? I wanted to find that story that Burroughs had written when he was a kid: "Autobiography of a Wolf."

Don't you mean *biography*? His teachers had prodded him.

No, he'd said. And again: Nope, no.

My phone was wiggling again on the table. I picked it up. Going to tell the Ass Dean to fuck himself, I said aloud.

But it wasn't him, it was a Connecticut number, one I'd erased a million times. *La Cocinita at 8?*

I began to sweat. We'd driven each other so crazy that I couldn't even remember when we'd seen each other last, that file was sealed. Three-day screaming matches (her idea), degrading sessions where I'd beg for her attention but only—I knew it as I was doing it—so that she wouldn't have to be alone... But now another memory was strolling back to me, some horrible blip of magnanimity (maybe after drinking) where my brain had said to my typing thumbs: yeah, sure, some margaritas, gaze at each other's faces again? Great.

I went into the bathroom and shoveled water over my head and shirt. Then I jogged to the car. If I left now I'd be late but tolerably late. Plus: I didn't care what she thought anymore.

I approached the passenger-side door. It was an embarrassing form of self-chivalry my car enforced. The driver's side could only be opened from the interior lock. But something was sticking between the door and the frame. As I pulled the door open, it plopped onto the ground. I bent down and flashed my phone on it. I couldn't believe it. More gore.

This piece was apricot-sized and seemed mostly made of fat. But there were some darker globs too. It reminded me of a bar I'd been to near Joshua Tree. I was driving east and the structure had seemed cool and friendly against the mid-afternoon blare. I gulped two beers and stretched and seeing no option besides a urinal, crouched with my shoe wedged against the stall. I looked down at my pubic hair and usually camouflaged crack with fresh hope:: "gross." When I sat back down I realized I was staring at a mostly disintegrated human foot floating on the bar top in a formaldehyde-filled jar.

Mexico? The bartender seemed unsure when I'd asked him where he'd gotten it. No, *Hawaii*. Or Nam, he said, hedging. Actually Ebay, he admitted later. You'd be surprised.

Huh? I said, snapping out of something.

I could tell you were a writer, he continued, so I had to get my story right.

Scientists have proven that matter doesn't exist, I said. You see a foot, but when you get past all that skin bone squishy stuff etc., nothing's really there.

Traffic had cleared and I accelerated over the Triboro. For some reason I couldn't stop thinking about the Assistant Dean. His life seemed pitiful to me. I couldn't imagine what he'd had to get home for. Or why, when we'd been talking and drinking wine, he hadn't understood that my problems, *and in fact this was my problem*, came from outside of me.

Welcome to Connecticut, the sign said, bulging into my headlights' view. The wheels thumped in misalignment. Plus a low drone had started to keep pace— every conversation we'd ever had was rapid-cycling through my head. *La Cocinita* was a hole. Mexican but smelled of years of French fries. I remembered a faraway night where I'd popped a tire on the curb and she'd psychoanalyzed my flaws while spinning the tire iron over the hub nuts. *That's talent*, I thought.

What's wrong, she'd said later, what's wrong?

It was raining very softly. My vision turned diffuse. Coffee. The Merritt Parkway only had a few gas stations but I'd seen a "Rest Stop Ahead." I drifted along the gentle curve of the exit. Lately my sleep had been abysmal and each morning I woke up feeling worse than when I'd gone to bed.

My narcoleptic friend described sleep as a seduction so druggy you'd never want to resist. No problem, I resisted nothing.

My phone buzzed again.

This is that sleep, I muttered. And suddenly drooling against the Datsun's steering wheel, I was gone.

In my dream someone who looked like the Assistant Dean was mowing the lawn.

You're such a control freak, they said, looking over their shoulder.

And that thing you were trying to tell me about, what a joke!

I felt like laughing back, but as hard as my body shook, no sound came out. I gestured to the mower that I'd lost my voice. They kept mowing, blindly. I guessed something was blocking me from sight. Trees. I was standing in a giant fir forest, thickly needled branches brooming my sides.

Something else was wrong. My pulse was ragged. My gut hurt. Then it gushed at me: I was hornier than I'd ever been. Feeling the mower near me, sensing him completely, cell by vacant cell, I was going to bust, discharge molten spunk, cave inwards, fuck anything in sight.

Was this how everyone else felt all the time?

I lumbered from behind the branches, my head swinging down. Black fur dragged with me.

DEAN, I bellowed. My lip curled on its own without meaning to.

He stared at me, terrified, steering the mower engine between us.

Just let me shave these down, I sobbed at my paws and their gore-smeared claws. I knew if I touched him I'd turn him to human paste.

But I was so full of love.

FROM *Transcription*

Eileen Myles

News of the dog: here's the fence again, and there's a willow tree probably Australian there's a tall blue and red plastic ride we fall into the shady bowl of it a sec. Aqua bench. Can a park be childless, their teen markings are all that signal we're on the earth, then up the tree into new bright green leaves and birds are singing and the dog is only ass, her forefront dipped entirely into the bushes. She has a score. It's like old people smoking. She can eat whatever she wants now. Shit, chicken bones it's hers. In fact she may choose her death. Did she.

Deeper in and she's gone. So we find on the other side her white maw thoughtfully munching on what could be a muffin or a leaf. She turns around her tongue hanging out her white face blazing in the sun and this is pure joy. She is fifteen. The sun highlights all the wrinkles in her barrel chest. A soft torso that used to be a strong one but the width and the heroic bone structure, ripples and inclines to say where the muscles were. She doesn't care. She wears her body like her favorite clothes. Age is a slight inconvenience on her way to sudden meals. Her paws and lower legs are white the upper a splash of honey. Above it is pink: inflamed, puffy, raw the sores of aging are here like the raw exposed joints of a stuffed teddy bear. Watching her is so much yoga. Each new attraction causes her head to drop so we see her white under maw which I used to call 'velvet' when she was a puppy and now I call it sort of washcloth. There's moments when all I can do (and I can't) (and I did) is rub my palm along the shifting grade of her butt, back, shoulders, it's a bit of a slide. She's moving in the wood chips round a circle of hot cement. It's dancer-like, like Merce being old, each paw falls deliberately rippling with the rest. She snakes. In a way only her tail is a testament to how uneven it all is, tadpole to the highly erratic path of her walk. She lowers her head to the base of a slender tree and the silvery bone her identification flickering from her neck her only jewelry. ID.

As if we're in another world the sidewalk is suddenly cool and blue and she's turning, to the right, walking away. She looks like she's walking into a restaurant she practically owns, she's that kind of man.

Moments are speechless, arrive in a patch of grass (remember pitch) shaped by cement and on the other side wood chips in the sun, two sworls and they contain grass wood chips sun and pit bull that's what it has. It's very still. Holding these events still seven or eight years ago even making a screen shot of some of the best ones like a lonely applause. A bird chimes in knowing. There's the here. A world of traffic outside my hotel window. I can peel the corner of the walk up. This is a risk. And I hear the rain of another country, another century. Not so grand. No this then. Pouring rain. It's really pouring here, no there, no ecce.

Yet I feel like this is the finest dog that ever lived. No ecce. Her head just dipped slightly a view from the back makes her ears just the humps of them be these shapes on either side of her head. Devil's or the uniform hats of the Guardia when they jumped on a train in Spain in the seventies holding their guns. Rain's pouring. No ecce.

Her attention is a statue. And then she moves among the children's things, joyous prisoner of her own adulthood. Past the benches and flagpoles and slides. She's looking up. She dips her nose in something white. Quick—again. Something black blocks our view and she's a flickering dog emerging between the aqua labeled bins of "TRASH" written in an odd stenciled early dot matrix font—cool—and another piece of baked earth furniture is emblazoned with a thin stripe of light and between these two urns flashes the fading black lipped face of dog bright and shadowed cheating towards us for a moment and what's this chains fuzzy chains in the foreground and she only as an image as an existence grows sharpened past the webbing a shroud of stuff fluttered through the way of the camera and now back to us through time dead center is this betrayal speak to me I do see my father now in his fading gaze but here in the vessel of dog story—birds sea birds outside if I peel the page—a motor—

One more moment's gaze like none of my words and thought have any power—on—

to the sniff at the root of a bush and an enormous dark shadow of self passes with its camera—acknowledged in a flash of white face then the three of us, only shadow dog the tall arms lifting the future eye vertical song and she looks at the shadow intrusive burden of the future this and some bushes and trees real and shadows complicate fill out beautifully the pattern. And now it's a course of shadows she's ambling through. My head round in the corner of the rectangle, the mitt of trees. A moment for all of it, dangling willow, bushes and smattering of a butterfly and out she comes into the boring compromised sun looking around. Holds statue pose for a second, horse in a painting, and moves into the spaghetti of darkness again, my bad movie. Trim. Plodding through the seaweed and the whole park today we look away colorful swings that look like helmets and I feel a dream. The slaughter of children in my head. The pounding surf of the internet. A baby deer slain. The quietness has no other. A broad panorama of park one dog. Composition serene. Human composition empty except for one nagging shadow. Back to the darkness, the miracle of dog trailing the shadowy edge of bushes, slow uneventful. A negotiating bear. I think today I will go on a boat.

She's huge now close. We're on her back. The physiognomy of dearness is unsurpassed. A neck and shoulders soft wide, held up by the bent flagging legs its own form wiggled in dark echo taller taller to its right. We just let shadow walk for a while. No dog only its repetition. Sentimental painting of the last Indian on a cliff. And then the two dogs the shadow dog and the white, the white and black and tan are feeding on something making an eight of legs, a thing and the tail arches to say it's time waving and she dips and pees and turns around. Okay she says impatiently tired blazing and yet. There is a tree that's mostly dark. I shall stand next to it. A tree that once around is bright and you shall see my bended head and the strange island of white on its blackness. Dead that's all you know now. My breath lingers on in your word. Look at the dry grey tan vegetation strewn surface of the earth. That's where you'll go. Enormous legs now enormous dog. The folds on the inside of one chicken bone leg a part of meat of calcified muscle, a folding a friend. And the dandruff in her fur, her skin is flaking. The tube of her, the tub of her the intelligence lifted and gazing. Always an aim before moving. Into the same wide procession of green, turning, going. Only two feet left. And we can almost feel the grass now with our own paw. The incessant shuffling. Stop, gaze, scan.

Back into the brightness and you're walking a friend, the other dog, then the world is staggering now bouncing complicated green and suddenly your limbs are blurry and close. Then it's simply traffic the exchange of public lawn and dog on and on for a while and we can think our thoughts. Dirt feels different. I'll say that. It's dirt, a lemon squished and the detritus of willow, a smattering of strands. We hold on the squished lemon half because the color is wild and we need that. And it's only green and dog legs entering for a moment. Shaking the jar. I think she wants to go home. She's shade and dog, dark posed one thing before the dark concrete and fence bright reflective in the sun. We're done. And she smells home half way through and smells. Stops.

I scribble when I bounce. That's the point of it. I'm impossibly calm but restless. I go all blurry on the fence like her exit's more interesting now. That long dead park. Each blade of dead grass gets ceremonial. Whiff.

Then it's that house, a first one. At first it looks like tree: tree but it resolves into dog small fuzzy dog beneath a messy grove before a beige house. Freeze it.

Go across the room sitting on the toilet looking at this worship. Permanent dog in the middle of a day. The best painting. Now. From the perspective of then. Which is it. The sweetness of allowing the past to roost in the present. I'm the dog. And the image fades. I touch—

There's goodies wherever we go. Goodies in the sun. Along a row of rocks. Sniffing. The glow of light on gravel. Luminous, somehow. Such a long reminiscence.

She turns at last a blazing, thirsty white-faced tongue out member of the dead heading home. White stripe of sun on her back.

Calling. Across the silence calling. I am your man. She turns and looks back still holding still. And then moves which means come. Come with your dumb camera.

The scratchy swirl of beige you can't not notate. Grass. Now her head peeks in like marginalia.

I get it. The other dog the corgie is here. Younger with an upright curious sympathetic face. Older dog she dwells. Standing in grass on her own. She jumps and it's her chubby legs we're locked on. Two dogs circling limbs in green grass. I thought we were home. Where did this corgie come from.

My dog's getting petted by a man. And you see the pile of hair loose on her back. You can see his pointed loafers now. His tumbled jeans. And the corgie is running around circling Rose.

And Rosie jumps up. She always has energy for love. He touches her shoulders. Her neck. He brushes the hair off. The corgie runs around. Rosie looks up. Right in the eye of the camera. I thought we were done.

What is that. A pole? A leash. Now it's just human legs a shadow walking across the grass. A tiny dog mid field. Oh yes coming home. Face close up. Weary. But it's me that's weary. Of copying, of writing, of filming. Of killing my dog.

She's nothing but a blur. I hold that insubstantial joy like a child. And now my head is out and her face is out. I give her a grey brown treat. A liver square and she engulfs it softly off my hand and I feel the wetness that accompanies the act. I get a lick.

That's me and its pleasure come home. And bougainvillea bright orange red filling the field. Just the field of vision.

But fast to her ass which is bustling just past in the bushes swinging her tail around—Rosie! I wake up and meet you each day. We examine a boulder with RTS painted on it like an ancient religion and wheaty dried grass straggled all around. But I want to get back to the bougainvillea. Jangly. Up and down making confetti with the screen cause it's moving and I'm high. It's red and I'm scribbling. Do you hear me. And now longingly up and down the length of a cypress bluing the sky. It's kind of a minaret. And a dog barks there and we see the composure of the neighborhood. Rows of popsicle stick a wooden fence crowds of bushes then Mr. Tall tree and a house eye open to the left. And there's the dog in the center of things smack dab like a medina or the first good thought I've had all day duplicated by her shadow. She's about ½ an inch tall. I'm waiting for her apparently and the day is hot and this is hard. Tongue out and kind of pale.

(I'm trying to duplicate ecstasy saying goodbye to the flowers and trees.)

The curb the cars the fences the day the burning grass and there's the dog waiting. Now waving, staggering, coming to me.

The other walk is hard. First I see the cat that is no longer mine. I'm looking down at you tugging forward on the leash and I guess we are going to the other park. (I remember this day when we meant to get everything.) We faced a spray of a very frondy tree. Lots of thin leaves on a single branch. We're sniffing in front of the punk rock (techno) house that has fights and Ernie precious jet black Ernie is with us. Everyone's smelling up a storm. Who pisses here. It's later in the day and the shadows are covering the street. The neighbor says hello but I think she's monitoring us. She laughs cause the cat's taking a walk with us too but actually I make her laugh in that friendly way and she dangles her baby out to take a picture of her too and now that baby is eight. She's walking around. She's reading. This is an everything but walk. Examining the glories of a very distressed yellow fireplug marked with the tell tale 'R'. It's not graffiti. It's the fire department turf. Meanwhile the gentle tap tap tap of the music of the house is still pouring out. One side of the fireplug is blue. Chalk blue. I want to say scrawl. The cat seems to get distracted I'm luring him in. He looks back at his other day. Another much more agitated than anything thι day can hold a white dog is barking and jumping up and down. The wall behind him is rose faded salmon and in sunlight goes to white. Blazing. It's my yard he barks. My sidewalk. We're close up and all we see is whiteness and fence. The entwined genius of chain link fence. Leg's barking a brindle head staring. Is it two dogs. I see anger but long stuffed yearning. Those dogs are fucked. Finally Rosie leading with her head. We're heading to the park. Fences here are covered in dried vines like strings of green leaves. Rose says sniff covered in piss. The way her fur has thinned there's one black stripe gleaming in the sun as it fades to the sides. She's clean as hell cause she's bathed a lot because of her skin. There's another dog. That poodle I think, white. Each dog animates a yard like a one man gang I'm here and what the fuck do you think I'm doing. Everyone's in when they'd rather be out—they're in out in their kingdom. But this is all ours mine and Rose. Cause of the ritual, cause of our walk. Cause of the camera. I remember when they built that strange web of supportive stone below the fence. Really fucking ugly. It raises the yard. It's a fashion in yards here. I think of the violent husband I met one day and I think this is the violent reward. The apology raised yard. It just makes me sad people's idea of beauty. Just a big apology. And you're watching this. This other dog's got button nose button eyes it lifts its head to show chin but it mostly stares. This dog wants to come, to play. I feel locked in this position. You continue to sniff. Now a baby squeals, the dogs barking and across the street on a low wall of brick are lions. I see lions. We look across the street and back. Bark bark bark. Thank god there you go with your sandy back. Oh now an empty bag of Lay's. I'm trying to duplicate what the dog sees like it's ecstasy but it's not. But there's a small purple flower the sweetest thing with its folds and its brighter pinker twin and you look in the flower and it's paler I can't just go white but the flower does. A silent blaring horn. There's four of you another bunch and I'm grateful for this. Finally you head with the white dab into the screen. Into the square. There's a walk along a row of leaves chewed on by bugs purple flowers cars telephone poles trees this is California. A little luxuriant a little condemned. You bent and sniffing along the row and this time of day your shadow mine are inescapable. Light on leaves. We're the stuff. Wand of the pole reaching beyond making this blue square active, wires, piles of green. Look what we did. When this was canyons and wild. That god. Only blue. That's intelligence. The wad of me walking then you. Head and shoulders. The little mayor with your neck and head covered in light now we turn to a street that is dirt.

ꜰROM **Dead Letter**

Jocelyn Saidenberg

Suspensed

We, who have turned our houses into ships, who float and haunt an added open to inwardness to what is oceanlike, like a closed beyond mirroring our traces, now are at ease among shadows. Among shadows I am at ease. I attach to objects, think object, and there it blurs what's telling what's thought. And it is mine, endlessly, and this is what exhausts me.

If I could unthought, be the unthinking thought me, nonthinking being me. If I could write me, you or he be my passive. Or if I could breach into the world as your or his failure. For you receive me, bereft of your own experience, floating, hauntingly. Yet I decline to be written, prefer not to be your copy, for inevitably your negligent husbandry abandons me like grass, sea grass, to grow chaotic everywhere, and there I leave the inwardness that is dark.

We who come from mistrust and air, forever losing, lost and losing because I remain that more unthinkable.

You see me only as your error, or better, an error, but see more now as an atmosphere of error as weather shadow cloud. You resist to think my thinking, refuse my difference, and in this we fail together, our error.

It's neither mine nor yours to expend fully, forgive, please, my absolute. I miss you terribly. That is, your must could only be my last word, your force of necessity assumes your grand, immanent, and insistent, what you've called, my weather. Love, gather together in the self-inhabited, suspended, exclusively to itself.

My door is locked to you, and there are no more windows, to say incapable of receiving.

Not yet.

That was me, being occupied, locked from the inside, that is, occupying myself, hardly, poorly. Then, please, read me both ways, as ambiguity, both ways, as unaccounted, for that endangers you and your recording promising whatever pleasure for you, your writing returns you to your own oblivion, not closer to me than ever. Nothing remains? I halt the need, nothing halts nothing but my flowing, stationary but floating, haunting. My error is our alibi. We remain faithful. Enlisted in each other. What do you need, want for me? What I for you? How, love, do we hate being both?

The speed of my pulse, measureless, an aspiration of blood circulating. Blood sharing. Addicted to our pulsations, aspiring for blood for measure. We do not write but addict, we will through repetition, involuntary need, for we desire desires addicted to their own attachments.

Not storming but a blankness onwards with no colors as if soluble, you would like for me to figure, as if a blankness that is classed as that which escapes classification. You like me, not willed, unrushed and involuntary, bewildered, when you're that will that cannot be hence a nothing to be read, nothing to be written, no color to be painted. We fall outside, an insoluble nothing, for we have fallen, are felled in our orchard. Love, could it be that what we prefer is nothing itself? Itself doing nothing?

You like me. In a pathless place for want of a road, muted and plain.

For you and I are suspended suspense and then finally what leads to love you said a suspended will suspends thinking, you followed, as if to suggest, I am your returned, everlasting ruin, absolute error, in a world that can't clothe me, yet fits not at all. Why are you trying to bury me living? Try, try. Our temple's assembled of ruins.

But when do I need them, do I not need emptied into empty? I figure to myself, bewildering thought returns self-thought, from circumference to center. You write stones and I retrieve myself, if never. I might have died save for summoning a path with no signs, a disaster of traces and pasts erased behind me. I am something you don't know. Get it? Not you, not yours.

But please do not think me insensitive, though indifferent to body, food, mind and even to you. I am not that I feel no pain, for it appears that my thought wishes this thought. Stone thought. Dream you.

Moving Day

Here I remain, the unaccountable, standing immobile in the middle of an uncarpeted room.

At times another attorney might come to us, having business with my attorney, and, struck by my peculiar aspect, would make a sinister observation, act of a contention. At other times, an attorney seeking an interview with my attorney calling at our office would find me alone and would seek precise information touching on my attorney's whereabouts. He would leave taking with him his idle talk of which I would have taken no heed, and also taking with him an himself no wiser than the he he was when he came. He for a time might contemplate me in my position, in the middle of the room, motionless, blank stare. Or if my room were full of attorneys, a reference underway, witnesses and workers, and business driving fast, and a deeply occupied legal man seeing me wholly unemployed would make a request of me unoccupied to fetch a document at his office, I would as you know decline with tranquility and remain yet idle. That attorney, staring, would turn to my attorney.

What could he say? He was aware that a whisper of wonder was running around, in reference to me, his strange creature, he kept in his office. I could see it worried him very much, being not any small item of rumor. But how could he rid himself of me, what he now called his intolerable incubus, me though sensitive, his sylvan spirit lingering in his orchard or woody faun by a pond.

He asked me again to quit him but after three days, from his view, of my consideration, I said I preferred to abide with him. And what he thought his conscience could not endure, speaking to himself he fancied letting me live and die in his rooms and masoning my remains into his walls upon my death. He considered to himself, more out loud than he noticed: Who is the incubus, the ghost, the vagrant that will not vagrant himself? He made no reply, had none to himself to make, so he logicked himself into quitting me since I would not quit him.

He conjured up new premises for himself, mere blocks from me, but making me thereupon a trespasser in our rooms, no longer ours. A common trespasser he figured me into. Common to him no longer.

One day he said, "I find these chambers too far from the City Hall"—liar—"the air is unwholesome."—liar, again—"In a word, I propose to remove my offices next week, and shall no longer require your services,"—liar, he needs me more than he needs air—"I tell you this now, in order that you may seek another place."

I made no reply and no more was said.
The wind dying down now to a hush.

On the appointed day he left me in the naked rooms, a motionless occupant, not frozen, but not folded up along with the huge folios. Offices no longer habited, emptied of unbalanced bodies and tables, the heedless and fiery, Nippers, Turkey and Ginger-Nut. My lawless fellows, thwarting objects and their unreadable smudges, all gone and departed.

"Good-bye: I am going—good-bye, and God some way bless you; and take that."

Whatever it was it dropped to the floor. I sensed he tore himself away from me the one he for so long longed to be rid of. Adieu, my love. I will visit you no more. Adieu.

Tenanting or Purification

I cleanse myself, of myself, of others, of nights of bodies, mine and others, yours. Love would think I am fastidious when finding under the sofa what love mistakes as personal. It is a ritual to cleanse oneself of life—not a matter of private hygiene—for a care neither to seduction nor self-identity.

Passive onto it, I am an immobile earth. I compress my time, near timelessness into this point in space. You color me with half-staved thoughts, half-formed, almost thoughts. We stand skinny there. Were you once my remedy for thinking, medicine against myself? I give no answer at the present.

My attorney stayed away, coming not near, as if some squeamishness withheld him, poor little fucker.

He misses me, our landscape, our window, that never changes, changes less. It doesn't give more or less, our eternal ruined view of a viewless and not deserted but rather if never dead empty. Only copies, I made for you these emblems of what is not any more, what offers no view.

Whisper to me from behind buried skulls and endless etymologies, whisper to me, give up give up give it up. Whisper to me an empty world or a world housing few whispering loss and losing, framed and walled up in it, incased in petals. Whisper with me and preserve me with your abstinence, with me ebb, wave with me, petrify in obstinate silence, vestige with me a trace in an orchard or our window.

I haunt our building, sleep in the stairwell, fitfully, sitting on the banister of the stairs by day, sleeping not sleeping, waiting while not waiting in the entry.

In vain you have left me, in vain you persist, in vain you imagine I am nothing to you or to anyone, but I am yours, and we are your terrible account. I your uncountable nothing, to you I am confidentially yours. Ever yours.

Find me on the banister at the landing, in confidence, there. I am as you find me.
Find me as I am.
Ever yours,
B.

"What are you doing here?

"Sitting on the banister," I mildly reply.

"Are you aware that you are the cause of great tribulation to me, by persisting in occupying the entry after being dismissed?"

No answer. I give no answer.

It is as you sensed the same either way, here or there, yet in vain no alternative. Your house or mine. Doesn't it, love, all come down to the same, no difference but all? I drown myself in it and invite you. We ask for not even what otherwise persists. Ask.

Why read, why copy, why thought, why others? Haven't you been trying to read my face—I caught you mid-act last night. Try, try. My suit, my voice, my profile, your open fields of what might be told, expanding but nothing works, or a work that has no form, found. Find me no form.

I am leanly composed. Dimly calm. A word without wrinkles. Brought to a standstill, a mutter of difference, or broken moaning, if you could listen. I had not forgotten how, living in the difference of that life that grieves. Not as you imagined it? Incapable, fucker, either of love or of grief?

Opium

Does desiring erase remembering? Insatiable forgetting, drugged by abandon, a vastness of what is not mine or me. All feeling. As if I could surprise myself, or better, surprise you out of yourself. A gift. Let hair become leaf, let leg become root, let sigh become windspell, birdhum, let my head become weather, my heart shadow, then cloud again. All felt. Yet temporary all as all weather shadow cloud.

Listen, an inner rhythm lives, an inner aching gathers to me, bundles around the formless. You need this, need me to be intimate, tonic to your grief, captured, returning, and back to myself. Any snug contrivance falls flat, limps along lame and drugged. How the leaving always comes back. Listen, there's a duet in the next room.

He tried, honestly tried, to find a way to it.
"No, I would prefer not to make any change."
A clerkship, more copying, a trip in the countryside, bill collecting, bartending, his propositions.
"Too much confinement about that. No, I would not like to do that; but I am not particular."
"Too much confinement?" he parroted.
"I would prefer to be doing something else."
European travel companion, entertaining a young man with conversation, others. "Not at all."

He next tried to frighten me, my immobility, into compliance, little fucker, he did.

He was precipitately leaving me when he turned toward me, a turn I had known, now desperate as much as despairing.

As if called back, he says in a tone quite kind, "will you go home with me now— not to my office, but my dwelling—and remain there till we can conclude upon some convenient arrangement for you at our leisure? Come, let us start now, right away."
An overture to which I could only state, or re-state: "No, at present I would prefer not to make any changes at all."

He answers nothing.

Sometimes I do things without knowing why, counterfeiting a semblance of knowing but not. If looking for an exit, slow or fast, I invite you to step overboard, slide out onto my draft, love, please, unroot my feet.

Pause at the door unattended. Step over the threshold unbidden, arrive in his presence unformed. Delivered outsideness, stationary, for I like to be stationary. Pause. I prefer to cleave to you, your inwardness to my apparition, your incubus, your manghost. Poor, pale passive mortal, I am yours. My unwonted wordiness once inspirits you. And yet you abandon me. Not the slightest obstacle in my pale unmoving ways. I did it for you. Silently. Though I repulse you, have transformed your melancholy, your pity into fear.

Listen. A pauseless person there I am always.

Plastic: an autobiography

Allison Cobb

White Whale

After I visited the plastic collection beach at Kamilo Point, Hawaii, I thought I would need to travel to every junk beach on the planet, just to see it—places where spinning gyres, currents and geography coincide, and the ocean vomits up some portion of its vast cargo: in the Pacific, the Pitcairn Islands, Hawaii, Malorrimo; Padre Island on the Gulf of Mexico; in the Atlantic, the Azores and Bermuda.

Then I would need a submersible to take me down three thousand feet into sea canyons in the Mediterranean, where plastic bottles pile up in the sediment like strange cylindrical fossils. Then across the seabed and downward, darker, colder, eight thousand feet below ice floes in the Greenland Sea, my arc of light reflecting off a clear plastic bag floating past in the black.

Then smaller and smaller still until microscopic to slide inside the gut of a lugworm, *Arenicola marina*, burrowed beneath beige sand at Dovercourt beach on England's east coast. A powerful suck from the worm's mouth swirls me inside it, slick and dark, along with sand grains and tiny plastic particles.

Its muscled gut walls contract, stripping from the miniscule bits whatever its cells recognize as food, whatever is organic—bacteria, algae, protozoa, and the laboratory chemicals that saturate the particles—polychlorinated biphenyls, dichlorodiphenyldichloroethylene, nonylphenol, phenanthrene, triclosan.

Working the plastic through its guts makes the worm tired and sick; its walls contract less and less. It rests. A bar-tailed godwit catches sight of the worm's dark tip, snatches with its narrow beak, swallows in two quick jerks. The worm and all it enfolds meld into bird cells. As for me, I am ejected, only imaginary, cast back on the beach in a tube of sandy worm excrement.

Ridiculous. I lay on the couch on a Friday, the 13th of January, thinking such thoughts. I'd failed. I felt incapable of writing this book, of expanding to the necessary scope. Of acquiring the time and money and breadth and depth of—what? I didn't even know what I was missing. *The Autobiography of Plastic,* a title I announced to my friends on a whim and kept repeating because people liked it—enough to give me a few thousand dollars in grant money. Enough to interest a book agent, who asked for chapter summaries. But I had no idea what it meant.

January in Portland means evening all day. It had rained, and it was going to rain. But for a moment the sun burned almost all the way through the cloud layer and turned the sky silver. I decided to stop thinking, get off the couch and take the dog for a walk. I opened the front door and there in the dirt sat a white plastic ring, gleaming. I picked it up. It was deeply worn and weathered, hard to tell where it came from, the mouth of a pill bottle maybe. It had teeth marks in it, definite marks from some animal's mouth.

It struck me: I am not lucky enough to be worm shit. Imagining piloting around, an explorer peering out from my safe suit of self—that is wish fulfillment, a fantasy. I am inside the worm still, the worm inside me, sloshing molecules back and forth. A house forms its own coast, a body does—skin, blood, gills, lungs—awash in the currents and whatever they bring, seeping through cells respiring, tidal.

The teeth that chewed on this plastic probably belong to my dog. He chewed on it, and swallowed some tiny plastic particles, and some drifted down into dirt, where in about one month, I will poke a few holes and tuck in pale peas that will grow into plants, vining themselves out of sun, water, air and nutrients pulled through roots from the soil.

In May I'll walk out and pinch off a sweet green pod, chew it up with my teeth, and swallow. Quincy the dog will do the same, he learned it from me, tugging pods with his mouth. I always plant too many, so I will fill bowls with peas and share them with neighbors, who will admire the sweet crunch in their teeth. In there, along with whatever molecules make a pea, there might be a few broken free from the plastic bits, and whatever else has washed this coast in its sixty years as suburban tract—particles of soot from car exhaust, bits of mercury fallen with rain drops, asbestos slivers from the house shingles. Here neighbor, let me feed you, let me feed you, dog, let me feed you hungry body.

I put the ring in my pocket and walked out the gate. I felt a little whisper of that vertigo. My neighborhood that had been familiar—kind of weedy and worn but tidy—turned up a new skin, studded with plastic: street, sidewalk, lawn, gutter. I picked up each piece and put it in my pocket. Then I couldn't stop. Every day, on every dog walk, with disgust, boredom, sometimes delight, I kept on picking up plastic. Like at Kamilo, I started to make lists, recording each piece and taking a photo. An ocean flooding my own shores, I absorbed every bit. I stored all the plastic in plastic garbage bags on the back porch.

In October the car part turned up in a corner of the yard, just outside the fence. It was four feet long, curved and black, one side flecked with white splash marks from mud or paint. It formed a complicated shape, wide at one end and tapered at the other, with holes and slats and ridges all along its length. The widest end contained deep score marks, some scratched all the way through the plastic. Without the car body to hold its curved shape, it folded in half like a wing at its narrowest point.

"That's your white whale," said Jen when I dragged it in. After several weeks she asked how long I planned to keep the car part in the living room. I moved it into the bedroom, on the floor near my side of the bed.

Works Cited

Location of junk beaches:
Ebbesmeyer, Curtis, and Eric Scigliano. *Flotsametrics and the Floating World: How one man's obsession with runaway sneakers and rubber ducks revolutionized ocean science.* New York: Harper, 2009.

On *Arenicola marina* and plastic:
Barnes, David K.A., Francois Galgani, Richard C. Thompson and Morton Barlaz. "Accumulation and fragmentation of plastic debris in global environments," *Phil. Trans. R. Soc. B* 364, 2009: 1985-1998.

Browne, Mark Anthony, Stewart J. Niven, Tamara S. Galloway, Steve J. Rowland and Richard C. Thompson. "Microplastic Moves Pollutants and Additives to Worms, Reducing Functions Linked to Health and Biodiversity," *Current Biology*, 23, 2013: 2388-2392.

Wright, Stephanie L., Darren Rowe, Richard C. Thompson, and Tamara S. Galloway. "Microplastic ingestion decreases energy reserves in marine worms," *Current Biology*, 23, 2013: 1031.

Against One Model Alone

James Sherry

"Is it now too fanciful to suppose that..."

— Ron Atkin

What do you expect we poets are going to say about the environment? Shall we reiterate, in a charming way, the nightly news about eco-disasters or describe its eco-beauties ad nauseam? Will natural pietism, where we love nature and think it does no wrong, usher in an eco-commodity polemical wave? Or can poetry enhance our correspondence with the non-human components of the biosphere, giving us a chance to adapt our culture to new conditions?

The environmental movement runs a great risk if it adheres to a moral or other single model of human interaction with the biosphere. If, for example, we focus only on blame and redress of grievances, we lose sight of the fact that the root cause of global warming is desire. We lose sight of the fact that we expect to develop a society that includes not only all the people and their interests, but the interests of the non-human components as well; what it is, from bacteria to redwoods. We seek restorative, not retributive justice.

If, as another example, environmentalists focus on a problem and solution model alone, we may fix a few things, move, as the saying goes, the deck chairs around, but recreate similar problems with new solutions, biofuels for example. The large scale concern remains our energy expenditure and its resultant heat, so a problem and solution model without cultural change drives competition among various interest groups—who gets to be hot?

From an essential point of view, human activity around the environment is often conditioned by a single myth about nature. Most writing around nature emphasizes either of two polarized and irreconcilable points of view. One is competition, "nature red in tooth and claw," the Tennysonian model. On the other end of the spectrum is a kind of number two, natural pietism that suggests nature is ultimately good and good for you. Don't panic, it's organic. You know the pitches. Rethink it for a minute.

We have a strong science around global warming. We can repair most of the damage with existing methods; we can arrest climate change, not a future ideal but, with a little extra cash, start today and improve as we progress. And it will become increasingly cost effective. We also have aggressive political systems that can implement solutions; both totalitarian and democratic governments can achieve results with the right negotiations with the 0.1%. The difficulty lies in convincing people to change. Our culture, our choices seem limited to a tired residue of 19th century imperialism on one side, the competitive view, and various naturalisms on the other.

Such polarity hoovers in denial because neither of the points of view includes enough of the biosphere or of society to amend them or to address the emotional maelstrom that the desperate information we already know about climate change provokes. Speaking to the flood of data, environmental culture operates across a range of tactics from representing a problem in order to increase awareness as the Canary Project photographs show to elucidating how to reposition humanity as part of nature as I suggest here. Works can focus on poetry itself, poetic relations with science or the politics required to establish the consensus required for sustainable change. Each person and group formation in the range possesses many insights and connections. And there are many species of thought each with its own perspective.

Based on this spectrum of forms, one might draw a matrix of viewpoints and interests that reflect our ecosystems as a set of embodied relationships rather than an array of things in a container where conveniently we can throw our unwanted. To support that matrix, multiple models can be made available and applied relevantly. The positions are not difficult to diagram, but we lack the will to change behavior. It is culture that supports our ability to act in an organized and coherent way rather than just act to survive. Poetry provides images for our aspirations.

But rather than use poetry as a metaphor machine, producing as many and varied images as possible, in an environmental poetry, metaphor might be engaged as an alternative practice, used when the logic of language and thought break down or become unhelpful. (see Frederic C. Bartlett's essay "Imagery in Thought,"1932) In science, for example, metaphor represents mathematical concepts that need translation to be understood in English. In politics metaphor characterizes a problem that we want to solve or a population to engage. The context is different but the tactic is similar; use metaphor as needed rather than fabricate as much as the market will bear. But what tools are available to modify our manufacturing model of poetry and culture in general? There are many; here are three.

SOCIAL STRUCTURE

As we see every few months in the news, the world as constituted by a competing set of essential views is collapsing around us. To quote Michael Thompson, "When people argue from different premises they will, in all probability, fail to agree … Attention is focused not on the facts of the matter but on the facts of the disagreement … In other words the discerning spectator begins by granting legitimacy to all these sets of contradictory premises. Nor does the fact that they are contradictory cause him any dismay. On the contrary, he sees social life as a process that depends for its very existence on the perpetual contention between these different sets of convictions about how the world is."

A physicist's world, for example, has resources in abundance, since matter is neither created nor destroyed, whereas an ecologist's world has limited resources and a poet's world; well, you know yourselves. The planet does not contain only one or two perspectives. We can build conflict into our creations, and as poets we know how to do that already. We can also build in association and interactions that show the many and simultaneous facets of the biosphere.

Thompson uses *Canterbury Tales* to provide a clear model of contemporary society. In Chaucer, the pilgrims and their relationships represent civil society—knights, managers, householders, priests—each with a unique point of view, story and set of interests concerning their venture. Their identities are, as ours today, based on their jobs, what they do. They are, however, united by a common purpose. Now imagine an environmentally-oriented social structure.

As a result of the stresses of climate change, an environmental model of the planet begins to take hold of society. And a new set of social classes emerges based on the individual's view of her surroundings. Thompson originally hypothesized five distinct cultural biases "each of which has associated with it a different idea of nature."

Social Being / Voice	View of Nature	Example
hierarchical	isomorphic nature	government, law, critic, experimentalist, formalist
egalitarian	accountable nature	activism, sects, political poet
individualist	skill-controlled cornucopia	entrepreneur, markets, romantic, innovative poet
fatalist	lottery controlled	ineffectual, victim, purist, avant-gardist
autonomous	freely available cornucopia	hermit, hobo, ecopoet

(Based on Michael Thompson's environmental social structure: http://projects. chass.utoronto.ca/semiotics/cyber/douglas4.pdf)

No single consistent point of view is likely to work for all conditions or metabolisms. Each of these social beings links to a part that you might take as your role in society changes from a worker on the job where you see nature as a threat, to your projects as a writer where you hope to enhance the virtues you perceive in nature, to your conflicts as a citizen voting for laws about conservation and then having live by them. I'm so busy, what do I do with my candy wrapper?

If we view culture not as a set of habits of mind but as a continually renegotiated ecosystem of social relationships, we can establish a construction of nature that makes sense and sustains our focus while disruptive conditions persist. This can be true for us at any scale, for poets even between disruptive thoughts.

Thompson proposes, and I support this approach for poetry, that the new models resist the urge to remove conditions such as complexity, goal ambiguity, contradictory certainties, conflict, institutional inertia and temporal change. All the issues addressed by innovative writing. The conceptions of policies preserve their "historical contingency." Thus the arts and sciences can represent their processes as evolving with, perhaps even invoking, the "imperfections inherent in any cultural unit." And political processes can be lubricated by more alternative technologies and more inclusive language constructions.

While we cannot make much progress in specialized knowledge without a rigorous taxonomy, we cannot make much progress in our relationships in society or the biosphere without art, science and politics that accommodate both peripheral beliefs: value and fact.

The implications of this concept for social policy and for input from the sciences and poetry show us an approach that moderates "specific debates so as to not erode general consent." Environmental change drives social change. That fragile edifice of difference that we use to buttress our egos must be reinforced by accepting commonality and interdependence into our repertoire, or it will all collapse around our pages.

HIERARCHY

Another tool to help position our human self-image in the biosphere is the addition of inclusive hierarchies to the evaluative hierarchies that start with oneself, differentiated from all else in the universe. If we don't distinguish ourselves from the world, of course, we would not be able to continue. Eating, drinking, even breathing are called into question.

Culture, on the other hand, carries this good thing too far by creating countless isomorphs of this fundamental creature dichotomy between oneself and the world, blocking similarities. Defenders of specialization attack obvious common ground between disciplines of thought reflecting the creature dichotomy. Group formations of identity politics, while establishing a necessary buttress against centralized control, unintentionally or by design, often transform into echoes of these defense mechanisms.

And cultural output reinforces those correspondences. My poetry is better than yours; our poetry is more important to the canon than yours; Alfred E. Newman is the best poet; Neo-gringo poetics breaks better eggs... You've been in these conversations overtly and in the more indirect but equally top heavy forms of one-upmanship. Or even the milder pressure of I like this poet and that poet, don't you? These evaluative hierarchies, while relevant, ignore the countless interactions, relationships and inclusions that are also mandatory for an individual's continued existence.

Rather than continue to focus solely on evaluative hierarchies in culture—like/don't like, good for me/bad for me, or even subtly good/better/best—environmentalism presents us with an additional tool: inclusive hierarchy.

Inclusion has far more applications than evaluation and occurs readily throughout the biosphere and society extending to the entire physical and energetic world. A garden can be used as a simple example. In the garden we see flowers, shrubs, and ground cover. The flower is neither better than the shrub, nor is the garden somehow superior to the flower by virtue of including it.

An inclusive hierarchy is easily represented:

garden
^ ^ ^ ^
flowers, shrubs, ground cover

Or as another example:

human genders

∧ ∧ ∧ ∧

male, female, gay, lesbian, bi-sexual, transsexual, queer

In this kind of hierarchy, no gender of homo sapiens is superior. The species is not better just at a higher level of abstraction. Or as a third example:

Contemporary Writing

∧ ∧ ∧ ∧

Poetry (essay, novel, etc.)

∧ ∧ ∧ ∧

speech-oriented, language-oriented, chance, appropriation

In a hierarchy based on form, poems, essays and novels are varieties of writing. We might list another level below to show different presentations of poems, essays and so on. And below is an inclusive hierarchy of a poem:

Inclusive Hierarchy of Poems

N-5: marks on the page, letters, punctuation, and numbers
N-4: phonemes and morphemes
N-3: words
N-2: phrases and sentences   some poems
N-1: stanzas, sonnets, and thematic forms ⟍ merge these
N: Poems   ⟍ two levels
N+1: books, MP3 and other audio files, readings, broadsides, and other media for presenting single and multiple poems. It may include analysis of single authors
N+2: anthologies and other definitions of poetry. This dimension also includes analysis of multiple authors
N+3: reading interpretation and meta-theories about poetry, models of what creativity means and how poems are created
N+4: notions of creativity, the mind, and poetry's place in society and the world exist for groups of people each in their own culture
N+5: In the eleventh dimension environmental poetics links poetry beyond human social structure to the non-human world, and defines a way for poetry to act as an environmental model

Many more complex hierarchies can be demonstrated with this tool called q-analysis, introduced by the physicist Ron Atkin (*Multidimensional Man*, Penguin, 1979). Atkin even goes so far as to describe physical dimensions in terms of q-analysis, inclusive rather than parallel dimensions. He claims that physicists accept this as a fair representation of mathematical dimensionality. Q-analysis supports models of physics, population and poetry, an environmental tool.

But lest we misuse its method, keep in mind that while inclusive hierarchy tends to value things and relationships more equally, it is more difficult to communicate from lower to higher levels of abstraction than from higher to lower. Within the garden, understanding the flower or the shrub, its form and function, is fairly easy. Among other things the flower provides color and the shrub provides shape. But if you're a flower, your understanding must travel much farther to grasp the function of the garden as a whole.

In this example, travelling from lower to higher levels of abstraction, inclusive hierarchy appears to work like evaluative hierarchy (higher is better). We see that difficulty frequently in social constructs, politics and science, but only if we establish simplicity of execution as preferable in every case to a more complex routing. Sometimes complex routing saves energy later on. The point is that to produce non-entropic results, we use imagination; we make poetry, and we need to travel from lower to higher levels of abstraction to understand climate change beyond immediate survival.

Normally, to persist as biomass we need to use as little energy as possible to execute a task such as acquiring food or writing a poem; such priorities improve our chances of survival during periods of scarcity. Hence we tend to look downward in a hierarchy at those who must work harder for their keep. But when the problem before us can only be addressed by using more energy, such as understanding the garden from the perspective of the flower or understanding a new poetic strategy from the perspective of our prior reading, we should not shirk from the effort involved in writing or reading such complex routing. In fact the extra mental effort significantly reduces overall energy output as we'll see in the next item in our cultural toolkit when we discuss manipulating ecosystems. In fact to change we must choose the more complex routing, and in this case we temporarily exercise a flow of energy contrary to the expected flow of biomass.

These tools of poetry can be immensely helpful with change. Besides metaphor that allows us to bridge logical gaps more readily, parataxis, onomatopoeia, juxtaposition and other rhetorical devices provide ways of jumping upward in an inclusive hierarchy from one level or image to another. The tools of poetry cool climate change. A thorough analysis of the tools available to solve problems arising from inclusive hierarchy is beyond the scope this discussion, but the grid of problems and solutions referred to at the start of this discussion isn't all that difficult to imagine.

Nevertheless, there continues to be a fundamental conflict between the biosphere taken as a whole and the survival and flourishing of any one species or group and further any group's survival versus the individual. Without such analytic tools as Thompson and Atkin provide, we cannot manage our civilized successes. Writing environmentally comprehensible poetry that adequately represents or furthers the methods and protocols of the biosphere becomes less likely if we continue to look at ourselves and our surroundings only through the lenses from the past. The great irony of our age appears as soon as humanity grasps the possibility of getting out from under nature's boots— plague and privation. At this very moment, we see the results of our having gone too far.

Thompson asks a fundamental question: How do we treat humanity and nature together as a single complex system? Only culture, our poetry, for example, can provide the will to change, to push against our heredity toward a commensal relationship with the rest of the planet. Without cultural change we can only appeal to self-interest.

EXTERNAL COGNITION

The separation of each individual from the rest of the universe, that structure of survival for each organism, infers an internalized thinking process that further separates each of us from the rest of the planet. Contrary to reductivist notions of Cartesian cognition, our interactions and interdependence prove our existence as much as our thought process.

In the *Discourse on Method* Descartes sought to achieve certainty about his existence, "that from the mere fact that I thought about doubting the truth of other things, it followed quite evidently and certainly that I existed." But Cartesian cognition does not deal either with ways of thinking that extend beyond the mind or that are less than certain such as any thinking about complex systems like the biosphere. He is simply trying to establish certainty.

So while we infer from Descartes' work and Bishop Berkeley's subsequent dissing of the senses that thinking takes place only in the mind with input from perception, we can look beyond the *cogito*, especially as we realize how certainty is no longer in the cards.

Environmentalism can only become effective throughout our culture if we develop a model of cognition to add to the Cartesian metaphor and its personalized vision that appears to sequester valuable thought within the individual. If we advance the notion of external cognition, the individual is no longer conceived as a monadic mental state surrounded by a feeble body.

In his article "Environmental Epistemology" (*Ethics & the Environment*, 10(2), 2005), Mark Rowlands, professor of philosophy at the University of Miami, redefines cognition as taking place both inside the body and "also in the manipulation and transformation of external information-bearing structures." Several functions take place externally, especially the function of memory, like an external disk array on your computer. "In certain circumstances, acting upon external structures is a form of information processing."

Many organisms exploit external resources in order to reduce their energy consumption and increase survival rates. Rowlands cites how a beaver's dam-building skills make food more accessible with less effort and less risk. The beaver might have developed longer legs and bigger muscles to run from the pond to the tree to eat its bark before the wolf could catch him. As an adaptation such a strategy would use far more energy than one that manipulates the ecosystem. Taking fewer risks and using less energy, the beaver, who adapts its surroundings, survives more often than the physically enhanced beaver.

Recent conceptual and found poetry for example uses a related strategy, appropriating prior texts, recontextualizing them and publishing them largely unchanged. An example of this strategy occurs in *Oops!* in the essay "How Language Poetry Got Its Period" written in 1995 where I take a biology text and make minor word changes to create a credible poetry text.

The success of new conceptual poetry, from the environmental point of view, is associated with low energy input producing many pages of output. Ironically, with little work applied conceptual poetry achieves a great amount of consideration compared to poets laboring diligently on the page. And predictably many writers flock to this low effort practice. Further conceptual poetry uses a visual art model, crossing disciplinary boundaries to capture poetry in an art net. There are didactic values in reimagining creativity, but few citations of conceptual texts occur. Once the idea is framed, reproductive value flags. Reusing the same information seems academic on the surface, but changing how we look at productivity, recycling, is an important alternative to the labor-based theory of production. It cuts both ways. And we need to keep both thoughts in mind to avoid reductivist evaluations.

Beavers aside, language also demonstrates external cognition. Let's say a cook is looking for spices in the rack. Rather than memorize the location of thyme on the shelf, the cook runs her forefinger across the bottles, reading the label on each bottle in turn until she finds the word thyme. Recognizing the position of the bottle that she wants takes place both inside and outside the mind, creating an environmental link where cognition takes place.

The cognitive operations used to acquire information about and to represent the world are themselves processes *of* the world. They possess, quite literally, worldly constituents, not just personal ones. And even those organs that legitimately can be regarded as located inside the skin of cognizing organisms cannot easily be identified independently of the world. Such vehicles will, in many instances, have been designed to operate only in conjunction with the "manipulation of environmental structures."

Such low cost strategies, even when they require more mental energy, make it more likely that organisms survive in conditions of reduced resources like the amount of money paid for poetry. Language helps account for human success. The drive toward social structure in towns is a good example although recently developed balance sheets of energy consumption raise questions about the efficacy of cities' economies of scale. Our social organizations like cities and governments exemplify external cognition, and the fact that we build cities proves the inadequacy of an internal-only model of cognition to account for existing conditions.

Rowlands cites the case of the adolescent sea squirt that has developed a brain that allows it to move about collecting food. In adulthood, to enable reproduction, totally unlike adult humans, it affixes itself to a rock and proceeds to eat its own brain as an energy-saving method when the food passing by becomes insufficient. How often in my life have I applied only certain things that I know in order to get a job done and not confuse conceptualizing with execution of the task at hand?

External cognition helps explain how our self-image is concerned with the condition of the environment. Establishing that ecosystems include self-interest extends the idea of environment to the mind itself, not as an abstract, impersonal value that we *ought* to support or a moral imperative that might not be shared by workers in natural resources. If we think of our surroundings and ourselves as composite, integrated entities then we might stop using our environs as trash bins and develop increased respect for other people.

EXEMPLARY TEXTS

Externalized cognition represents a vital step toward environmental perspectives. Writing in multiple contexts turns out to be an example of such externalization.

In *Cheerleader's Guide to the World: Council Book*, Stacy Doris constructs her work from internal *and* external components rather than by analyzing a core event or idea through internally consistent logic. The book "…sandwiches Popul Vuh Patterson / Tibetan Dead Jigme Linpa Pindar // Rah rah." (The quotation is followed by a chart of a football play as if drawn for a sports team.)

"The good old idea

was that corn growth

+ tax cuts make leisure."

(Roof, 2007, p10)

By juxtaposing these elements physically on the page Doris establishes a variety of connections between internal and external components of varying strength and usefulness. Some of them associate subconsciously, some through our knowledge of history and some through their inherent connections such as shared content. In all cases, the exercise establishes a cognitive/cognizing link between a person and external components in an ecosystem. These links reach out from the mind to the page and back. We read them again and they change; we are thinking outside as we read.

Compare Doris' lines with Milton's sonnet "On His Blindness" where, emanating from god "...thousands at his bidding speed / and post o'er land and ocean without rest..." all with the same interest, passively waiting to execute His will. While each differs, they agree on a common master. Each individual of thousands operates by linking to each other through God's will. The poem reifies the notion of internalized cognition. The world is within the mind of God but thought, within the mind of each person, extends to God, mirroring the family, the household, the clan, each with external links extending to the next level of hierarchy.

While the materialization of God contains some contradictions with its centralized source of value rather than a distributed ecological model, even in Milton's case the material of language focuses the reader on the words on the page as much as what is already in the reader's mind. Milton's poem talks about internal cognition but is read using a combined process evident of external cognition.

Doris' synthesis reveals another kind of agreement. Greater than the sum of its parts, her synthetic poetry requires more than the components of its construction to be read and absorbed. In this sense, poetry is externally understood. Meaning goes beyond the poem on the page to the experience and assumptions of the reader.

Interestingly, poetry dealing with the materials of writing, from Mallarme's *Le Livre* to Silliman's *The New Sentence,* includes a great range of external subjects and materials, expanding poetry from a few monolithic subjects like love and war to complex and simultaneous concerns. Writing strategies that use diverse materials and practices open the door to an extended poetry that addresses real-world problems. Such environmental writing practice reestablishes poetry as a valid knowledge-creating process. Focusing on culture this way also reduces the limitations of innovative culture's narrowing focus on the materials of construction in a tantalizingly dialectic manner.

Like the beaver dam, Doris' synthetic poetry expands our access to resources that common usage would exclude. By juxtaposing the different texts, *Popul Vuh*, "Patterson," etc. they arrive together in the present in the poem. Collapsing time represents one tool Doris uses to deliver cultural change and expand the possible solutions to our climate problem. By showing readers past, present and future together, new correspondences develop. She also jams separate texts together. But synthetic poetry requires more than juxtaposition to operate as an ecosystem.

Working synthesis also means matching solutions to the complexity of the problems they are intended to address. For example, matching a multi-dimensional poetry or ecosystem to a one-dimensional value solution, such as the facebookian like/don't like (or financial considerations of renewable energy isolated from the costs of the wars fought to obtain fossil fuels), makes a mockery of the difficulty of any poetry, even the simplest verse. Yet how often for convenience do we suggest that a poem is good or bad? How often to convince do we play emotional tunes when we know the problem of climate change requires far more than moral outrage. While simplification helps reduce energy output, does symmetry help assure that the problem gets solved?

Asymmetry provides the centrality/peripherality
Criteria that serve to separate the prescribing
Entrepreneur from the prescribed ineffectual.
A personal strategy aimed at the deliberate
Avoidance of all three types of order in nature—
Randomness, chaos, and order—
Resisting, unresting, complicit—
Can viably conjoin
Social context and cultural bias.
The author need not take it literally,
But reading materializes.

The Longest Division

Kate Colby

I write a lot about place. And from it to the extent that I can. I know I'm really in it when I hear the feedback looping out from and back into my head. But these moments of utter occupation are hard-won because place flickers and moves from beneath you, like a fuzzy gray dot at the intersections of a black-and-white grid. Just when you get there it's gone to the corner of your eye.

One way that I try to get at place is through its people. For the last year or so I've been collecting components for a project about Isabella Stewart Gardner and her eponymous museum in Boston. The museum is located on the Fenway, the first in a series of city parks designed by Frederick Law Olmsted and known as the Emerald Necklace. The museum opened in 1903 and was designed by Gardner herself in the style of a 15th-century Venetian palazzo that she flipped inside-out—the cold, hard facade contains its opulent interior like a geode. Tiers of Italianate balconies and arched windows rise around a skylit courtyard filled with palms, fountains and Roman statues. The galleries are lit low like private rooms and layered with plunder—tapestries, fireplaces, altarpieces, antique furnishings, gilded ceilings, wall coverings and stained-glass windows that Gardner obsessively collected during her world travels. The outermost layer consists of her vast art collection, works ranging from Titian to Degas to Whistler.

Each room is jam-packed and just-so. There is a sense of completion to her arrangements that makes isolating and contemplating any one element difficult and disruptive. She imposes her contextual constraints on annunciations, pietàs and Vermeer's belabored attempts at perspective, damping the works' resonance, bending their associative trajectories around into the ring road of the city of herself. Her motto, *C'est mon Plaisir*, ripples beneath a phoenix on the museum's emblem.

Gardner tried to hermetically seal her world by making it a condition of its bequest to the city nearly 100 years ago that no element or artwork ever be added, removed or moved from its place in the museum. Nonetheless, there are leakages. In the second-floor Dutch Room a self-portrait of Rembrandt in a feathered cap faces a blank space on the opposite wall where the painter's *Storm on the Sea of Galilee* used to be. In 1990 thieves made off with an estimated $500 million of artworks and objects that have not been recovered. The spaces create an imbalance in those rooms—they gape and swallow your eye. But because of Gardner's rigid stipulation, the art can't be rearranged to fill them.

The museum is a large-scale, lifelong installation project, whose self-containment deeply satisfies what a friend once called my "completist panic," a condition that I've since realized is the leading impetus for all of my work (not to mention the greatest source of my frustration with raising two small children). The exhausting availability of information and the speed at which it continually shifts and flattens the perceptual landscape of our cultural present makes me want to zip myself into Gardner's close round world. I can breathe my own air there, smell my own breath. And yet, even though they endlessly debate and explain loopholes into it, the museum board and staff mostly continue to obey Gardner's stricture, and so the stolen artworks broadcast their own punctures in her project. This dos-à-dos-à-dos of perfection, its theoretical impossibility and actual undoing is what consumes me.

I recently gave a reading with Susan Howe, whom I'm often compared to because of our common interest in the early history of New England. To writers of other origins New England is a brand, and with good reason—the depth, intensity and entrenchment of its borrowed lyric tradition make for a lot to lug around and plug yourself into if you choose. I think of the locus of my work both as a place among many others and as a challenge because of its particular baggage. But it is first and foremost the place that means me and that I mean to mean back. This reciprocity is what Susan Howe and I have in common. After the reading she told me that she is also working on a project about Isabella Stewart Gardner.

In *Civilization and its Discontents* Freud compares the human mind to a city with all of its ancient and modern structures simultaneously intact and available: " ... the observer would need merely to shift the focus of his eyes, perhaps, or change his position, in order to call up a view of one or the other." In *The Midnight* Howe writes, "In relation to detail every first scrap of memory survives in sleep or insanity." In both cases the fine points of memory are theoretically accessible, but there is a fundamental difference in how they are accessed. Freud's mind-place is an impossible palimpsest of static, equally extant layers. Howe embodies hers in her tireless multimania, only her place is made in the process of breaking into it, so details are intermittently available and always recombining, swallowing each other up and changing the view in a dynamic vat of past and present. While Freud's conceptualization of the mind is utterly subjective, Howe's is of a piece with the world—it is inextricably bound up with history. But she removes the connective tissue of the historical record and lets the past's clippings, offal and picked bones lie looking like themselves and the minds that left them there. If Freud's mind is a perfectly preserved place with actual parameters, Howe's borderless place is made of fractured ruins of many minds and memories that run away like grid-dots as you get near them.

Like Freud's wishful vision of mind and memory as discrete artifact, Gardner's project fails both because and in spite of her great effort to keep her collection intact and impervious to change. Howe, on the other hand, works just as hard to undo what she's doing at the same time as she's doing it—while she acts on the urge for completion with her rigorous work, the work is always its own product. It's a pilgrim's continuous progress toward where she already is and what she already knows, but with a resulting deeper understanding of why she knows it. With collage and visual components she introduces chance and dimensions of subjectivity that deepen and soften her field of inquiry, allowing her searching roots to push further.

The Midnight is patched together from pieces of and reminiscences related to old books, poets, historical figures and Howe's mother, an Irish actress named Mary Manning. One of its more prominent themes is the history of bed hangings, curtains that were once draped around beds in order to keep certain things out (cold, ghosts, prying eyes) and other things in (heat, noise and nebulous qualities of sleep). Other than a grave, the place where one sleeps is as local as it gets. It's a location to which one gives oneself over. Sleep is a state of being both fully present and realized and also absent and mere witness to oneself, where one's endlessly combinatoric fragments are called forth in inscrutable relationships. *The Midnight* exists in such a dreamplace and roughly woven location with the warp of time removed. Picking through and heaping up the weft, Howe never presumes comprehension or comprehensiveness: "Thinking is willing you are wild / to the weave not to material itself."

And yet, "Non-connection is itself distinct / connection" and neither does Howe prevent patterns from forming. But when she suggests or allows a connection, she makes sure to point out her own hand in the sleight, the "intersection of realities" she sets up, leaving room for the reader to call out the contrivance. The intersection remains nonetheless. In the course of the book a thread of performance emerges, binding Mary Manning to A *Midsummer Night's Dream*, Jonathan Edwards, Japanese Noh, and Howe's own visit to Harvard's library to research Emily Dickinson wherein her consciousness of her attire and its loud signaling threaten to subsume her purpose in being there. Curtains contain both the bed and the stage. AMTRAK makes a number of stops along the way, bringing her places together—and/or choosing them—including Howe's current home of Guilford, Connecticut, where the train's whistle keeps her awake at night. Olmsted describes his own childhood sojourn in Guilford during his own bout of insomnia. But just as you begin to give in to the shapely web of connections she drops a reminder that "little relocated facts epistemically relocated tell very little." This struggle between binding and rending and the difficult work of doing both and neither is the tensile strength of her project.

Howe manifests sleeplessness, indulges the desire for exhaustiveness while demonstrating its futility. She enacts the maxim of her fellow re-visioners of New England, delivering content by the bucket-load and letting form be taken. Isabella Stewart Gardner, on the other hand, says, "That is enough." In her impervious sphere, form and content complete one another like a call and response to prayer. So, what will Howe do with Isabella? I see her dropping a microphone into the depths contained by the empty frames on the wall and recording what she hears there. Those gaps are the cataracts in—and the chance to escape from—Isabella's circumscribed vision. While I am interested in the premises and attempted hermeticism of the vision itself, Howe is holding her listening glass to the chinks. But we are both Rembrandt boring holes into his missing masterpiece, the beautiful thing we know we could make if we would only stop unpainting it. Our parallels derail themselves, their vanishing point a maw.

•

I was born in Boston and grew up twenty minutes away in Wayland, Massachusetts. To get there you take the Mass Pike to Route 128, the city's ring road, whose formal name is the Yankee Division Highway. Drive north about two miles, then take Exit 26 and follow the Post Road to the town center. Growing up I was within biking distance of Walden Pond, The Wayside Inn, the Alcotts' Orchard House and the Concord battlefield. My grandmother frequently took me and my brother on picnics at what's known locally as the Rude Bridge, thanks to Emerson's dedication, which it bears on a plaque at one end. There is a small visitors' center at which you can try on mobcaps and three-cornered hats.

At the center of this classic factual New England landscape was my family, which is of the traditional congregational sort. You talk about anything but what you're talking about, then have a few cocktails and forget both. Textbook Puritan derivatives, my relations tend to be parsimonious to the extreme, so they don't waste a lot of time on the tangle of human psychology. This innate economy manifests in a practical anti-parsimony principle when it comes to the material, where time is infinite and resources are discrete. When my great aunt Dodie died, found in her decrepit Providence manor house was a box labeled, "Pieces of String Too Small to Be Useful." My parents will drive thirty minutes from home for wholesale groceries. I joke they'd drive fifty miles for cheaper gas. I've gained from them these horn-locked notions that time is precious but can't confer advantage because we are all in it.

This is one version of the original Puritan paradox of hard work versus predestination that a dispositional New Englander somehow ignores or reconciles and lives with. But I'm at odds, as a would-be completist who feels the press of time like a bundling board. I explore this perpetual state of emergency by doing my best to divide things down to their essence, even though I'll never get there. And I try to include everything and also different kinds of it, in addition to every bit of it. All the time. Every end of string. My poetic practice has shaped itself accordingly around Zeno's and Kant's paradoxical state of kinetic suspension—I want but can't have it all, so I keep to my place and divide mitotically.

Place is what clings most closely to the body that is not the body itself. For me, writing about where I've been and where I live is both an indulgence and a form of resistance—I can voraciously parse my own impetuses while thwarting my yen for hermeticism. I love to close loops but stop believing in them as soon as I do. In place and its attendant events there is always more to excavate and to try to synthesize. The ground keeps deepening and dividing beneath my feet.

•

After eleven years in San Francisco Rusty and I moved to Providence in 2007. If space is what the body displaces and place is what it occupies, then I'd been beside myself, taking up space for over a decade. California's high sky and unbounded landscapes pulled me out of my own brain and body and the delimited conditions under which I was born and became myself. The removal gave me contrast in abundance. It also made my mind feel more perceptibly mechanical, like my synapses had grown and their firings slowed. But while this sense of relativity was exhilarating, in time it began to feel like a never-ending spacewalk. After a few years of floating I started pulling myself back in, writing increasingly about New England and using description to put me in my body there:

> The summer I was seven, the gypsy
> moths infested, caterpillars wriggled
> from the sky, tangled in my ratty
> hair, formed knots, crawling skin,
> shivers, peristaltic on the sidewalk.
>
> Stinging nettles, tiny hairs
> of hooked skin, throwing
> burrs at others' backs, sticks
> stabbing though your thin shirt
>
> —Unbecoming Behavior

In the year before we moved back I wrote Unbecoming Behavior, which is about expatriatism and physical displacement—my own and that of the writer Jane Bowles. It was an exploration of the removal from a home and an experiment in remotely accessing it. One way I tried to reinhabit Massachusetts was by evoking its particular locating discomforts, especially the sticky summer heat that California lacks. I wanted to swell and itch.

> hives   buzz
> at night   induced
> by heat   pocked skin
> throbbing   cicadas
> shrieking   bites
> the night   the glowing
>
> bug zapper

From 3,000 miles away I stabbed at my "You Are Here" dot, counting on never quite getting there lest it disappear or I adapt to it. I needed to stay suspended somewhere just in front of it in order to maintain the contrast necessary to think. And so moving back East was fraught—I worried that I wouldn't be able to write there. What I've since realized is that "there" was a place of my own making and different from "here". Here is where I am, no matter where and where else I'm pointing at.

From Wayland, return to 128, drive south one mile to Exit 25 in Weston and get on the Mass Pike. About seventy-five miles west is the Quabbin Reservoir visitors' center in Belchertown. (Due to the proximity of Athol, my uncle used to refer to this region as the "digestive tract of Massachusetts." A map is a maw.) Most of Boston's water comes from Quabbin, which was built in the 1930s by damming the Swift River and drowning the valley. The residents of Enfield, Prescott, Dana and Greenwich were relocated and the buildings were razed. More than 6,000 gravesites were moved. The disincorporated towns no longer appear on the map, but their streets and stone walls are still there. Supposedly you can see them from the air or when the water level is low.

I wrote *The Return of the Native*, which is partly about Quabbin, after driving back across the country to Rhode Island. The book is named for Thomas Hardy's, which I read right before we left. The jarring shift of that move had me thinking about the abstract and unstable qualities of maps, as well as about their revision, appropriation and erasure—how Hardy drew his Wessex map on top of the real one, how Quabbin wiped out a chunk of the Massachusetts map while adding a significant feature to it, and how even after all that time living there I still pictured California as a place on the U.S. map. When I called my parents, say, I actually saw myself *in* the map with a phone to my ear. I didn't think about Massachusetts that way. Massachusetts made me think of the feeling of being in it, and that is what makes me native, maybe.

Maps are one way we locate ourselves, relatively. But if anyone knows how to locate his characters by giving you the feeling of being in a place, it's Hardy. Each novel is contained within a real place that Hardy makes and that functions as its own social petri dish. Together, his carefully wrought characters and landscapes evoke the genius loci of nineteenth-century rural England, a place that in its self-containment is remote from this highly mediated moment. But rather than let them be, Hardy dulls and abstracts his places with a map, when the novels' respective settings don't even overlap and have little to do with the pseudonymous places to which they are retroactively assigned. London glares above the fake-medieval place names of Wessex like an over-bright and disorienting beacon.

Hardy was a completist and perhaps he panicked. It was not enough to have created a cluster of beautifully consummate things, he needed to bring them all together under an umbrella whose cheapness he either ignored or couldn't see. I retroactively assigned the chapter titles from Hardy's book to sections of my own *Return of the Native* in an approximation of the heavy load his map placed on his places. I was indulging the urge to undo what one has done well by trying to do more on top of or around it. While the titles forced narrative frames and a strong connection with Hardy onto my book, in most cases they also wound up feeling weirdly appropriate to their respective sections of the poem (and therewith swallowed the whole point in an analogous demonstration of cartographic peristalsis).

But if Hardy's map seems beside the point at best, other than as a brand, it does make me think about how one might merge relative and innate[1] qualities of place into a completely representational map depicting all of a place's factual and subjective history layered like innumerable vellum overhead-projector transparencies.[2] I once explored this sort of experiential mapping in writing, in a Charles-Ives-esque long poem I've since retired, which, among other things, I stuffed with bits of songs and hymns and American folklore. About it, I once wrote, "If these walls could talk they'd sound just like this."[3]

•

Conflicting perceptions of the world as built versus the world as received might be the defining conflict of New England self-identity—the original Yankee division. A Puritan insists on having it both ways and fuzzes over the dissonance. A Transcendentalist does the same. Emerson says in *Nature*, "Build your own world" and also "I become a transparent eyeball. I am nothing; I see all; the currents of the universal being circulate through me." But there is no room in the purview for the largesse of paradox. I wrote about Fruitlands because I was interested in the inability to act and move that an extreme philosophical position can induce. The inhabitants were so intent on receiving and refusing to intervene in the physical world that they nearly starved after only seven months together.

---

1 I mean innate for each person—things both adherent and inherent to place. Just don't ask me which is which.
2 I worry it's starting to look like everything I mean is only the internet.
3 They didn't.

Puritanism, Transcendentalism and other utopic New England test-tube worlds—Hopedale, the Shakers, the domain of Sylvester Graham—were created under pressured laboratory conditions of a nation's short gestation and vast amount of amniotic space. The philosophical deadlock of action and reception inherent to all of them touches off panic in the completist—if both everything and nothing depends on me, then I'm stuck, suspended like Achilles, who not only can't get ahead, but can't move at all as space and time subdivide around him like an endlessly shuffling deck of cards. And yet it is not possible not to move and act and be in time, and this again might be what furnishes the tension in poetry—deconstruct versus "make it new"—"theory at war with phenomena" (*The Midnight*). As a locus of poetic struggle, New England makes sense.

•

Exit 29b off Route 128 puts you on Route 2 West, which passes through Concord on its way to Acton, childhood home of Robert Creeley. A book that I return to repeatedly is *Robert Creeley and the Genius of the American Commonplace*, the greater part of which, according to the jacket, consists of an "interactive biographical essay culled from conversations between the poet and Tom Clark." Creeley talks a lot about the enduring influence of the Puritans' ideological conflict on his upbringing as well as about the intrinsic physical qualities of his native place that helped him to work outside of—or freely within, at least—the terms of that paralyzing inconsistency.

Think.
Slowly. See
The things around you,

Taking place.
—"Massachusetts"

As things are allowed to take their places—to adhere themselves there—place becomes a way to apprehend them. In regard to what Creeley considered an ideal location from which to observe and write, Tom Clark quotes him as saying, "It is where one feels an intimate association both with the ground under one's feet and with all that inhabits the place as condition." He doesn't write about woods and fields and houses, but those places loosely enfold his poems the way a lantern holds light. A word that Creeley uses frequently when describing where he came from and that is central to my thinking about the role of place in writing is "immanence."

> **Tom Clark**: You've spoken of an enlivening presence you felt in the landscape, the local woods. There's a sort of allegorical or emblematic landscape also evoked in the hymnal, perhaps not dissimilar to the lyric landscape of your poetry—not the lush greens of classic pastoral, but a bare, stripped woods of winter, all light and shadow.

> **Robert Creeley**: Yes...the language of the hymns brings back for me that still small voice, that curious immanence. I *did* know it as some immanence, or qualification, in the sense of the physical staging of the place. A hushed evening, twilight, say—the physical terms were not just evocative, but like, say, the way water sounds.

The way water sounds. That embodiment of immanence, inscape, physical presence has propelled me through many a sticky moment in my work. When exhausted by subjectivity, I fold into the qualities of place and find a momentary objective center in what emanates from there.

> I see love and need you
> to hear it: listen,
> I did once love someone
> who told me that

> he and some other boys would climb onto a roof over Main Street and cast claim-baited hooks into the air, where the seagulls would catch and swallow them. The boys would then fly the gulls like kites over Main Street. The dying birds would have seen the harbor and returning trawlers, their compatriots swarming like flies over fish heads with eyes in them, fish tails, the dilapidated Manufactory

> — *Beauport*

Even if it is only a desperate throe of perspective, this panoramic quality is not something you'd find in Creeley. Clark describes Creeley's work as having the "fated limitation to a condition of sight without perspective". His flat affect has a cinematic *verité* anticipated by Emerson's transparent eyeball: "I am nothing; I see all." The condemnation to vision is ironic, given that Creeley had only one working eye and another made of glass. But if he lacks the mechanical perspective afforded by two working eyes, he's also spared the cognitive dissonance in the difference between what is seen with the right eye and the left that others' brains fuzz over. While his poems are *about* lack of perspective—collectively they feel like a struggle to escape from a sack—they are born of a stable place.

The perspective Creeley's poems are fighting for is denied by another kind of dissonance that refuses to resolve—the inadequacy of speech to express and thus facilitate understanding of the horrors of human existence. "Speech / is a mouth," gaping and flapping and always only uttering itself: "I think to say this / Wrongly." You get the sense in Creeley's poems that if only everything were effable then we might fruitfully assimilate it. He palpably, precisely manifests the dullness of words and the fumbling that we do with them, showing that meaning is possible in language, even if that meaning is another kind of its-own-mouth.

In my own fight for perspective I keep trying to describe what achieving it feels like to me—weightlessness, punching through a self-healing wall, the screech of feedback. The success is momentary by nature because there's no permanent state of perspective to be had. Even the most sweeping prospect must accommodate pervasive change, but perspective also requires a vantage place. Susan Howe clips and collages the past into piles then climbs on top for a small view, drops microphones into cracks and calls up faint voices, digs deep into the bottomless hole of history in pursuit of her perspective. She works with the assiduousness of a Puritan. Creeley is more of a Transcendentalist, reclining in a sharp bed of pine needles. Howe writes *into* New England, Creeley writes *from* it. Neither tries to contain it. I try to contain it over and over again in fits and moments, like jars of fireflies jammed on the nightstand.

Howe's accretions resist closure in every possible way, including formally—whether she's working in series of tiny text boxes or swathes of prose, the work digs into and piles up on itself in a way that wants to go on forever. She makes heaps of scree, sometimes purposeful, sometimes accidental, and I can't think of anything she's written that wants to be beheld and admired discretely. Her writing to date feels continuous, but not contained. It is still building and splitting and smashing and sweeping itself up in new ways. She voices the immanence of history, which is as contingent and unclosed as a thing can be, since there are an infinite number of ways to organize it. And so her focus on New England is necessary—not the location itself, but the locatedness—because it allows her to keep drilling down toward the unreachable core and pull out more. She's done Jonathan Edwards over and over again but is still not done with him. Her work is to make more work for herself by unstitching time, one after nine.

Creeley's poems are formal objects to the utmost, but he never closes the loop of his exploration of subjectivity and language and the way they speak or don't speak to one another. Each poem is a whole but is also only one piece of conduit in an endless subjective plumbing project. It is also a clog, backing up all over itself in an almost defeatist reflexive maneuver. What allows him to have it both ways—open and contained—might be his terminal zingers, in which subject and object are the same, taking turns with the verb, and prepositions refuse to resolve into one way of meaning:

> And all our nights be one, love
> for all we knew.
> > — "Old Song"

> We break things in pieces like
> walls we break ourselves into
> hearing them fall just to hear it.
> > —"The Answer"

> One comes to a place he had not thought to,
> looks ahead to whatever,
> feels nothing lost but himself.
> > —"The day was gathered on waking..."

Creeley's last lines resonate, but inwardly—the poem absorbs its own vibrations. The poem is the mallet and the gong and the hand that stops it.

•

Continue north on 128 and take Exit 26 to get to the Peabody-Essex Museum in Salem (note: this is a different Exit 26 from the one off which I grew up—128 is full of such loops for which to throw you). When I was just starting to write poetry and looking for a way to think about it, it was here that I encountered a Chinese puzzle ball. Painstakingly carved by hand from a single piece of ivory, a puzzle ball consists of nested concentric spheres of different symbolic motifs that move freely inside one another. By gently manipulating the ball with a fine tool, the spheres' corresponding holes can be lined up to allow you to see into the ball's center.

This seemed like a useful analogy. I could close my loops while nesting worlds within worlds interminably. The idea and its shape have stayed with me, from "the set of all sets that is a member of itself" in *Fruitlands* to the antique glass buoys that *Beauport*'s Henry Sleeper collects: "The small glass globes of purple, amber and blue are a solar system when the sun shines. Worlds orbit worlds and vanish into the rest of it when he squints through their empty centers." While I want my poems to do and undo things both individually and collectively, creating a self-contained object does require some sort of closure of each poem's system. By nesting them and letting them reflect and refer back to one another incessantly I can have my terminal zingers and have them eat one another, too. These inter-referential relationships between the poems and me are facilitated by our common place.

•

Route 128 terminates in Gloucester, where I grew up spending summers and where my parents now live full-time. The city's perilous fishing trade and concomitant attraction for artists and writers helped to create the romantic New England sea trope that was once so central to American self-identification. Winslow Homer, Fitz Henry Lane, Kipling, Longfellow and T.S. Eliot depicted Gloucester fishermen at sea in iconic works suffused with salt and readymade for the canon. A local fishing shack has been the subject of so many quiet works of art it's known as Motif #1.

And yet Gloucester has kept tourists at arm's length and gentrification efforts often fail, so the place feels less self-conscious than many. It's that one-to-one relationship of the city to itself that makes artists want to depict it, which, in turn, has made it an artistically self-conscious place and one of poetry's zingiest locations. It is challenging to write about Gloucester, since it's a place that's simultaneously extra "real," objectified and abstracted, and because someone has already written about it to the max. Charles Olson spread himself over it like plastic wrap. I admire his ambition, even if it didn't leave a lot of room for the rest of us. In the Maximus poems he came as close to completing a project as might be possible or desirable, and the manifest tension between his push toward catalogic exhaustiveness and a metaphysical resistance to it influenced my own sense of what is impossible and undesirable in poetry.

Olson's solipsism bothers me, but please. Look at me. Still, there is a difference that I am still splitting into. Olson and I are both containers, although on different scales—he tried to encapsulate Gloucester in all its dynamism while I've tried to capture certain frozen moments of it. But we both poke holes in the bag, Olson with metaphysics and counter-colloquial cultural reference, me by creating and closing another container around it. The biggest difference in our projects might be one of ontological assumption—Olson's solipsism seems wishful and mine is fearful. I need there to be more, whereas he seems to hope and half believe that he is enough. In either case, the innumerable points of entry into place provide an equal number of ways to triangulate back to the self.

•

While I'm still hovering toward exhaustiveness, I've learned to keep my place, whether it's where I come from or where I am. For now they're the same and I feel fortunate—as the locus of the original and fundamental American war with place, New England has a defining relationship to itself as a physical location. The first English settlers tried to harness it and the place resisted. They learned to give in to the exigencies of the land at the same time as they continued to inscribe on and erase a whole other cultural conception of place from it. It is a place that was taken and then deliberately and dramatically made. Also, as the crucible of Anglo-American lyric tradition, New England is fertile ground for innovative appropriation. Howe, Creeley and Olson are my founding fathers of linguistic landscape architecture and I continue to consider my relationship to their place and respective places and my own place in them. I mean consider in the sidereal sense—to write like punching backlit holes through tin.

I regularly drive the length of 128 between Gloucester and Providence. My earliest colonial ancestors also lived and are buried here and this sense of original place gives me a specious but pleasing feeling of having returned to and arrived somewhere—of physical indivisibility and containment and home. If I never get out of here it won't be for lack of trying to stay.

Place is made and becomes itself. Autobiography is a dead end. But bloodlines do begin me at my body and for now this place means me, matters me, because I am in it.

A Meditation, in three parts, on Martha Ronk's *Partially Kept*

Elizabeth Robinson

Partially Kept by Martha Ronk
Nightboat Books 2012

Or

A precarious word, "or." As though there were an alternative, or a correspondence, that this small conjunction could mine:

the stalks of mint set in glasses with the root end upward & out of the water

sending forth sprouts without the aid of roots

or a thought, reasonable enough, but not even a thought

of a face never to be seen again

a configuration drawn with thin ink,   a face and she had seen it too

the root stripped from the leaves (13)

In "Partially Kept," the first section of her book of the same name, Martha Ronk gives us a rootless growth; she conjoins it with a thought that then self-cancels: "not even a thought," and not even a face, for it is never to be seen again.

"Or" stretches out that configuration, what one thinks she may have seen or heard, the pattern that suggests presence. But the correspondences that "or" makes possible exist in a state of artifice. They stretch time—to make immediate or to make distant: "Signs lodged below the surface, or/into the past, garbled, hushed."(25) Their surface is another configuration, a garden that floats before us: its fertile "if."

"If," one says, and that perch is all that exists of the thought (not even a thought) (not even a sentence)—

the sentence itself an integument of flexible green, evoking

beginning and end

a half mirrored   a whole   a half and beginning again—

The fragile tethers of "or" and "if" connect us to an empirical world that is ever ready to become a chimerical world. And what is better, Ronk asks, to enter the daylight that transcends our daily "just plain going about things"? Or to discover within that glare that our final understandings are only shades, resemblances, correspondences that cannot stand up to the order we want of them?

In this series of poems, Ronk is preoccupied, almost obsessed, with hearing and seeing—

—and listening as if I were listening in // as closely as I never can—(15)

—what I see, what I can't and haven't the names for[...]glimpsed in time-lapse, seeing into and close up, sight unraveling at this distance—(16)

It is almost as though to see and to hear will tell us where we are, for sense is also context. And sense is, if not proof, then a kind of justification, a way of reclaiming the reality of what is irretrievable, " a form of another entirely relegated to if not related to / *the particular state wherein you reside*."

Light   Aftermath   Relic

Light again. Light is always beyond itself, beyond the eyes by which light makes seeing possible. In that way, light is related to the practicality of vision.

But in "No Sky," the second section or sequence of *Partially Kept*, light is also a measure of duration. Its passage, since it is never still (change suggesting itself as a synonym for loss), becomes elegiac.

> a sense of fading into the distance, the strokes feathering off at the end
> everything in attendance in the atmosphere's exchange of air and tree
> as novel in its entirety as any preconceived idea. (36)

Tangled in its daily or seasonal pattern—which Ronk accepts, too, as mostly random—light, like memory, impinges on loss by insisting on time. But where does time go? What is its progress? Why are we not permitted to hold onto our losses as immutable?

> Impingement as slight pressure
> as slight as her glance, distracted,
> from where as a slice of light in and out of the slats
> the consequence measured but the source traced back,
> waning. The window hard,
> the light impermanent and unquestionably deft.
> A slight thing transparent as wings trapped against the glass,
> shifting as the intermittent light,
> lost in its own pledge to it. (35)

The poet is pledged to something that cannot commit itself to durable presence in time. Aftermath occurs as an event or entity that exists in a peculiar suspended state between antecedents and consequences.

Polarities that would anchor us in the aftermath—but the aftermath of what?

Daylight makes its transit through sky, or no sky. Headlights propel light into shadow "driven by the demarcation of time." Aftermath is "needful," that is, both necessary and in need. Where all stabilizing contradictions collapse, where the light shifts again, aftermath is the site where one struggles to go on "without knowing whose experience is having whom or to whom."

a left-over stripe of silver across the sky

Then what if the aftermath of experience, as with the fading of light, is doubt? A lack of certainty resides at the heart of memory; the result is that doubt becomes our relic ("as the day faded in the original of which this is only a copy / calling up what never was in the tonal variations of gray / as the house is only a material copy of *house* writ large." (39)

Doubt: recursive and precious:

What does not take place must occur over and over again as one continues to wait for it and if one wants it deeply enough one must actually work to prevent it lest by its happening it be reduced and delimited. (53)

Diffusions of time and illumination filter into these poems, spookily. The speaker, clutching memory and doubt as relic, as the consolation of some (escaping) object, abandons order for aporia and enters into

an unspoken agreement to allow oneself to be encircled by whatever ensues

neglecting what came before and what is to come for the purpose of perfecting

form (52)

Having arrived

=

Remembering the acts of oblivion

Say the world were divided into inside and outside. How does the mind discern which is the closer, which the more distant? One proceeds through this indeterminacy, and memory arrives, bearing with it its deficits—one cannot be certain what is or was true. Just that:

all that one wants is the repetition of it, not so much to ask

not so much

And yet, in this final, brief section, "August," Ronk's poems acknowledge "the material archive against which our memories rest / ardent postures, guises, ruses." Here again is a form of the inside / outside tension: the ostensible emotional earnestness of the ardent juxtaposed against the social artifice of posture.

The rhetoric of one's posture—a sort of conscious comportment—haunts these poems, but as a kind of muted bewilderment: "Who said what I am said to have said"?

Ronk describes the poem as "a cylinder   enclosing silence" but elsewhere writes "let rhetoric take over the silence." Then the social persuasiveness, the tidy formulae, of rhetoric serve as a protective garment over the impingement of poetic untidiness, the "future's invasive," "the ones at risk, the vulnerable."

Say that one re-reads a poem, a memory, a day. Then one could be reassured that things recur, that the present leads to a future because, after all, having read before, one has already proceeded into the present. Re-reading holds memory as something we can read again, knowing its future.

Summer will come again, and August within it. Yet our readings of experience, our projections to a future lapse into an inside-outside dilemma. Is it loss or is it discovery? Ronk's syntax has a strange simultaneity that returns rhetoric to silence to rhetoric to silence, &c. That is, her language arrives as lyric and demolishes the expectation of experience.

You have to write what you don't yet know and hope

that in another time you might. (57)

FROM **The sea, the limit**

Tierry Hentsch

Translated by Nathanaël

To consent to the world, is not to accept it indifferently in all of its states. Still, how is one to consent to that which is without accepting the unacceptable. There is no formula. There is only the possibility of my attention to the world, the possibility of rejecting in it not its things, but several among them. The capacity for refusal that I share with others is part of the world. To consent to the world, is to consent also to that which I reject in it, is to consent to the refusal I oppose to it. In this world there is the glimmer, wavering and tenacious, of the capacity for discernment.

To discern. To riddle. From an Indo-European root, *krei, krinein* in Greek, to separate, slice, choose, decide, judge, interpret. From which are also derived: critique, crisis. And, through Latin: crime, excrement, certainty, concert, discretion and secret. To give but a small idea of the list of words which share the same origin. Of a word, etymology does not give the true meaning (which follows from usage), but it indicates its depth, its sources, its ramifications; it gives to dream the multiplicity of the senses which sustain and frequent it. Discernment also leads us to classification, to interpretation, to discrimination and waste (*excrementum*). The only gaze, on any one thing, is discriminatory. Indeterminacy provides no hold, for us it doesn't exist.

Perhaps it is this first obviousness which impels Anaxiamander, Ionian philosopher of the sixth century B.C.E., when he says, in that famous and enigmatic fragment of his which has remained with us, that things, with time, grant themselves justice in their mutual discordances. An idea one finds in Heraclitus, who celebrates the fertility of conflicts and the harmony of opposites. Without opposition, without contrasts, without shadows, as has been shown by the traumatic experience of prisoners subjected to sensory deprivation, man is affected in his mental health and equilibrium. The limit, the boundary, the delimitation, the territory are among the primordial conditions of animal and human existence. And for men (I don't know what it is for animals), the faculty to discern is not only nor even principally exerted with regard to the physical space which surrounds him but in that other, internal, landscape he carries everywhere with him and which is also called the imaginary. Our mental representations are just as necessary to us as the hollow of the hand, without them, the mind, consciousness would lose itself in the sands.

A world without boundaries is a forest without trails, a desert without dunes, a sea without shores. No more imaginable than a painting without edges. I cannot remember who painted a white square on a white background, pictorial representation of the absence of representation—though even that absence itself necessitates a frame (wall, living room, museum) which gives it to be seen. The exploit cannot be repeated, at best plagiarized in other tones. Unless one sees in it a sort of Zen exercise. I ignore everything about Zen. It is possible that Zen leads to the mental equivalent of a world without boundaries, a sort of perfection in absence, an experience of a non-consciousness—epitome of the void. I don't know. To say anything about it is already too much. If there is a wisdom there, it is forever inaccessible to me. And if I had the slightest access to it I wouldn't even think of speaking of it. I live inside finitude.

Finitude is my condition. But I live in a time and a place which has trouble bearing it. The Occident cannot stand the limit. It can't stand the limit and covers the world in scars. I am living in an era in which every limit runs the risk of being barbed, in which every wound threatens to envenom itself. Wounds in space and in time. We are also great sectioners of time, adders of historical sections, dividers of eras that engender and contradict one another: Antiquity, Middle Ages, Modern Times. As though History had nothing better to do than to place eras end to end, to cement the central conduct of the main sewer, in order to "prepare" us. No other end than our own advent. Advent always postponed, put off until later. The present is never for us anything other than the past of a missing time *to come*. As Pascal says so well, "The present is never our end: the past and the present are our means; the future alone is our end. Thus are we never actually alive, but hope to live; and since we are always planning how to be happy, it is inevitable that we should never be so." (Manuscript 21, Brunschvicg 172).

The procrastination of the present has something to do with the refusal of the limit. That which, with the joy of the instant, is ceaselessly postponed, is nothing other than the presence of death. I am living in a civilization that is so refractory to finitude that it goes as far as offending death. It denies it and insults it all at once, it obliterates and does battle with it. Formidable incoherence in the belief that one is confronting what one is fleeing and rejecting what one denies. Death, thus deported, becomes a matter for the other: directly or indirectly, the other puts our own existence in danger, his suppression, or his distancing, is the condition of our longevity. *Live and let die.* Barbed wire and the refusal to die go hand in hand.

No. I must be mistaken: that which suffers no limit could not enclose or exclude. The battle against death, the battle for civilization concerns all of humanity. In principle, it excludes no one. If the civilizing œuvre progresses unequally, if it encounters suspicions, resistances, it is that it remains yet largely unassimilated, misunderstood. A matter of historical dislocation. Comprehension, inclusion, take time. The disparities of history will end up resorbing themselves ... Perhaps. But how many decades, how many centuries will yet be necessary for these enchanted tomorrows to fulfill their promise? No one has the slightest idea. The idea of progress, of happiness for all, the civilization of leisure, the eradication of illness, the failure of aging, all those hopes, all those projects feeding the limitless fable that guides us and in which no one, in the end, believes. To which the spectacle of the world offers every day the most cruel disavowal. The absence of limits is a bad hope in a world barded with fences.

Because the limit is not a fence and the absence of limits does not make one free. Excess is not freedom. In itself, the limit does not exclude. And every exclusion isn't necessarily bad. Whereas the need to include everything—that sick need to reduce all foreignness to the known—leads to the most radical exclusions. The boundary is only a closure if it is unthought. What closes, is the refusal to think. Refusal or laziness, it doesn't matter: prison of the imaginary, in which I am at once prisoner and guardian.

We have all more or less heard talk of those detainees chained up in a cave. Their necks caught in shackles which do not allow them to turn their heads and they only see the shadow of the simulacra of an invisible fire, at their backs, projected on the wall facing them. One could believe they are the slaves of a cruel master. But no. They are there doing nothing, watching the shadows pass. One might easily think them in front of the television set. Nothing enslaves them but themselves, riveted to their bench of their own volition. Plato goes so far as to say that whoever wishes to free them from their chains runs the risk of dying from it (the Athenians did, after all, condemn Socrates to death and even did so democratically). Boetius speaks as well of voluntary servitude, but by describing that haste as though tied to the miserable hope nurtured by each to climb an echelon in the repressive hierarchy. In Plato's allegory the idea of some gain isn't even evoked. No hierarchy, everyone aligned at the same level of stupor. The limit to which each seems to acquiesce is internal, we see to our own enchainment. The cave is our own cranium.

The allegory incited so much commentary that it seems to have exhausted its evocative force. I wonder whether that wear doesn't come from our admiration of the cave from outside, as though it offered itself to the gaze as a vertical section, like those façade-less models that make visible the internal arrangement of their spaces. By operating this magisterial sectioning, the architect would make us see from an improbable exterior, at a magical, "superior," angle, the state of man and of knowledge. The allegory, diabolically deceitful, establishes a limit which separates from it in a perfectly illusory way. Oh, if it were only a matter of that simple distance, we would be sages at the simple sight of the spectacle it offers us and we would hold the truth cheaply! The cave, of course, we are in it, in the company of the philosopher, who himself has not left it—for what improbable star? But at least the philosopher undoes himself from his chains; he sees the fire, sees the wheel of simulacra. He is the one who finally discovers and takes the long and tortuous road that leads laboriously to the open air. From there to believe he has arrived, arrived at the kingdom of Ideas, in contemplation before the Intelligible, there is only one step to take.

Wrong. The light of day devours his eyes, he sees nothing, without even mentioning the sun. He must, so to speak, remake a cave with his hands and, very slowly, open his eyes, his fingers. What one glimpses with difficulty, in this light, is that the world it illuminates is none other than this very world, this world we inhabit so little, so poorly. The bounds in which we maintain our minds prevent us from seeing things and deprive us of their beauty. The cave, its visible wall, draws a screen against reality, it is the habit in which laziness drowns all things. Reality is not given, too many automatisms cover it over. If it were given to us to bask in it in our earliest childhood, we have forgotten it, by dint of learning. What makes experience—what is also called culture—a fertile soil, is turning it over, undoing it, it is making it into an always loose earth, ready to receive. Seeing is a lengthy task.

This task is both without limits and a tributary of our finitude. Junction of the extreme and of measure. There is no limit to the desire for beauty and the exercise of this desire is only possible within the limits of the "human machine." We must always return to the cave, which we never are really able to absent ourselves from—it would be like leaving our own mind, going mad, perhaps. But the mind can apply itself to rendering its walls more porous. If the doors of perception were cleaned, said William Blake, everything would appear to man such as it is, infinite. But those pores remain for the most part opaque. The infinite they withhold and that at most they allow to be gleaned by intervals is never more than a call. It is the call of *Eros* so dear to Plato, the one whom Socrates says to his friends, lovers of adolescents, that he has it from a woman: tension between what I have—desire—and what I am missing—everything. Lack is my condition. Lack is in me without limits, like a bottomless well that no pleasure can fulfill. If I fulfill my desire, I smother it. If I exacerbate it, it exhausts me. The incessant quest for more pleasure and the means necessary to its attainment manufactures my servitude. Putting oneself in a state of lack, as is said with regard to drugs, is making oneself into a prisoner of the ephemeral, a slave of the tyranny of the senses. For the senses, there has never been enough. That very lack, physical, installs dependency.

For Plato lack is a force. It is the most powerful lever of thought. Others might say that Plato invents sublimation. A rather pejorative term since Nietzsche, since Freud. And it is true that Christianity (so wrongly named the "Platonism of the people"), by curbing, by canalizing its impulses, has much contributed to placing those limits whose absence I may earlier have seemed to have been regretting. But religion, as an institution given to maintaining order, does nothing but erect one servitude against another. The limit is external, imposed, suffered. Plato, on the contrary, considers it from outside. A cave man, he reflects on the boundary within himself, he positions himself there and he thinks it. He thinks of the game played out in man between the limited and the unlimited. This game must be thought if man doesn't want to become its toy. Man has the possibility of being a player, the subject of his own game. Or he is more often contented to be its object. It is that the game is a difficult œuvre, a long-term demand.

Man is the possibility of the infinite within finitude. We are in all respects limited, in time, in space, in our means, in our powers of comprehension. But, in this limited realm comprised of one's life and one's person, the very idea of our finitude projects thought beyond its boundaries. The simple question of a beyond the universe, a beyond death, the sole fact that we ask it, is the mark of the infinite in us. Finitude of the senses, infinitude of the mind: the mind conceives what exceeds it, mathamatizes the infinite. By opening infinite spaces to reflection the mind foils the trap of the senses, it dissolves the obsession with pleasure and possession; it liberates us from performance, whether in love, work, sports, play, drugs—whatever the vial, provided there is drunkenness …

Is it a matter of being sober? "Be drunk without respite!" said my favorite Baudelaire. "On wine, on poetry, on virtue—take your pick." Have I forgotten? Have I abdicated?

Somatics and Experimental Prose: An Unfinished Essay

JH Phrydas

for Bhanu Kapil

PART I—EXPERIMENTAL PROSE

1.

> Prose is about time ... Prose slows down the excitement,
> it redistributes the tension of certain words and certain emotion ...
> [it] redistributes the tension at levels we can endure.[1]

~

I will begin with prose: why prose, especially experimental prose, the place of the sentence, the paragraph, the "novel"; in effect, why do some of us write prose instead of poetry, or music, or architectural blueprints? In a world of limitless possibility, only tempered by the temporal and spatial reality we inhabit, one that is constantly in flux, both emerging into and receding from view, our view, what does the sentence *do* or *enact* differently than other types of representation? Nicole Brossard speculates, in the quotation above, the temporal as prose's main valuation: she posits an inherent grammatical and syntactical structure of the sentence that *slows down*, that *redistributes*, that *lessens tension*. The elastic ability of the sentence to contain a time-stamp we can *endure* seems vital for Brossard in a way that creates another type of tension—this time internal—with regards to genre.

What is genre but a category to define the limits of how we approach and react to the infinite ways language can shape, delineate, utilize, aestheticize, etc.? Brossard comments on this cognitive splitting that imagines these limits not as chasms but as no-(hu)man's-lands, the grassy areas between the road and the fenced-in carnival: the potential space of running amok. In the same interview, Brossard *wonder[s] how far the poetic can go before it becomes prosaic and*

---

1   Nicole Brossard, from "Delirious Coherence," an interview conducted by Susan Holbrook, published in *TCR, The Capilano Review: Narrative*, 9.

what suddenly gives the prosaic a poetic dimension.[2] A sentence suddenly becomes poetic when it wanders far afield. The *suddenness* seems to creep up: an abrupt nuance, an embedded shift in the sentence one assumes is *just* a sentence before pop!, it's poetic. Maybe this isn't a Brossardian ease of tension but a reinvigoration—a means to bring tension to its extreme—where the sentence buckles and turns away: a type of revenge.

I'm interested in this space, in this pop: or rather, in the sentence before the pop. Most readers assume sentences are *easier* to read than fractured lines of poetry and approach them with a trust inherent in preconceived notions of understandability: the sentence couches the reader's comforts. Thus, when the sentence defies expectations it performs something else, an unknown feeling that creeps up on the reader and enunciates new types of anticipations: the *poetic(s)* of prose.

There is no law defining reaction: the sentence *is*, and one may follow it or stop in one's tracks. This cessation is choice: the human ability to attempt to foreclose a space before it influences, or in the very act of intended influence, in relation to what may be *unendurable*.

And yet, still, what is this *sentential poetics*, this question of traction, of method, of sway?

It excesses form and aligns more closely with syntax, cadence, and tone.

~

... complexity and seismography...[3]

2.

In the field of our thoughts, in thinking of existence (being-existing) in time and place, we have the most absolute of mirrors: the sentence.[4]

---

2   Ibid., 8.
3   Ibid., 14.
4   Renee Gladman, "The Person in the World," *Biting the Error: Writers Explore Narrative*, 46.

~

I'm fascinated by the act of reading, of the decisions that go into choosing to sit at a cafe or stand on a train and picking this text or that article to read. Jennifer Miller, a medieval scholar at UC Berkeley, told me in 2004 that we read texts in anticipation: how the text indulges or manipulates that anticipatory desire is just as important of a methodological tool as form or content. Readers *want* something out of the act of reading, and this desire is economic as much as affective or intellectual.

Does the sentence, then, act as a more democratic or catholic site of inclusion, where the reader can let their guard down, open the page, and read the coziness of a beautiful, well-thought-out metaphor? Is the sentence assumed as an escapist ruse for distraction, entertainment, disassociation from the space around the reader? If the reader feels soothed by the linearity of the sentence, what happens when that calm is disrupted, literally, by a breach? A syntactical re-orientation? A quick curve in an unforeseen direction?

Words, when spilling onto more words, enact a different type of linearity, one that fractures and accumulates, that slips in route to dead ends and refuses to bypass dark alleyways.

It is possible that prose has a privileged position in relation to disruption: in seducing the reader to assume regularity, the ambush could be quite jarring as well as sublime. I am reminded of Vladimir Nabokov's *The Defense*: the protagonist Aleksandr Luzhin, whose mental breakdown turns his life into an insidious chess match he cannot win, is stunned to find that, when opening the door to his hotel room one day, it leads *somewhere else*: a backyard, a kitchen, someone else's room. Is the character or the sentence losing its mind? Is the reader equally implicated?

Although Nabokov reveals an aporia that emerges in the durational space of the sentence, his writing practice does not go far enough: it remains, in effect, *fiction*.

~

...fiction is too burdened by a system of expectations (e.g., entrenched characters, well-developed storylines, conflicts and resolutions) to allow for the wandering and sometimes stuttering 'I' that I associate with discovery.[5]

---

5   Ibid.

3.

...how might our work as artists, writers, or teachers probe
the submerged relations between our bodies and
the social forces that channel their potential?[6]

~

New Narrative and Canadian experimental prose has done rigorous research into the *political* ramifications of non-normative sentence structure and subversive prose over the last thirty years. Much of this writing refracts through individual experience, distrust in linear and historical ideologies, and a resistance to oppressive State and Media apparatuses, ones that erase local identities for political and economic gain.

Experimental prose, then, is a *protest* against the written historicity of given scripts, preconceived concepts, the world as inherited and necessary *to endure.* What does prose do that opens the space of possibility, that reminds the reader of limitless potential, that performs as well as transmits anti-colonial affective language: that which resists as it enacts?

It may lie in the fractured sentence; the prosodic accumulation; the non-normative structure of experimental syntax. As Bhanu Kapil writes:

> Syntax has the capacity to be subversive, to be very beautiful, to register an anti-colonial position: in this respect. I think of the semi-colon: how it faces backwards and is hooked, the very thing a content [shredded plastic] might be caught on. A content, that is, that might never appear in the document of place. Perhaps the poet's novel is a form that, in this sense, might be taken up [is] by writers of color, queer writers, writers who are thinking about the body in these other ways.[7]

And then: to move from this space, to open up the topography of politics, underlying all types of written and spoken discourse.

---

6   Rob Halpern, from "Rob Halpern: on 'Somatics,'" conducted by Thom Donovan for the Harriet Blog, *The Poetry Foundation*, April 26th, 2011.
7   Bhanu Kapil, "A Converstion with Bhanu Kapil: The Poet's Novel," conducted by Laynie Browne, *Jacket2* Blog, April 26th, 2013.

~

> Can a poem arouse a form of embodied social sense whereby a body's relation to its occluded intimacies becomes perceptible?[8]

4.

> For a life to count as a good life, then it must return the debt of its life by taking on the direction promised as a social good, which means imagining one's futurity in terms of reaching certain points along a life course. A queer life might be one that fails to make such gestures of return.[9]

~

My writing practice centers around building, quite literally, a queer space, one that is not separated from *the world as it is* but is enmeshed in it, transposed upon it, always occurring simultaneously with it. In experimental prose, queer space emerges not as necessarily strange or Other but rather insistent and pervasive: *subtly present*. The pull of desire, the unintelligible need for touch as incessant and demanding, shapes the sentences, drawing forward the topoi of cruising—the need for contact.

Desire affects the spaces we inhabit: this is pivotal, vital, unavoidable. In a way, we exteriorize our inner systems, following streets to make certain synapses in our brains fire; like illuminated lines reflected off rough concrete.

To write the bend. To enact the bend. Does the bend transmit? Do we turn, in the writing, when reading this text? In following a line of sight it seems natural we must contort our bodies likewise.

What does it mean *to queer*? Texts may *be queer*, or evoke a *queer* space, but in the reading, in their reception, something other may occur: total failure of a transmitted *turning*.

I see this as a Gladman-like *reach*—the sentence's desire for touch. Again, we might look to syntax: to map breathing, the waiting body, the oscillation of a moving chest, leaning against a tree, all senses open to possible encounter.

---

8 Halpern, "on 'Somatics.'"
9 Sara Ahmed, *Queer Phenomenology*, 21.

~

Deviation leaves its own marks on the ground, which can
even help generate alternative lines, which cross the ground
in unexpected ways. Such lines are indeed traces of desire;
where people have taken different routes to get to this point...[10]

5.

Speech has a function that is not only representative but also destructive.
It causes to vanish, it renders the object absent, it annihilates it.[11]

~

The space of non-reproductive desire maps along city streets and urban parks. Similarly, my texts fall into repetitions of a walk from cement to dirt: the space of potential touch, but also, the space of writing.

It's important not to forget that writing enacts that which it is *not*—actual living-in-the-world. The text must be aware of this contradiction, comment upon this distance. Longing. The long-to-touch of the sentence itself, straining to make a connection. So that, the text, in enacting the cruise, will continue to repeat via different attempts[12] until some type of contact occurs.

The ellipsis of elision: ...

The end of the book.

The sex is elided. Once contact occurs, there is no more reason to write, and therefore no more reason to read. It is completion and consummation of the text; and yet, the ellipsis may initiate the first page—as a post-coital remembrance—as a gesturing back.

This, of course, is the intention: what occurs in the writing may be completely

---

10   Ibid., 20.
11   Maurice Blanchot, *The Work of Fire*, 30.
12   The word *attempt* signifies, already inherent in its connotation, in the realm of failure.

different. I know I sometimes make intellectual errors; ones you may notice cropping up along the sentential path. Some texts veer off course in my desire to experiment with grounding. I wanted to write a *grounded* text that does not mention the ground, and thus, a writing arises that tends towards an uneasy type of abstraction. Here, the writing escapes intention, but also *intuition*.

And thus, a return to my original artistic aims: of clay, of language as a plastic art, through the failure of gestural inadequacies.

~

He devotes all his energy to not writing, so that, writing, he should write out of failure, in failure's intensity.[13]

_____

13   Maurice Blanchot, *The Writing of the Disaster*, 11.

Works Cited

Ahmed, Sara. *Queer Phenomenology: Orientations, Objects, Others.* Durham: Duke UP, 2006. Print.

Blanchot, Maurice. *The Work of Fire.* Trans. C. Mandell, Stanford: Stanford UP, 1995. Print.

—. *The Writing of The Disaster.* 2nd ed. Trans. A. Smock. Lincoln: U of Nebraska P, 1995. Print.

Brossard, Nicole. "Delirious Coherence." Interview by Susan Holbrook. *TCR The Capilano Review: Narrative* Winter 2013.

Gladman, Renee. "The Person in the World." *Biting the Error: Writers Explore Narrative.* Ed. Mary Burger, et al. Vancouver: Coach House Books, 2004. Print.

Halpern, Rob. "Rob Halpern: on 'Somatics.'" Interview by Thom Donovan. *Harriet Blog.* The Poetry Foundation, 26 April 2011. Web. 5 May 2013.

Kapil, Bhanu. "A Conversation with Bhanu Kapil: The Poet's Novel." Interview by Laynie Browne. *Jacket2 Blog.* Kelly Writers House. 26 April 2013. Web. 5 May 2013.

Louis Bury

5/14/13

(me) I'm not sure I'm prepared for the amount of freedom & unconcern for standards I'm about to grant myself in this project
, as in poetry,
I can fail but ^ there are few
consequences to the failure
—if what I first write isn't good enough, I don't
have to worry about making it better, getting it
right, but, instead, only producing more, until
things click

▶like a monkey w/ a typewriter
marking time until things fall into place

—a ?: Do I take notes in different notebooks or put everything in one place?
—argument for different notebooks: makes it easier to find things
—I can envision, à la Mathews' *The Journalist*, starting dozens of notebooks,
each based on an elaborate, and ultimately impossible, taxonomy of note taking
—by the end of the project I'd have to walk around w/ a briefcase full of
notebooks in order to be able to get through the day w/o misplacing a note

---

Sontag. *Reborn: 1947-1963*

xii — Sontag & remaking herself: it's partly accident that I started w/ Sontag but it
feels auspicious given what Rieff says about self-invention through notes

what I essentially did when I switched from Business to English in college:
took notes, addressed to myself, on the person I wanted to become

5/15 (at the gym)

(me) in a way, this entire project is an elaboration of the Steinian insight (or, more
precisely, the insight you can have reading GS) that there is no wrong way to read

▶in this respect, I like the idea of just keeping one long unending notebook rather than trying to set up a (taxonomy)

on the side of order, rightness, coercion

Roubaud. *Poetry, etc.*   define: ...

109-10 — what he calls memory-effects, which happen in all writing, are, in poetry, primary, the point, whereas in other forms of writing, they are considered as either "negligible" or "parasitic"
                              while reading
▶ to take notes ^ is to prioritize the memory effects of your own reading, is to read poetically, as though you were reading poetry

(me) writing things down helps w/ retention, it's true, but at this point I've written down so many quotes from so many books that I think I write them down not to remember them but to ∨ forget them, w/ dignity & thereby open myself up to future shocks   give myself permission to

---

   ▶this is the case for my writing in general but doubly so here: I will have to find ways to make this book relevant to others beyond just myself
      ▶at the same time, I do think it's the case that unless you're pleasing yourself in the writing (again, Stein), the results will be stilted in some important way

   Notes: commitment to private pleasures, privates uses of knowledge

Imagine: academic work in which you could completely & entirely read what you want ▶ would it still be academic work?

DH Lawrence: "I don't care what a man sets out to prove so long as he carries me away in doing it."

(Roubaud)
280 — "The accusation of [poetry's] incomprehensibility is associated in an implicit way w/ the demand of *immediate* understanding."

(me) notes don't presuppose an immediate understanding—on the contrary

▶ notes are time capsules rigged out to meet the demands of non-immediate understanding: maybe, in future, when these artifacts get unearthed, a new kind of comprehension can take hold

▶ at the same time, part of the function of notes, filing cabinets, databases, notes are a form ⟵ storage systems, etc. is to store something so as to be able to forget it: of planned amnesia   most likely, the thing stored will remain, b/c safe and secure, unused

---

(me) consider how to make this project something other than mere notes, b/c the only notes that are considered worthy of interest are the notes of people we already care about
    ▶ rarely are notes perceived to have merit on their own

(me) how—and why—to incorporate humor in notes to yourself?
        (me) I remember re-reading old college lecture notes & on the back of one notepad I wrote that the professor's voice "rides me like a sleep pony"

I have to remember that I don't have to get every word right, that I can go back later & dress things up a bit, arrange the fossils of my reading into a skeleton, or, better, that I don't have to arrange or re-create anything other than the energy animating my most excited digging, that the mere act of accumulating trinkets & bones, in whatever order, is sufficient for producing a skeletal criticism, that the archeological site itself, with its tents, half-dug holes, exposed findings & scattered tools, might enclose a knowledge every bit as useful & important as the fleshless, reconstructed beast

skeletal criticism: piecemeal, incomplete, shot through with gaps, absences, metonymic echoes, a criticism that doesn't try to say everything that can be said on the subject but instead leaves some things implicit, to the imagination

notes naturally assume poetic shapes, contain stops, gaps, vectors of energy ▶ builds intrigue into the writing, visual energy, irrespective of content

Sontag. *Reborn*

30-1 — thankful she didn't let herself slide into the academic life
38-40ish — the journal gets more entertaining, less mawkish, when it gets
fragmentary & scattered

(me) something exciting about unsustained effort, ambition
sullied by life
40-3 — gay & straight slang

_____

(me) deluded fantasy of this project: that you can get things right the first
time, be utterly brilliant when spontaneous, brilliant <u>b/c</u> spontaneous

_____

on the phone
describing this project ^ to my sister:
    her: it's like a snapshot of a mind in motion
    me: the problem is that the only notes anyone would ever want to read
        are notes by
        someone important enough that people would be interested in such
    a snapshot
    her: so basically   if you do a good enough job on this book you'll have
    to write another
        version of it in the future

_____

(me) as productive as I've been these first several days, I've been quite down
about the project: even by my standards, which are out there, I'm exploring
territory that's particularly useless, unmoored from discursive context,
uncategorizable

almost
▶otoh, one thing that pleases me about this project is that it prospects
territory that is ^ completely uncolonized—uncolonizable ▶maybe my
projects have this tendency, w/ their concomitant feelings of uselessness,
b/c there's so little terain ~~in the world~~ in literary studies left uncolonized
(which is different than saying that there's nothing new that can be done)

5/17

the other nice thing about this project: no thoughts came today & I didn't have to try to force any

___

5/19

(me) maybe narrow the project down to just the notes of poets, that way the scope is more manageable, the audience clearer, & the subject becomes the relationship b/t notes & poems

(me) if this does get published, 2 ways of doing it:
1) include everything: ie, make it a narrative: "it started as x but evolved into y and z"
2) boil everything down to its absolute pith: maximum efficiency and excitement rather than involved backstory

obv makes it more readable but also makes it more suited to the digital attention span

already well suited to it
- an argument for option 1: literature is one of the last bastions expansiveness, slowness, dilation: few cultural spaces are left for them, literature more than ever needs to adopt that function
- an argument for # 2: stop trying to be being boring & overly precious about your own droppings, your own waste: if you want to be read, you have to be both good and engaging, no one, not even the most generous reader, has the time or attention span for anything less

— how to become a writer: get good at writing
— how to become a good writer: get relevant, too

at least how it's gone for me—if you start w/ considerations of relevance, you can't easily get good b/c relevance, esp. widespread relevance, is inimical to quality

—if you start w/ considerations of quality, you can't easily become relevant b/c quality in its purest form is intrinsically motivated

––––––––

(me) very little of this is about notes so far! even less of it is relevant!

––––––––

(me) what usually happens w/ notes is that you take so many that they become almost unusable for their intended purpose or, alternatively, that you take so few that they're of little help
> maybe what I'm really doing in this project is taking notes w/ a commitment to review them that would ordinarily be abandoned when they became unmanageable

▶ Reynolds: At a certain point in the research process you need to take notes on your notes.

(me) why do I keep referring to this project as a "project"? ▶ connotes my need to feel like I have something ongoing that I'm working on & my feeling of purposelessness if I don't
▶ "project" also puts significantly less pressure on the outcome than "book"

––––––––

5/20
Sontag. *Reborn*
(me) remarkable just how formative books are to SS's sense of self

71 — "an intellectual vampire"

— gets engaged to Rieff in the space of 2 weeks!

79— "the assumption that intellectual decisions only confirm subjective (irrational) preferences"
81 —"speech is social + erotic + has more incentive in the feared"

(in contrast to writing in a journal)
83 —"The best it [marriage] aims for is the creation of strong, mutual dependencies"
96— "One criterion of interpretation is that it doesn't allow *enough* meaning (sense) to the text."

(me) maybe I started w/ Sontag b/c I imagine this project to be in some sense a refusal of interpretation

98 — "One sense of interpretation: making allowances for."

A friend & colleague proposed a writing group for this coming summer, after Graham Greene, in which every day, first thing in the morning, we'd each write 500 words, good or bad, then be free (his word) from writing for the rest of the day. And I realized: I don't want to be free from writing, from the sense of obligation to write, I want it, always, as something I should, or could, be doing. The condition of *not*-writing seems like the writer's self-torturing curse but is actually the condition necessary for being a writer. If you're not *not*-writing—if you're not feeling guilty about not writing—you're not orienting your life in a way that makes writing possible.

Sontag. *Reborn*
101 — Goethe declared that "only insufficient knowledge is creative"
105 — "Aristotle is right: happiness is not to be aimed at; it is a by-product of activity aimed at—"

5/22

315 W. 57
Ste 405

Sontag
135 — "Much of morality is the task of compensating for one's age."
136 — "Emerson: A man is what he thinks about all day."

Sontag
150's — even here principles of selection & concision are used to eliminate the dross & filler from S's notes

▶ note takers are hopeful alchemists, convinced that on the next page
the formula will be happened upon that transmutes
------------------------------------way too bombastic!
here's what I want to say: after I've taken all my preliminary notes, when I come to take notes on these notes I will have begun to write the public version of this book ▶ the

*
* * notes, in other words, are, as they always are, a blueprint an outline, a rough draft for some future, latent poem

a block of untouched marble, awaiting the sculptor's hand
however, unlike in sculpture, w/ notes the writer builds the ⌄ block
that she

undifferentiated

intends to later chip away at

look up if there's a technical
term for this

After/words: an editorial exchange

E. Tracy Grinnell & Jen Hofer

Each of us felt compelled to write—yet unable to begin—an editorial note for this final issue of *Aufgabe*. We decided that being in conversation might be the easiest way to draw out some of our thoughts and reflections on the past fifteen years of producing this journal.

• • •

JEN HOFER: One of the things I most appreciate about *Aufgabe* is its multiplicity. What are some metaphors or images that multiplicity calls to mind, for you as a person most deeply at the center of the project? How have those metaphors/ images metamorphosed between 2001 and 2014?

E. TRACY GRINNELL: Initially, I thought of *Aufgabe* as a vehicle for my own exploration of and engagement with contemporary innovative/experimental poetries and eventually as a porous space through which the literary "multiverse" could move—a way of recording currents and landscapes, a poetic ecosystem comprised of writers, artists, translators, editors, and those who moved between those modes. The first issue was released maybe three months before September 11, 2001, so working on the second and subsequent issues took on a heightened urgency in the aftermath of that event and the wars it spawned. I considered it a space of resistance to the jingoistic distortions, the euphemizing newspeak, and the racist foundations of U.S. foreign and domestic policy that flourished during the Bush years and seem sadly to continue unchecked. While I still consider the journal to be a space of and for resistance, I would say that the urgency for me in recent issues has shifted again to a tending to the poetic ecosystem—I think of Bernie Krause's recordings of forests before and after "selective" logging, a type of logging that is meant to preserve the forest. In his recordings you can hear the extent of the damage—where a forest may look unaltered, it is actually deeply and sometimes irreversibly harmed in its biodiversity. I think of the dynamics and complexities of the literary multiverse (necessarily international, beyond borders) in this way—a rich but subtle and nuanced reality that must be tended to, protected, championed.

Similarly, I'm interested in what images or metaphors you might use for the process of editing and translating. You edited and did translations for the Mexican feature in 2003, in our third issue, and have stayed on as a contributing editor and translator for Mexican, Central, and South American poetries since then. How interconnected are editing and translating for you?

JH: Concretely, in terms of process, editing and translating are totally distinct for me. But conceptually they are linked in the sense that both help to create spaces where I can do more than would be possible for just one tiny Jen Hofer alone. Both are exteriorizing impulses, community-constructing impulses where I'm actively interested in doing something very different, and much more, than simply creating and promoting my own writing. And another similarity, I suppose, is that both are grounded in deep reading processes, the way teaching is also grounded in deep reading (and is also an exteriorizing activity). That is, when I read as a translator or read as an editor, I enact a much more lush engagement with the work in question than I'm able to when I'm reading for pleasure (though both translating and editing are deeply pleasurable). Another link between editing and translating is that both respond to a passionate sense that particular work should be in the world, and I want to do whatever I can to make that happen. In terms of images or metaphors, I think also of tending, but of much more constructed spaces than forests or other natural terrains (though is there any "natural" forest left anymore?). I think translating and editing are more gardening sorts of activities, where you're being very intentional, very purposeful (if not methodical) and yet still unexpected "volunteers" might spring up, or some things die that you'd intended to keep alive and others that you hadn't realized could live in your climate grow wildly. I also think of translating and editing as a kind of geometry— exploring the properties and relations of various points, lines and shapes, putting different elements into proximity with one another and plotting the distinctions and interconnections among them.

What does the "multi" in "multiverse" open up, in your view or experience, that the "uni" in "universe" constricts? And given the range of ways that our cultural fields and forests have been "selectively" logged, what sorts of listening do you think are possible now?

ETG: I have always felt a tension between the social experience of poetry, based so largely on proximity and inclusion, and the discovery of formal and poetic affinities that emerge through reading and which can evolve into friendship and a more expansive sense of community. So, creating a space for the "multiverse" has always come from a desire to keep the doors open, to encourage reading across cultural realities and familiarities, to allow for engagement with differing, sometimes starkly contrasting, or surprisingly parallel, trajectories of innovation. What emerges then is a more complex and varied community, precisely that which is obscured when we limit ourselves to social cliques and coterie poetries that can function like closed circuits to those outside of them. And I do think, unfortunately for the real forests, that our cultural fields, forests, and gardens are much more resilient than the environmental ones. I think that there is immense potential—given the technologies at our fingertips (some of our fingertips)—for listening now, but as always we must be actively engaged, critically and constructively, with the ways in which that happens. Questions of access seem to me to be paramount.

I'm wondering about the boundaries and limitations you confront as an editor—realities the journal consistently lays bare—how have you approached editing/curating for such a vast physical, social, and literary space?

JH: I've approached it as I approach most things—haphazardly, incompletely, intuitively, with both gusto and trepidation. I have never seen any aspect of my work as panoramic or exhaustive, and I cringe when I hear people talk about me as an "expert" in anything. There is always so much more to learn, so much more to do, so much more to make. It was never a goal, for me, to represent "what's happening in contemporary writing" from Mexico, or from anywhere. Rather, my editorial choices have been based in my excitement over the work other translators—and especially emerging translators—are doing, and a desire to provide space for that work to flourish. It's an interesting inversion, in a sense, where I'm able to do "local" research (i.e. research within contemporary USAmerican Spanish-language translation poetics) with the result of learning about wonderfully non-local writers. I've also been very excited to work on a project that considers *all* of America—not just USAmerica—when selecting "contemporary American poetry" to include in its pages.

I don't think this is the place to lay out post-*Aufgabe* plans for Litmus, but I wonder if you might offer a list of 3-5 words that might point to your inspirations or your thinking about the trajectory of some of the impulses and ideas described above, in the future?

ETG: flex-breath, slipnet, arch•ambryonic*>, migrate, locule, deanimalesparecequecadacosaasumanera

(selected from poems in *Aufgabe* #12)

• • •

It would not be possible to list everyone who has contributed to the editing and producing of *Aufgabe* since its inception in 1999. Instead, we extend endless gratitude to the over 200 editors and translators who have made these thirteen issues not only possible but beautifully varied, and the over 700 writers and artists whose work has appeared in these pages. Each of them is listed in their respective table of contents in the digital versions of *Aufgabe*; issues #1 – #6 are currently available for free download on the Litmus Press website. The remaining issues #7 – #13 will be available online by 2016.

Onward!

– Brooklyn, NY

June 8, 2014

Contributors

Molly Zuckerman-Hartung, "The Impossible"
2012, oil, glitter, screws, ribbons, globe scrap, and wire, on cheesecloth, 24 x 12 inches
Collection of the Walker Art Center, Minneapolis, MN

Contributors' Notes

MOHAMMED ISMAÏL ABDOUN was born in 1945 in Béchar, Algeria, and is professor of literature at the Institut des Langues Étrangères at the Université Alger-Bouzarea. He specializes in the works of Kateb Yacine and Henri Michaux.

SAMUEL ACE lives in Tucson, AZ and Truth or Consequences, NM. His books include *Normal Sex* (Firebrand, 1994), *Home in three days. Don't wash.* (Hard Press, 1996), and, *Stealth*, with Maureen Seaton (Chax Press, 2011). Most recently his work can be found in *Versal, Rhino, Volt, Mandorla, The Volta*, and *Troubling the Line: Trans and Genderqueer Poetry and Poetics.*

ETEL ADNAN was born in Beirut in 1925, educated in France and the United States, and lives in Paris. She has published poetry, fiction, plays and essays in French and English, including the acclaimed novel *Sitt Marie Rose* (first published in France, Editions des Femmes, 1978; reprinted by Post-Apollo Press, 2011). Adnan is also known in the world of the visual arts for her paintings, ceramics and tapestries.

WILL ALEXANDER is a poet, novelist, essayist, playwright, aphorist, philosopher, visual artist, and pianist. He is a Whiting Fellow and an American Book Award recipient. Author of over 20 books, he is currently typing up his second book of plays.

ANVAR ALI is a poet and screenwriter, whose collection of twenty-seven poems *Mazhakkalam* (Kottayam: D. C. Books, 1999), won the Kanakasree Award of Kerala Sahithya Academy in 2000.

ALEXIS ALMEIDA lives in Denver. She teaches creative writing at the University of Colorado, where she is currently at work on an MFA in poetry. She has written reviews for *The Volta*, and her poems have appeared or are forthcoming in *Unsaid, Likestarlings, La Vague*, and elsewhere. She is the poetry editor for *Timber Journal.*

NADIA ANJUMAN was an Afghani poet and the author of *Gul-e-dodi / Dark Flower* (2002) and *Yek Sàbad Délhoreh / An Abundance of Worry* (2006). She died in November 2005 after a physical altercation with her husband at the age of 25. In 2007, Anjuman's complete works were published in the original Persian-Dari by Iran Open Publishing Group.

JESS ARNDT is a fiction writer and co-editor of the prose experiment, New Herring Press. She was most recently published on BOMBSite and in *Matchbook, PARKETT* vol.91, *The Diner Journal* and *GLU Magazine*. She lives in WA state and Brooklyn.

DIANA ARTERIAN is the author of the chapbook *Death Centos* (Ugly Duckling Presse, 2013), and her writing has appeared or is forthcoming in *Black Warrior Review, Two*

Serious Ladies and *The Volta*, among others. She is a Poetry Editor at Noemi Press, and creator and Managing Editor of Ricochet, a publisher of poetry and prose.

Poet, translator and editor, OANA AVASILICHIOAEI's books include *We, Beasts* (Wolsak & Wynn, 2012, winner of the QWF's A. M. Klein Prize for Poetry) and *feria: a poempark* (Wolsak & Wynn, 2008). Her most recent translation was *Wigrum*, a novel by Daniel Canty (Talonbooks, 2013) and she was the editor of the Quebec poetry feature in *Aufgabe 12* (Litmus Press, 2013). "Mouthnotes" is from her current work-in-progress *Limbinal* (Talonbooks, upcoming 2015). She can be found at oanalab.com.

BABLA and KANCHAN are the names of the husband-wife Mumbai based duo who performed folk and chutney music and are renowned throughout the Bhojpuri speaking diaspora for their contributions to overseas Indian music until Kanchan's death in 2004.

SUBHRO BANDOPADHYAY (b. 1978) is a polyglot poet who speaks four languages, including English and Spanish, and writes in two. Closely connected with contemporary poets from Spain and Chile, Bandopadhyay is also a prolific translator. An associate editor of *Kaurab*, Bandopadhyay has published six books of poetry in Bengali and two in Spanish. He was awarded the Indian Sahitya Academy Youth Award (2013) and the Beca Internacional Antonio Machado de creación poética (2008). Bandopadhyay currently teaches Spanish language and literature at Instituto Cervantes in New Delhi.

JESSICA BARAN is the author of two poetry collections: *Equivalents* (Lost Roads, 2013—Winner of the Besmilr Brigham Women Writers Prize) and *Remains to Be Used* (Apostrophe, 2011). She lives in St. Louis, Missouri, where she teaches at the Sam Fox School of Design and Visual Art and is the director of fort gondo compound for the arts.

JENNIFER BARTLETT is co-editor of *Beauty is a Verb: The New Poetry of Disability*. She is currently writing a biography on the poet Larry Eigner. She lives in Brooklyn with her husband, son, and four animals.

Born in 1968, MATTHIEU BAUMIER is a French author of novels, essays and poetry. His poetry is featured in journals and magazines in France and other countries including: *Agora* (Spain), *Ditch* (Canada), *Polja* (Serbia), *Poezjia magazine* (Croatia), *Word Riot* (United States), *Poetry Quarterly* (United States), *The Literary Review* (U.S.A.), *OVS* (U.S.A.), *The Inflectionist Review* (U.S.A.), *The Indian Review* (India), *MadHat* (U.S.A.), *Sand* (Berlin), 3:AM magazine ... He is currently editor-in-chief of the international online poetry review www.recoursaupoeme.fr, the first issue of which was published on May 15th, 2012.

GUY BENNETT teaches at the Otis College of Art and Design and is the author of several collections of poetry, various works of non-poetry, and numerous translations, including *Approach to the Desert Space* (Seeing Eye Books, 2001) by *Souffles* founder and contributor Mostafa Nissaboury. Recent publications include *Self-Evident Poems* (Otis Books, 2011) and a translation of Mohammed Dib's *Tlemcen or Places of Writing* (Otis Books, 2012).

LAYNIE BROWNE is the author of nine collections of poetry and two novels. Her work appears recently in *The Norton Anthology of Postmodern American Poetry* (2013) as well as in *Ecopoetry: A Contemporary American Anthology* (Trinity University Press, 2013). A new collection, *Lost Parkour Ps(alms)* is forthcoming from Université de Rouen in 2014.

WENDY BURK is the author of two chapbooks, *The Deer* and *The Place Names The Place Named*, as well as the translator of Tedi López Mills's *While Light Is Built* and *Arcadia in Chacahua*. She is the recipient of a 2013 National Endowment for the Arts Translation Projects Fellowship to translate Tedi López Mills's *Contracorriente*.

LOUIS BURY is the author of *Exercises in Criticism: The Theory and Practice of Literary Constraint* (Dalkey Archive Press, 2014) and a Language Lecturer in the Expository Writing Program at New York University.

MARGARET CARSON translates fiction, poetry and drama from Latin America and Spain. Her translations include Mercedes Roffé's *Theory of Colors* (belladonna*, 2005) and Sergio Chejfec's *My Two Worlds* (Open Letter, 2011). She is currently translating the writings of the Spanish artist Remedios Varo.

CHAMAN LAL CHAMAN (1937-1999) was an influential poet renowned for his expertise in the traditional genre known as *nazm*. He also worked as a Journalist with the Urdu daily *Aftab* and served as an editor for the Kashmiri-language magazine *Sheeraza*.

ABIGAIL CHILD is the author of 6 books of poetry, among them A *Motive for Mayhem* and*Scatter Matrix* as well as a book of criticism *THIS IS CALLED MOVING: A Critical Poetics of Film (2005)* from University of Alabama Press. An award-winning filmmaker as well as a writer, Child pushes the envelope of sound-image and text-image relations with humor, liveliness and complex montage. Her newest book *MOUTH TO MOUTH* (2014) will be out this spring from Eoagh Press.

RYAN CLARK, a native Texan, has dedicated years of his life to homophonic translation and is particularly interested in the reparative potential of appropriative writing, including how poetry responds to violence and subjugation, symbolic and otherwise. His work has appeared in *Smoking Glue Gun, Tenderloin, Seven Corners, Similar:Peaks, Fact-Simile,* and *Something on Paper.* He currently teaches composition at Savannah State University.

ALLISON COBB is the author of *Born2* (Chax Press, 2004) about her hometown of Los Alamos, New Mexico, and *Green-Wood* (Factory School, 2010) about a nineteenth-century cemetery in Brooklyn, New York. She is at work on *Plastic: an autobiography*. She lives in Portland, OR.

KATE COLBY is author of four books of poetry, including *Beauport* (Litmus Press, 2010) and *The Return of the Native* (Ugly Duckling Press, 2011). *Fruitlands* won the Norma Farber First Book Award in 2007. She is a founding board member of the Gloucester Writers Center in Massachusetts, and is currently based in Providence, where she was a 2012 fellow of the Rhode Island State Council for the Arts.

AJA COUCHOIS DUNCAN is a Bay Area writer of Ojibwe, French and Scottish descent. Her writing has been anthologized in *Biting the Error: Writers Explore Narrative* (Coach House Press) *Bay Poetics* (Faux Press) and *Love Shook My Heart 2* (Alyson Press). A fictional writer of non-fiction, she has published essays in the *North American Review* and *Chain*. Her most recent chapbook, *Nomenclature, Miigaadiwin, a Forked Tongue* was published by CC Marimbo press. In 2005, she was a recipient of the Marin Arts Council Award Grant for Literary Arts, and, in 2013, she received a James D. Phelan Literary Award.

BISWAMIT DWIBEDY is the author of *Ozalid* (2010), *Hubble Gardener* and *Erode* (forthcoming) from 1913 Press . He was born in Odisha, India and lives in Bangalore. He has a MFA in Writing from Bard College, New York and lived in Iowa City for many years. In India, he works for Ogilvy and Mather, and is the founder and editor of Annew Press.

SHONNI ENELOW is an assistant professor of English at Fordham University, who writes for and about theater and performance. She has recently published articles on the literary aesthetics of performance documentation (*Theater*, 2013) and James Baldwin's dramatic writing (*Theatre Survey*, 2012), and is the co-author of *Research Theatre, Climate Change, and the Ecocide Project* (Palgrave Macmillan, 2014). Since 2010, she has been working on a series of performance lectures, which she has performed in and around New York.

P. M. GOVINDANUNNI won the Edassery Award for his collection of poems in Malayalam, *Amaratharakam* in 2010.

TEJI GROVER (b. 1955) is a Hindi poet, fiction writer, painter, and translator. Her poems have been translated into a number of Indian and foreign languages, including Assamese, Marathi, Bengali, Panjabi, English, Swedish, Norwegian, Polish and Catalan. Her novel *Neela* appeared in Polish in 2010. As an activist, she works extensively in rural Madhya Pradesh, developing innovative pedagogy and, conceiving and producing books for children.

OLIVIA C. HARRISON is Assistant Professor of French at the University of Southern California. Her current book project analyzes the representation of Palestine in Moroccan, Algerian, and Tunisian literary works from the 1960s to the present. In addition to her editorial work on the translation of *Souffles-Anfas*, she has translated poems and essays by Abdellatif Laâbi, Abraham Serfaty, Abdelkebir Khatibi, and Etel Adnan.

ROBERTO HARRISON's books include *bicycle* (forthcoming from Akrilica Press), *Os* (subpress, 2006), and *Counter Daemons* (Litmus Press, 2006). His latest of many chapbooks is *Bridge of the World* (cannot exist, 2011). With Andrew Levy he published and edited *Crayon* magazine from 1997 to 2008. He also publishes and edits the Bronze Skull Press chapbook series. He lives and works in Milwaukee.

COLE HEINOWITZ is the author of *Daily Chimera* (Incommunicado, 1995), *Stunning in Muscle Hospital* (Detour, 2002), *The Rubicon* (A Rest, 2008), and the critical study, *Spanish America and British Romanticism: Rewriting Conquest* (Edinburgh UP, 2010). She is the co-translator of Mario Santiago Papasquiaro's *Advice from 1 Disciple of Marx to 1 Heidegger Fanatic* (Wave, 2013) and is currently translating the work of Alejandra Pizarnik.

TIERRY HENTSCH (1944-2005) is the author of several books including *Raconter et mourir. Aux sources narratives de l'imaginaire occidental* (Pum, 2002), *Le Temps aboli. L'Occident et les grands récits* (PUM, 2005), *L'Orient imaginaire* (Minuit, 1988), translated as *Imagining the Middle East* (Black Rose, 1996) and *Les Amandiers* (Kaplan & Co, 2002). *La mer, la limite* was published posthumously by Héliotrope.

KEVIN HOLDEN is the author of two chapbooks, *Identity* (Cannibal Books) and *Alpine* (White Queen Press)—his book *Solar* recently won the Fence Modern Poets Prize and will be released in 2015. His poetry has appeared in such places as *Conjunctions, 1913, jubilat, Harp & Altar, Colorado Review, Typo*, and *Little Red Leaves*, and was included in the recent anthology *The Arcadia Project* (Ahsahta Press). He also translates poetry from Russian and French, and that work has been published in *Aufgabe, Double Change*, and other journals. He lives in motion between the Connecticut and Hudson Rivers.

Novels by the Moroccan writer TAHAR BEN JELLOUN (b. 1944) include *The Sand Child* (Johns Hopkins, 2000) and *The Sacred Night* (Johns Hopkins, 2000), for which he won the Prix Goncourt. His poetry is collected in *Poésie complète [Complete Poetry]* (France, Seuil, 1995). A long-time resident of France, he has taken on issues of discrimination against immigrants in France in such texts as *Racism Explained to My Daughter* (The New Press, 2006).

PIERRE JORIS' recent publications include *Meditations on the Stations of Mansur al-Hallaj* (poems) from Chax Press and *The University of California Book of North African Literature,* coedited with Habib Tengour. Forthcoming are *Barzakh—Poems 2000-2012* (Black Widow Press), *Breathturn into Timestead: The Collected Later Poetry of Paul Celan*

(FSG), & A Voice Full of Cities: The Collected Essays of Robert Kelly, co-edited with Peter Cockelbergh (Contra Mundum Press).

SONAM KACHRU is a research fellow with the project Zukunftsphilologie (Future Philology) at the Forum Transregionale Studien, Berlin. He is interested in the history of philosophy and literature available in Sanskrit which he pursues awake to the trials of thought elsewhere but without an interest in comparison alone. When not translating Sanskrit or Kashmiri he issues vague threats about composing his own fiction. Fortunately such threats have not materialized. His most recent publication is a translation and commentary of the utterances of the fourteenth century visionary poet Lal Ded for Spolia Magazine: The Medieval Issue (New York, 2013).

JAYAN K. C. is a poet and filmmaker who has published four collections of poetry in Malayalam. His experimental shorts and documentaries have been shown in many international film festivals and have won several awards. He currently lives in New York.

SACHIN C. KETKAR (b. 1972) is a bilingual writer, translator, editor and critic. His translations of contemporary Marathi poetry has been published as Live Update: An Anthology of Recent Marathi Poetry in 2005. Along with numerous recent Gujarati poets, he has translated the fifteenth century Gujarati poet Narsinh Mehta into English. He won the Indian Literature Poetry Translation Prize in 2000 and currently lives in Vadodara, Gujrat.

MOHAMMED KHAÏR-EDDINE (1941-1995) lived a tumultuous life that traversed Morocco, the south of France, and Paris. The author of numerous volumes of poetry, his novel Agadir (France, Seuil, 1967), which won Jean Cocteau's "Enfants terribles" prize, describes the dire consequences of the earthquake that struck the eponymous city in 1960. Khaïr-Eddine contributed to Les Lettres nouvelles and Présence africaine and co-authored the manifesto Poésie-toute with Mostafa Nissaboury.

ABDELKEBIR KHATIBI (1938-2009) trained as a sociologist and was one of Morocco's most celebrated writers and theorists. The author of several critically-acclaimed fictional texts, including Love in Two Languages (Minnesota, 1990), he was also a respected critic of art and literature, as evidenced in volumes including The Splendors of Islamic Calligraphy (UK, Thames and Hudson, 2001), and Maghreb Pluriel [The Plural Maghreb] (France, Denoël, 1983).

JENNIFER KRONOVET is the author of the poetry collection Awayward and the co-translator of The Acrobat: Selected Poems of Celia Dropkin.

In addition to founding Souffles and Anfas, ABDELLATIF LAÂBI (b. 1942) is a prolific poet, novelist, essayist, playwright, and children's author. He has produced numerous translations of seminal Arab-language writers, including Mahmoud

Darwish, Abdelwahab al-Bayati, and Ghassan Kanafani. He is the editor of the seminal anthology *La poésie marocaine, de l'indépendence à nos jours* [*Morrocan Poetry from Independence to the Present Day*] (France, Editions de la différence, 2005), which brings together over fifty Francophone and Arabophone poets for the first time.

KIMBERLY LYONS books of poetry include *Rouge* (Instance Press, 2012), *The Practice of Residue* (Subpress, 2012), *Phototherapique* (Portable Press, Ketalanche Press, 2008), *Saline* (Instance Press, 2005), and *Abracadabra* (Granary Books, 2000). She lives in Brooklyn NY, where she publishes Lunar Chandelier Press and works at the Brooklyn Women's Shelter.

FATIMA MAHJUBA is a poet from Azad Kashmir, in Pakistan.

GHULAM AHMAD MAHJOOR (1885-1952) was, along with Nadim, one of the greatest vanguards of modern Kashmiri poetry. He is known for his evocative use of folk genres to explore new themes in poetry, and the new uses to which he put the traditional *ghazal* and *nazm*.

Writer, feminist and activist MALATHI MAITHRI (b. 1968) is recognised as an important contemporary Tamil poet. She hails from Puducherry State in southern India. Her very first short story, "Prayanam," was published in *Kaniayazhi*, a premier literary magazine, in 1988. This has been followed by the publication of three books of poetry and a collection of essays. She has co-edited *Paraththal Adhan Sudhandiram* [*Flying is Its Freedom*], an anthology of literary works, and *Anangu* [*Woman*], a collection of essays.

BIBIANA PADILLA MALTOS was born in Tijuana in 1974. She is a writer and conceptual artist closely tied to the Fluxus movement. She is the author of *Equilibrios* (1992), *Intrucciones para cocinar* (2001), *Los Demonios de la Casa Mayor* (2002), *Los Impersonales* (2002), *25 ScoreS 25* (2009), *Mini Poemas* (2009), and *MCA-Chicago Scores* (2011). Co-founder of AVTEXTFEST and AVTEXTPRESS experimental literature projects, Padilla Maltos holds a degree in International Affairs and a Masters in Marketing.

A major force in contemporary Malayalam poetry, ROSE MARY was born in 1956 in Kanjirapally, Kerala and has published three books of poems and four memoirs.

LUCY R. MCNAIR holds a PhD in Comparative Literature from CUNY Graduate School. Her translations include Mouloud Feraoun's Algerian classic, *The Poor Man's Son* (University of Virginia Press, 2005), Samira Bellil's inner city memoir, *To Hell and Back* (Bison Books, 2008), and poetry by Andrée Chedid, Venus Khoury-Ghata and Amina Said in *The Poetry of Arab Women* (Interlink Publishing Group, 2000).

TEDI LÓPEZ MILLS was born in Mexico City in 1959. She has published ten books of poetry, several of which have received national prizes in Mexico: *Cinco estaciones, Un lugar ajeno, Segunda persona* (Premio Nacional de Poesía Efraín Huerta), *Glosas, Horas, Luz por aire y agua, Un jardín, cinco noches (y otros poemas), Contracorriente* (Premio Nacional de Literatura José Fuentes Mares), *Parafrasear*, and *Muerte en la rúa Augusta* (Premio Xavier Villaurrutia). Her most recent book is a collection of essays, *Libro de las explicaciones* (Editorial Almadía, 2012).

CHHANNULAL MISHRA, an internationally acclaimed Hindustani Classical singer was born in Azamgarh, Uttar Pradesh, India. With over thirteen albums recorded his awards include the Padma Bhushan, India's highest civilian honor in January 2010. His renditions of Kabir's (the 16th Century poet-saint) poetry are performed in *Benaras Gayaki* style.

Poet, translator, and editor ANNA MOCHOVAKIS is the author of two books of poetry, *You and Three Others Are Approaching a Lake* (Coffee House Press, 2011), and *I Have Not Been Able to Get Through to Everyone* (Turtle Point Press, 2006). Her translations from the French include Albert Cossery's *The Jokers* (New York Review Books, 2010), Annie Ernaux's *The Possession* (Seven Stories Press, 2008), and Georges Simenon's *The Engagement* (New York Review Books, 2007).

Poet and translator RAJIV MOHABIR, a Kundiman and American Institute of Indian Studies Language fellow, received his MFA in Poetry and Literary Translation from Queens College, CUNY and is currently perusing a PhD in English at the University of Hawai'i, Manoa. He translates folksongs through the lens of translation-as-transformation-and-adaptation. More of his translations can be found in his chapbook *na mash me bone* (Finishing Line Press, 2011).

AKTHAR MOHIUDDIN (1928-2001) was one of the most distinctive, original, and influential prose writers in the Kashmiri language who used the short prose form to write about the history of violence in the Kashmir valley. He is the author of about six collections of short stories and forty radio plays.

JENNIFER MOXLEY is the author of *Clampdown* (Flood, 2009), *The Middle Room* (Subpress, 2008), *The Line* (Post-Apollo, 2007), *Often Capital* (Flood, 2005), *The Sense Record and other poems* (Edge, 2002), and *Imagination Verses* (Tender Buttons, 1996). She has translated Jacqueline Risset's *Sleep's Powers* (Ugly Duckling Presse, 2008), *The Translation Begins* (Burning Deck, 1996) and Anne Portugal's *absolute bob* (Burning Deck, 2010).

ARYANIL MUKHERJEE (b. 1964) writes in two languages—essentially and originally in Bangla sometimes transcreating them to English. He has authored twelve books of poetry and essays on poetics and translated scores of international poets on both hemispheres including a 234 pg. book-length translation project on John Ashbery. His five collections of Bengali poetry include *Sunaamir Ek Bachchar Par* [One Year After the Tsunami] (2008) and *Smritilekhaa* [Code Memory] (2013). Anthology appearances include: *The HarperCollins Book of Indian Poetry in English* (2011), *La Pared de Agua*, a Spanish anthology of contemporary Bengali poetry (2011), *Indivisible: An Anthology of South Asian American Poetry* (2010).

These poems, which are from JOHN MYERS' *Event Staff*, use some words of Ariana Reines, Joseph Campbell and William Maxwell. Other recent work is forthcoming in *Denver Quarterly*, *Animal Shelter* and *H_NGM_N*. John grew up in the Endless Mountains. He lives in Tucson where he makes art and watches.

EILEEN MYLES is the author of many books of poetry and prose, including *Snowflake/ different streets*, *The Importance of Being Iceland*, and *Inferno (a poet's novel)* now available on iTunes in her own voice. She lives in New York and is the recipient of a 2014 Foundation for Contemporary Art Award in Poetry.

DINA NATH NADIM (1916-1988) Perhaps the most influential poet of the 20th century in Kashmir, Nadim not only contributed to broadening the possibilities of Kashmiri lyric forms but also encouraged the use of the Kashmiri lexicon, foregoing for his new verse the stable poetic lexica and tropes of Persian, Urdu and Sanskrit.

NATHANAËL is the author of a score of books written in English or in French, including, most recently, *Sisyphus, Outdone. Theatres of the Catastrophal*, *Carnet de somme*, and *We Press Ourselves Plainly*. Her translations include works by Hervé Guibert, Édouard Glissant, Danielle Collobert, Catherine Mavrikakis, and Hilda Hilst, the latter in collaboration with Rachel Gontijo Araujo. Nathanaël lives in Chicago.

PETER NEUFELD is the author of a handful of poems. He was born in 1971 in Reedley, California. He lives in London with his wife, Marie-Claire, and his daughter, Livia, where he works and writes.

A co-founder of *Souffles*, MOSTAFA NISSABOURY (b. 1943) is the author of the poetry collections *Plus haute mémoire* [Highest Memory] (Atlantes, 1968), *La Mille et deuxième nuit* [*The One Thousand and Second Night*] (Shoof, 1975), and *Approach to the Desert Space*, translated by Guy Bennett (Seeing Eye Books, 2011).

MARINA OMAR was born in Afghanistan and has worked as an interpreter for Afghan refugee families. She is currently a doctoral candidate in Foreign Affairs at the University of Virginia.

Of the few who attempted to refurbish the language of everyday Bengali poetry, PRONOB PAL (b. 1954) stands out as unique and undaunted, with his prolonged and austere experimentation with poetic language. His important books include *Magic Canvas* (1991), *Bhashhaabadaler Kabitaa* (Poetry of Language Alteration, 1994) and most famously *Shaastraheen Chalaar Bedanaa* (The pain of striding outside the manual, 2004). Pronob lives in Howrah and teaches High School.

GHULAM ROSUL POMPUR (?-2011) Poet and critic, celebrated for his work with traditional forms.

JH PHRYDAS is an MFA candidate in the Jack Kerouac School of Disembodied Poetics, where he was the inaugural recipient of the Anne Waldman Fellowship in 2012. Phrydas is the founder of Fair Warning! Press, co-founder and editor of TRACT / TRACE: an investigative journal, and has been published in Gesture Literary Journal, Bombay Gin, and Berkeley Poetry Review. His chapbook Levitations is forthcoming from Timeless, Infinite Light.

DOUGLAS PICCINNINI is most recently the author of an encoded chromagylph, FLAG (Well Greased Press, 2013), and co-author of the bilingual, collaborative text Δ (TPR Press, 2013). His first full-length book of poems, Blood Oboe (Omnidawn, 2015), is forthcoming.

ALEJANDRA PIZARNIK (1936-1972) was a leading voice in twentieth-century Latin American poetry. Born in Argentina to Russian-Jewish immigrants, Pizarnik studied at the University of Buenos Aires and the Sorbonne. In Paris, she was influenced by the works of the Surrealists and participated in a vibrant expatriate community of writers that included Julio Cortázar and Octavio Paz. Known primarily as a poet, Pizarnik also published reviews, translations, theatre, and short works of experimental prose, and left behind a literary diary that reflects her debt to Kafka, Artaud, and Michaux. She died of an apparent drug overdose at the age of thirty-six.

Poet and critic ABDUL RAHMAN RAHI is an expert in Kashmiri and Persian literature and teaches at Kashmir University, where he founded the department of Kashmiri Language. Influenced by Nadim in the beginning, Rahi's work has long since found its own way, its unique voice, seeking connections across a bewildering variety of languages, histories, and peoples.

PINTU RAI identifies as a Bhojpuri speaker. He was raised in Ghazipur, Bihar. He relocated to Varanasi, Uttar Pradesh to continue his work and training as a folksinger at Benaras Hindu University (Varanasi). He is currently married and performs traditional and original folk compositions around the city.

RIZIO YOHANNAN RAJ is a bilingual writer, translator and educationist. Her works include two collections of poetry in English, Eunuch, Naked by the Sabarmati and Other Guna Poems, and two novels in Malayalam, Avinasom and Yatrikom, the first of which is translated into English as A Tale of Things Timeless (HarperCollins 2012). She has translated major 20th century Malayalam writers into English and introduced seminal works from other languages into Malayalam.

P. P. RAMACHANDRAN has published two collections of poetry in Malayalam, *Kanekkane* [Seeing, Seeing], which won the Kerala Sahitya Academy award and *Rantay Murichathu* [Cut into Two], both published by Current Books, Thrissur. He teaches in a high school and lives in Vattamkulam, a small town in Malappuram district of Kerala.

P. RAMAN was born in 1971 in Pattambi, and has published two collections of poems in Malayalam, *Kanam* and *Thurumbu*.

JOAN RETALLACK's *Procedural Elegies / Western Civ Cont'd /* (Roof Books) was an ARTFORUM best book of 2010.

ANA RISTOVIĆ is a Serbian poet who has published seven collections of poetry. Her most recent book is *Meteoric Debris* (2013). She has won many awards for her work both in Serbia and Germany. She was a featured reader in Southbank Centre's Poetry Parnassus in 2012. She has read her poetry across Europe and Latin America. ELÉNA RIVERA's most recent books are *On the Nature of Position and Tone,* (Fields Press, 2012) and *The Perforated Map* (Shearsman Books, 2011). She won the 2010 Robert Fagles prize in translation for *The Rest of the Voyage* by Bernard Noël, published by Graywolf Press (2011).

ELIZABETH ROBINSON is, most recently, the author of *On Ghosts* from Solid Objects, and *Blue Heron* from the Center for Literary Publishing. She is a co-editor of Instance press and the literary periodical *pallaksch.pallaksch*.

MERCEDES ROFFÉ is one of Argentina's leading poets. Widely published in Latin America and Spain, her poetry has been published in translation in Italy, Quebec, Romania, England, and the U.S. In 1998 she founded Ediciones Pen Press, an indie press dedicated to the publication of contemporary poetry from around the world. She has been the recipient of a John Simon Guggenheim Fellowship (2001) and a Civitella Ranieri Foundation Fellowship (2012). Translated into English, her poetry has been published by Shearsmann Books (Exeter, UK).

CAMILO ROLDÁN is a poet and translator who currently resides in Brooklyn, NY. From 2011 through 2013 he co-curated the Triptych Reading Series and is currently editor-in-chief for DIEZ. Among other journals, his work has most recently appeared in *Mandorla, West Wind Review, Lungfull!* and *Sun's Skeleton.* A new chapbook, *La Torre,* is forthcoming from Well Greased Press.

JOCELYN SAIDENBERG is the author of *Mortal City, Cusp, Negativity, The Dispossessed* and *Shipwreck. Dead Letter* is forthcoming from Roof Books in 2014. She is the founding editor of Krupskaya Books and has curated events and performances for New Langton Arts, Small Press Traffic and Right Window. She lives in San Francisco and is currently working towards a PhD at UC Berkeley writing on the poetry of Lucretius and Catullus and anthropologies of violence.

MOTI LAL SAQI (1936-1999) was a poet and critic, and a reputed scholar of the history of religions, folklore and folkmusic in the Kashmiri language. Apart from his groundbreaking work in, on and for the Kashmiri language, he was also awarded the *Padmashree* by the Government of India for his work in Urdu.

SARJU writes a column in the Malayalam magazine *Nalamidam* and has published a collection of poems *The Sea Where God Washes His Hand*. He is also a translator and his work has appeared in Arabic and English anthologies of Malayalam poetry.

YVETTE SIEGERT is a poet and translator. She has edited for *The New Yorker* and currently teaches comparative literature at Baruch College, The City University of New York. Writing has appeared in *Circumference, 6x6, St. Petersburg Review, Guernica, The Buenos Aires Review,* and elsewhere, and her work has received recognition from PEN, NYSCA, the Academy of American Poets, and the Andrew W. Mellon Foundation. Her translation of Alejandra Pizarnik's final collection, *A Musical Hell* (New Directions, 2013) was nominated for the Best Translated Book Award; she will publish Pizarnik's collected works with New Directions and Ugly Duckling Presse later this year.

CARLOS SOTO-ROMÁN is the author of *Philadelphia's Notebooks* (Otoliths, 2011), *Chile Project [Re-Classified]* (Gauss PDF, 2013) and *Alternative Set of Procedures* (Corollary Press, 2013). He is a translator and the curator of the cooperative anthology of U.S. poetry Elective Affinities. He lives in Philadelphia, PA.

V. R. SANTHOSH is a leading young poet in Malayalam who has published several volumes of poetry and translation, including a book of poems based on the paintings of Vincent Van Gogh. He is also a lyricist for songs in Malayalam movies.

SABYASACHI SANYAL (b. 1973) began publishing poetry in *Kaurab* at the turn of the millennium. An associate editor of *Kaurab*, he is the author of three books of poetry, *Neel Gramophone* [Blue Gramophone], *Haripadagiri* [Being Haripada], and *Bracketshahar* [Bracketcity], and a book of poetic prose, *Aprilata* [Aprilness]. Sabyasachi has traveled extensively around the globe and was educated in India, South Korea, and Sweden. A molecular biologist, Sabyasachi teaches and works as a research scientist at the Central Drug Research Institute in Lucknow, India.

K. SATCHIDANANDAN is a major translator, critic and poet in Malayalam. Born in 1946, he has been instrumental in introducing the work of Lorca, Vallejo, Celan and Brecht to an Indian audience through his translations. The author of numerous books of poetry, criticism and translations, he won the Sahitya Akademi award in 2012, and a film on him, *Summer Rain* was released in 2007.

VYOMESH SHUKLA (b. 1980). Besides writing poetry, he writes reviews and criticism, and has translated works by Edward Said, Raymond Williams, Terry Eagleton, Harold Pinter, Howard Zinn, and Eliot Weinberger's book *What I Heard About Iraq* into Hindi. He was awarded the Ankur Mishra Smriti Puraskar in 2008.

RAHUL SONI is a writer, editor and translator. He has edited *Home from a Distance* (Pratilipi Books, 2011), an anthology of Hindi Poetry in English translation, and translated *Magadh* (Almost Island Books, 2013), a collection of poems by Shrikant Verma, and *The Roof Beneath Their Feet* (HarperCollins, 2013), a novel by Geetanjali Shree. He was a Charles Wallace Visiting Fellow in Literary Translation at the University of East Anglia in 2010, and received the Sangam House Fellowship in 2012. He lives in India.

SUKIRTHARANI was born in Lalapet, in Vellore district of Tamil Nadu, where she still lives and teaches. Her first book, *Kaippatri En Kanavu Kel* was controversial for its so called "obscenity." She is the author of four collections of poetry.

STACY SZYMASZEK is the author of *Emptied of All Ships* and *Hyperglossia*, both published by Litmus Press. Her third full length collection, *Hart Island*, is forthcoming from Nightboat Books in 2015. She serves as the Director of The Poetry Project.

STEVEN and MAJA TEREF are the translators of *Assembly* (Host Publications), the selected poems of the late Serbian poet Novica Tadic. Their translations of Ana Ristović's poems have appeared in *Asymptote*, *Conduit*, and *Rhino* (winner of their 2012 Translation Prize). Their translation of her poem "Circling Zero" was published in the international poetry anthology *The World Record* (Bloodaxe Books).

DAN THOMAS-GLASS is the author of DAUGHTERS OF YOUR CENTURY (Furniture Press, 2014), *The Great American Beatjack Volume I* (Perfect Lovers Press, 2012), *Kate & Sonia (in the months before our second daughter's birth)* (Little Red Leaves Textile Series 2012), and *880* (Deep Oakland Editions, 2009). He is a middle school principal at a progressive school in Los Angeles, CA, where he lives with his wife Kate and their daughters Sonia and Alma.

PETER VALENTE is a poet, translator, and filmmaker. His poems have appeared in journals such as *Mirage #4/Periodical*, *First intensity*, *Prosodia*, and *Talisman*. Valente is the author of *Forge of Words a Forest* (Jensen Daniels, 1998), and *The Artaud Variations*, forthcoming from Spuyten Duyvil. His most recent translations include the work of Pier Paolo Pasolini, Sandro Penna, and Antonin Artaud.

TERESA VILLA-IGNACIO is Andrew W. Mellon Postdoctoral Fellow in the Humanities at Tulane University. Her current book project, *Poethical Import: Translationships in French-American Poetic Exchange*, examines the centrality of ethics in relations of translation and collaboration among France- and U.S.-based contemporary experimental poets. In addition to co-editing the *Souffles-Anfas* anthology, she is producing *Sounding Translation*, a podcast series featuring poet-translators.

FLORENCIA WALFISCH was born in Buenos Aires. She writes and makes textile art. She has participated in various individual and group shows, interdisciplinary projects, and poetry readings. With Ana Lafferranderie, she curates the reading series at Fedro, a bookstore and cultural center in San Telmo. Her poetry has appeared in various journals and anthologies. In 2004, Sopa de Ajo y Mezcal received the Jaime Sabines prize from Coneculta in Chiapas. She lives and works in her hometown.

MATVEI YANKELEVICH is the author of the poetry collection *Alpha Donut* (United Artists Books, 2012) and the novella-in-fragments *Boris by the Sea* (Octopus Books, 2009), and the translator of *Today I Wrote Nothing: The Selected Writings of Daniil Kharms* (Overlook/Ardis, 2009). He is one of the founding editors of Ugly Duckling Presse and a member of the Writing Faculty at the Milton Avery Graduate School of the Arts at Bard College.

About the Artist

Chlorophyll Bluess

Plants
but everything really, all shivering life
displays the colors it can't absorb
cloaked in excess
florid and shimmering spectrum

Secret heliotropism
the past strives to turn toward that sun which is rising in the sky of history.
The silent and subtle leaning of the plant. Toward
Photo-
synthesis

Plants convert carbon dioxide into air, absorbing the hot acidic and releasing
the fresh and breathy. Process the cool blues of grief and melancholy, the
hot reds of rage and struggle. The -ess in Bluess is a suffix appended; a
subordinate fastening. Something stuck to the posterior of a word; chewing
gum lifted from hot pavement to the seat of one's pants.

-ess makes the word
Feminine
(giggling   hungry   silvery quivers remembering stolid and heavy-sitting)
from Blues to Bluess
Sorcerer
to
Sorceress

Buddhists have a practice called Tonglen.
It is like this: breathe in the texture of claustrophobia. The sensation of all caught
up. Breathe out the texture of
relaxation
or spaciousness
or letting go

Breathe in
the blues
Breathe out
fresh
cool   light

Viridescence. Greenness.
becoming
energy
Sea change

This is why foliage is so ecstatically green: Non-Absorption
People say "you are what you eat" but this is not all there is to see. When a self-
consciousness of viewing exists,
absorption is compromised, and theatricality results.

So I am an actress of the source
Pulsing
From anxious to erotic to diffident to hypnotic, we never leave reality but neither
do we ever
exhaust it

— *Molly Zuckerman-Hartung*
www.mollyzuckermanhartung.com

Molly Zuckerman-Hartung, "Bird & Bird (Broad advisory, transactional and contentious capability)"
2011, oil, spray paint and painted leather connecting two paintings, left: 15 x 13 inches, right: 15 x 12 inches

do you Aufgabe?

Aufgabe #1, edited by E. Tracy Grinnell and Peter Neufeld, with guest editors Norma Cole (covers and content pages of small publications from France) and Leslie Scalapino. (out of print)

Aufgabe #2, edited by E. Tracy Grinnell, with guest editor Rosmarie Waldrop (German poetry in translation).

Aufgabe #3, edited by E. Tracy Grinnell, with guest editor Jen Hofer (Mexican poetry in translation, bilingual). (out of print)

Aufgabe #4, edited by E. Tracy Grinnell, with guest editor Sawako Nakayasu (Japanese poetry in translation).

Aufgabe #5, edited by E. Tracy Grinnell with Mark Tardi and Paul Foster Johnson (special issue dedicated to Norman O. Brown's lecture "John Cage") and guest editors Guy Bennett and Jalal El Hakmaoui (Moroccan poetry in translation). (out of print)

Aufgabe #6, edited by E. Tracy Grinnell, Paul Foster Johnson and Mark Tardi, with guest editor Ray Bianchi (Brazilian poetry in translation).

Aufgabe #7, edited by E. Tracy Grinnell, Paul Foster Johnson, Mark Tardi, and Julian Talamantez Brolaski, with guest editor Jennifer Scappettone (Italian poetry in translation).

Aufgabe #8, edited by E. Tracy Grinnell, Paul Foster Johnson, Julian Talamantez Brolaski, and Rachel Bers, with guest editor Matvei Yankelevich (Russian poetry & poetics in translation). (out of print)

Aufgabe #9, edited by E. Tracy Grinnell, Paul Foster Johnson, Julian Talamantez Brolaski, Jen Hofer, Nathanaël, and Rachel Bers, with guest editors Mark Tardi (Polish poetry & poetics in translation) and Laura Moriarty (A Tonalist Set).

Aufgabe #10, edited by E. Tracy Grinnell, Paul Foster Johnson, Julian Talamantez Brolaski, Jen Hofer, Nathanaël, and Rachel Bers, with guest editor Cole Swensen (French poetry & poetics in translation).

Aufgabe #11, edited by E. Tracy Grinnell, Julian Talamantez Brolaski, erica kaufman, Jen Hofer, and Nathanaël, with guest editor Christian Nagler (Salvadoran poetry in translation).

Aufgabe #12, edited by E. Tracy Grinnell, erica kaufman, Jen Hofer, Tyrone Williams, Jamie Townsend and Nathanaël, with guest editor Oana Avasilichioaei (poetry in translation from Quebec).

WWW.LITMUSPRESS.ORG

Back issues of *Aufgabe* may be purchased through Small Press Distribution. Issues #1 – #6 are currently available for free download from the Litmus Press website. By 2016, all issues will be available through our website and via Reissues on the Jacket2 website.